The Bankers

The Bankers

How the Banks Brought Ireland to Its Knees

SHANE ROSS

PENGUIN

IRELAND

PENGUIN IRELAND

Published by the Penguin Group
Penguin Ireland, 25 St Stephen's Green, Dublin 2, Ireland (a division of Penguin Books Ltd)
Penguin Books Ltd, 80 Strand, London WC2R 0RL, England
Penguin Group (USA) Inc., 375 Hudson Street, New York, New York 10014, USA
Penguin Group (Australia), 250 Camberwell Road, Camberwell, Victoria 3124, Australia
(a division of Pearson Australia Group Pty Ltd)
Penguin Group (Canada), 90 Eglinton Avenue East, Suite 700, Toronto, Ontario, Canada M4P 2Y3
(a division of Pearson Penguin Canada Inc.)
Penguin Books India Pvt Ltd, 11 Community Centre, Panchsheel Park, New Delhi - 110 017, India
Penguin Group (NZ), 67 Apollo Drive, Rosedale, North Shore 0632, New Zealand
(a division of Pearson New Zealand Ltd)
Penguin Books (South Africa) (Pty) Ltd, 24 Sturdee Avenue, Rosebank, Johannesburg 2196, South Africa
Penguin Books Ltd, Registered Offices: 80 Strand, London WC2R 0RL, England

www.penguin.com

First published 2009

5

Copyright © Shane Ross, 2009

Set in Bembo 13.75/16.25pt
Typeset by Palimpsest Book Production Limited, Grangemouth, Stirlingshire
Printed in Great Britain by Clays Ltd, St Ives plc

A CIP catalogue record for this book is available from the British Library

ISBN: 978-1-844-88216-8

www.greenpenguin.co.uk

Contents

Acknowledgements

I am a cranky curmudgeon at the best of times. I spend my life complaining about the mistakes, impatience and inefficiencies of others. Other people are mostly impossible, lazy, unhelpful and rude.

Writing a book makes matters worse. All human beings become intolerable. Neighbours become nuisances. Friends become enemies.

At some stage in the middle of writing this book the penny dropped. As everyone I encountered became thoroughly obnoxious, I was reminded of an incident from my long-ago drinking days. At some time during that fuzzy period I turned to a drinking companion and let rip: 'The more I drink,' I declared loudly, 'the more objectionable you become.'

Today I happily acknowledge that it was I, not my companion, who was the problem in those distant days. It is harder, with the benefit of full sobriety, to suggest that everybody I met in recent months could have suddenly turned into poisonous old foul-mouths. Yet that is the only alternative to the less than palatable truth: writing a book turns angels into devils, saints into sinners, sane men into monsters.

So it is probably appropriate to apologize first and to acknowledge second. Or to do both together.

This book has been a pleasure to write. Even some of Ireland's most despised bankers have been helpful in enabling me to put the pieces together. Happily I have been able to speak to many of the key players in this dark story. Some refused. Many have not wanted to be quoted directly but, suffice to say, there is no bank where I have not interviewed at least one director. In several cases it has been more. Senior politicians of all parties have assisted me in establishing the truth; even the walls of the Central Bank and the Department of Finance have been penetrated. Let me thank all those who wished to remain anonymous but who spent hours telling me about the shenanigans inside their workplaces.

To my employers in the *Sunday Independent*, special thanks for allowing me six months off to write the book.

More specifically, to those who laboriously helped to compile it, a deep expression of gratitude. To Nick Webb, deputy business editor of the *Sunday Independent*, heartfelt thanks for reading the book – chapter by chapter – and making valuable suggestions.

To Nuala Walsh, my personal assistant, for putting up with days of intolerable tension and for giving of her own time to dig up valuable information.

To Elizabeth O'Brien, for her patience and diligence in supplying research which provided priceless background.

To Paul Kearney, for his calm endurance while checking the book for accuracy.

To my good friend Ralph Benson, who took four weeks off from his job to share his expertise in a field where I was sorely deficient.

To David Conachy, photographic editor of the *Sunday Independent*, for helping to select and assemble the photographs.

To my editor at Penguin, Brendan Barrington, who made my task much more difficult by his conscientious insistence that it was important to back up my instinct for sweeping generalizations with tiresome evidence. His criticisms and suggestions have improved the story immeasurably. I am deeply grateful to him.

To my wife Ruth, who never complained about my long absences – a tendency which, on reflection, could be a cause for alarm, not gratitude. She was endlessly indulgent of my latest little obsession and listened patiently when I complained of the daily spat with whoever crossed my path.

I dedicate the book to my younger brother Connolly, who died suddenly in December 2007, and to my great friend Paul Tansey, who would have written it much better. Paul died equally sadly in September 2008. They are both badly missed.

Prologue

26 November 2008
It was the bankers' last supper.

The banking crisis was at fever pitch; the nation's finances were in peril; but Ireland's banking elite was celebrating in a private room in a discreet hostelry near Dublin's St Stephen's Green.

The occasion was ostensibly to mark the retirement of the chairman of the Financial Regulator, Brian Patterson. At the time the watchdog was in the wars, but Ireland's bankers wanted to give Patterson a good send-off. Patterson had, in fact, retired seven months earlier, but his departure was a good hook for a meeting of allies under siege.

Dinner with the watchdogs was part of the job; but it was important that no news of the party leaked to the media. Nor did it. The bankers were all careful not to be spotted as they entered and left. Any media story that the regulators were living it up with the bankers would have been dynamite. A view that the two groups were far too cosy was gaining credibility with the public by the day.

Patterson's chief executive at the Financial Regulator, the beleaguered Patrick Neary, was another guest of honour at the dinner. During the previous six weeks Neary had been the target of a wave of media criticism for his handling of the unfolding crisis that had caused the government to guarantee the liabilities of the Irish banks.

Not used to the spotlight, Neary had made matters worse. A disastrous interview on RTÉ's *Prime Time* programme on

2 October had exposed the normally camera-shy regulator to tough scrutiny. Two weeks later Neary had been grilled by an Oireachtas committee. Calls for his resignation were surfacing as he tried to explain his failure to cool the bankers' lending to the property market. Michael Casey, a retired economist at the Central Bank, had broken ranks with his former employer and exposed the watchdog's flaws. In the *Irish Times* of 14 October he had highlighted the crux of the problem: 'Close relationships between regulators and banks – difficult to avoid in a small country – will have to be ended.'

The hush-hush dinner was a sure sign that the relationship was still close, despite public unease about the mutual admiration between bankers and regulators. Pat Neary was in his comfort zone that night as he tucked into the strip loin of tender beef. Mary O'Dea, Neary's high-profile number two, and Con Horan, the watchdog's prudential director, were happily mixing it with those whom they so often supervised. Jim Farrell, Patterson's successor in the chair, was there too, dining at the only table in the room, laid for twenty-two. Farrell was a popular choice of successor for the bankers as he himself had been one of their own over a thirty-year career with Citibank.

Brian Patterson was not the only diner in the departure lounge on that November night. Within months many of the invitees would find that this was their last bankers' supper.

Eugene Sheehy, the smooth-talking head of AIB, was enjoying the evening, exuding his trademark calm amid the turmoil in the industry. According to one of those sitting close to him, 'Nothing seemed to be ruffling Eugene.'

Sheehy would be gone from AIB within six months, having been forced into a humiliating climbdown from his proud boast that AIB would not accept government funding.

Close to Sheehy sat Richie Boucher, the Zambian-born

chief executive of Bank of Ireland's Irish retail division. Barely three months later Boucher would succeed Brian Goggin as chief executive after Bank of Ireland too accepted a state bailout.

Irish Life sent along its top man, Denis Casey, a workaholic with an inscrutable manner. Casey was no great partygoer, but dinner with the regulators was a diplomatic and political imperative.

Within three months Casey was out of a job.

Fergus Murphy, the new chief executive of the EBS, attended this gathering of the oligarchy, nursing the fear that his own building society was another that might soon need a leg-up from the state. Murphy, untainted by EBS's disastrous move into commercial property just as the market was peaking, would later emerge as one of the few survivors of the last supper.

His rival at Irish Nationwide Building Society, Michael Fingleton, sent his apologies. Around the table the diners speculated that the controversial 'Fingers' was a no-show because he was smarting from a recent humiliation. He was the only Irish banker ever to have been fined by Neary or any other watchdog. A month earlier, provoked by constant taunting about his softness on the banks, Neary had fined Irish Nationwide €50,000 after Fingers's son – a London employee of the building society – had referred to the Irish government's guarantee of bank liabilities in an email seeking deposits from UK-based customers. His action was politically sensitive because Minister for Finance Brian Lenihan had already faced down opposition from the British government over its claim that the guarantee would give Irish banks an unfair competitive advantage. Lenihan made his displeasure known, and the fine followed swiftly; but it was a one-off, a token gesture.

Anglo Irish Bank chief executive David Drumm, a regular at bankers' bashes, accepted the invitation but pulled out at the last minute. A few months earlier Drumm had attended a similar event to honour the retiring chairman of the Revenue Commissioners, Frank Daly. In a weird twist of fate, before the end of the year Daly was to be appointed a director of none other than Anglo. On this November night, two months on from the state guarantee that was generally viewed as having been enacted to save Anglo, Drumm sent along a senior director, Peter Butler, in his place. Within four weeks Drumm would resign from Anglo when it was discovered that his chairman, Sean FitzPatrick, had been playing ducks and drakes with his personal loans from the battered bank. The Financial Regulator had never noticed.

FitzPatrick was not invited to the dinner as it was not for chairmen like himself, AIB's Dermot Gleeson, Irish Life's Gillian Bowler, the EBS's Mark Moran, Irish Nationwide's Michael Walsh, or the clubbable Richard Burrows of Bank of Ireland.

All bar Bowler would be shafted within months.

Pat Neary was one of the most popular people at the party. He had been assuring all those around him that Ireland's banks were well capitalized and that the Financial Regulator was working effectively. Neary was in denial.

In fact, denial was the common dish at the dinner, happily shared by both bankers and watchdog. Two months earlier, on 18 September, Neary had done the bankers a big favour when he banned short selling of bank stocks. But he could not save himself. Six weeks on from the congenial bankers' dinner he would be smelling the roses as he surveyed the carnage he left behind him.

The dinner was hosted by Pat Farrell, the president of the Irish Banking Federation. Farrell, a former Fianna Fáil general secretary, was believed to have the ear of the Minister for Finance. Farrell welcomed everyone, uttered a few kind words about 'Brian' and handed over to Patterson. The departing chairman defended his tenure at the helm, insisting that the 'principles-based' system of monitoring the banks had encouraged overseas banks to come to Ireland. In fact, it was a euphemism for a policy of letting the bankers run their own shows.

Here was the Irish banking aristocracy in action, wining and dining their regulators in undisturbed luxury just as a local volcano was erupting before their eyes.

1. Before the Bubble

Rogue bankers were not sudden arrivals to the Ireland of 2008. Regulators being fêted by bankers was nothing new. There had been bailouts before, and small cliques had frequently seized control of banks – all to the detriment of taxpayers. Nor were today's bankers the first buccaneers to create a culture of the cavalier pursuit of quick riches. They were the inheritors of that culture.

Ireland has a shameful banking history, not a proud one. For over thirty years Ireland has been cursed by banking scandals. While the smaller scandals and the smaller banks have come and gone, the activities of the larger ones suggest that banking skulduggery is endemic.

For many years the two big banks in Ireland had a free run. The formation of the Bank of Ireland Group and Allied Irish Banks – AIB – in the late sixties virtually shut off commercial openings for many outsiders. A retail duopoly was born.

AIB was formed in 1966 as a merger of three well-established banks: Provincial Bank of Ireland, Royal Bank of Ireland and Munster & Leinster. The Bank of Ireland formed the second part of the duopoly by way of a takeover by the old Bank of Ireland of the Hibernian Bank in 1958 and of the National Bank in 1965. The size of the two big banks' balance sheets and branch operations made it difficult for others to break their stranglehold over the retail network until the foreign invaders arrived in the 1990s.

However, the door was not completely closed. Reputable transatlantic banks –such as Citibank, Chase Manhattan and

Bank of Nova Scotia – entered the Irish market, but only in niche areas. The state banks, together with ICC and ACC, meanwhile plodded along with specialist roles. ICC was set up as the Industrial Credit Corporation to assist industry, while the ACC was established to provide credit for agriculture. Alongside them the building societies lived for decades in a shadowy world of their own.

It is often forgotten that, in the thirty-odd years prior to the crisis that enveloped Irish banking in the autumn of 2008, several small Irish banks went bust and one of the major players – AIB – was rescued by the state in 1985. AIB was too big for the state to countenance a collapse, but the same could not be said of less sizeable sinners.

Ken Bates, Joe Moore and Patrick Gallagher are names that hardly hold an honoured place in Irish banking history. All three managed to own or operate banks in Ireland in a manner that foreshadowed the career of Sean FitzPatrick. Like Fitz-Patrick, all three dominated the banks they ran. And like FitzPatrick, all three went belly-up.

Ken Bates is a character who could not be invented. He is most famous worldwide for selling Chelsea Football Club, which he had bought in 1982 for £1, to Russian oligarch Roman Abramovich in 2003, but he had a long and colourful career in a number of different ventures before that. Born in 1931, he enjoyed early success in the concrete business, selling his company for £545,000, a staggering sum in 1963. He moved on to the exotic financial waters of the British Virgin Islands, and emerged with his pockets bulging from a massive settlement from the British government after the failure of a development project there.

In 1971 Bates managed to bag a banking licence from Ireland's sleepy regulators. In considering Bates's application, the Central Bank inexplicably failed to discover a readily accessible time bomb: Bates had been connected to a publicly quoted UK company, Howarth of Burnley, that had gone into receivership – and he had not emerged favourably from the receiver's report.

With the Irish Trust Bank, Bates followed a well-worn path. He offered depositors higher interest rates than his competitors and attracted enough cash to make some risky investments, mostly in property; he also targeted the middle-sized Irish business market.

The Central Bank eventually found out about Howarth of Burnley and tried to remedy its mistake by forcing Bates to resign as an unsuitable director of a bank. Bates took the Central Bank to the Four Courts, where the judges ruled in his favour. Among his opponents in that case was one of Ireland's most celebrated civil servants and central bankers, Ken Whitaker.

As the recession of the early seventies began to bite, property prices tumbled and Irish Trust Bank started making losses. Bates's earlier battles with the Central Bank ensured that the regulators were lying in wait, ready to ambush him. They discovered anonymous offshore borrowers and large loans to companies controlled by Bates himself while Irish Trust Bank was in the red. These discoveries, combined with a lack of transparency, made them question the bank's solvency. In February 1976, the High Court revoked Bates's licence. At the high point of the drama, the day that the liquidation was due to come into force, a defiant Bates was arrested for re-entering the Irish Trust Bank's headquarters and removing files. He later returned them under orders from the court.

The Irish Trust Bank was dispensable: it had not established itself as a vital artery of the Irish banking system. Depositors in Bates's bank were in danger of losing their money. But happily for them, a general election beckoned. Fianna Fáil's shadow finance minister, George Colley, offered to bail out the lucky depositors if his party was returned to power in 1977. It was. And Colley delivered.

According to Simon Carswell's excellent book *Something Rotten: Irish Banking Scandals*, as recently as 2005 Bates reminisced that his 'only regret' about his days in Ireland was that 'we didn't make Irish Trust Bank into what Anglo Irish Bank is today. We tried to merge them at one point and call it the Anglo Irish Trust Bank.'

The mind boggles.

Bates has little contact with Ireland nowadays. By chance, former Irish Life & Permanent chief David Went bumped into him in Cape Town in January 2009 and told me, 'Bates is in fine fettle, still telling tales of how he took on the Central Bank back in the seventies.'

If Bates slipped into Dublin's banking swamp below the radar, Patrick Gallagher was a starry-eyed local youth who ended up in a Northern Ireland prison, a convicted thief.

In 1974 Gallagher inherited Merchant Banking Ltd from his father, Matt Gallagher. He was only twenty-two and hadn't a bull's notion about banking but simply ran his Merchant Banking as a personal fiefdom to fund some high-wire property plays and his infatuation with horse racing.

Gallagher was a sad case. He was hugely impressed by his late father's buddy, Charles J. Haughey, and was one of the first businessmen to put his hand in his deep pockets to bail out the Fianna Fáil Taoiseach when he faced a crisis with his bankers early in his premiership.

Gallagher was besotted by the high life. He was regularly seen wearing his loud blue pinstriped suit and smoking a cigar in the high-society Bailey restaurant in Dublin's Duke Street or in the Royal Hibernian Hotel. He kept the company of big developers, auctioneers and politicians. Initial success went to his youthful head. He contracted one of the worst doses of folie de grandeur to infect any of the mohair-suited brigade of the sixties and seventies. Within eight years his family business had incurred unsustainable debts of £28 million. He was bust.

Bad personal property investments were his downfall. He had bought the Phoenix Park racecourse, Straffan House (now the K Club) and other trophy properties in an orgy of self-aggrandizement and speculation. His vehicle for the purchases, the Gallagher Group, was being funded by, among others, Merchant Banking – a private piggy bank for his own use and in some cases to help out old friends, such as Charlie Haughey. When Merchant Banking collapsed, it emerged that Haughey owed the failed bank over €17,000. No effort had ever been made by Merchant Banking to seek repayment over the six-year life of the loans. Gallagher's other creditors closed in and put the Gallagher Group and Merchant Banking into liquidation. Patrick Gallagher ended up serving a two-year jail sentence in Northern Ireland for theft, having pillaged clients' personal accounts to bolster his doomed ventures.

Gallagher's story is a personal tragedy of a young man, infatuated with the trappings of wealth, whose head was turned by the glamorous lifestyle and powerful connections handed to him by his father. He paid a lifelong penalty. In his later years he was seen around Dublin, sometimes intoxicated, broke but lacking in bitterness. He would often inhabit old haunts like the Shelbourne Hotel, regaling acquaintances with fantasy plans, one of which was to build a Charles Haughey Memorial Hospital. He died in the spring of 2006 aged just fifty-four.

The lesson of Gallagher's unhappy story was not lost on
the critics – and the beneficiaries – of a loose banking regime
in Dublin. Although Gallagher had been sentenced to prison
in Northern Ireland, he was never charged with as much as
the theft of a paperclip in the Republic. Paddy Shortall, the
liquidator of Gallagher's companies, reported that Gallagher
had broken the law in over twenty places. In his findings
Shortall included accusations of false accounting, fraudulent
statements and both bribery and corruption. His report to
the Director of Public Prosecutions listed seventy-nine possible criminal offences. No prosecution was ever taken.

Patrick Gallagher's friend Charlie Haughey was to resurface
yet again in the story of Joe Moore. Wherever there was
money or a dodgy bank, Haughey turned up like a magnet.

During the seventies and eighties Moore built up Ireland's
largest motor insurance company, the Private Motorists'
Protection Association (PMPA). Moore was a staunch republican. His original business ideals were driven by a strong
dislike of British domination of the Irish insurance market.

He started life as a consumer champion but ended up as a
staunch Haugheyite. In 1979 Moore campaigned for Haughey
in his Fianna Fáil leadership battle against George Colley. He
was vindictive in victory; David Andrews, a Fianna Fáil junior
minister under Jack Lynch and fiercely antagonistic to Haughey,
was a victim. Andrews, a barrister by profession, returned to
the Law Library after being sacked by Haughey. Moore had
lobbied Andrews to vote for Haughey in the leadership battle;
after Andrews voted for Colley instead, Moore withdrew
Andrews's PMPA briefs – and much of his livelihood – for
three months as a punishment. When he was not causing political chaos, Moore was offering cut-price car insurance and
carving out a formidable share of the insurance market.

PMPA owned a bank known as PMPS, the Private Motorists' Provident Society. It took deposits and lent money to small borrowers. Buyers of shares in PMPS were offered cut-price insurance in the parent company. PMPA borrowed heavily from PMPS. The bank was at risk if the insurance company ever folded. PMPS was regulated not by the Central Bank but by the Registrar of Friendly Societies.

PMPA's strategy of cutting premium prices to attract new customers proved fatal. PMPA began paying off claims with new premiums. It could survive as long as enough fresh premiums kept coming in to meet current claims; but it became insolvent when the economy deteriorated. Claims rose and premiums dwindled.

It was unfortunate for Moore that Haughey, his spiritual champion, was out of power when the PMPA crunch came. He had no political friends in the Fine Gael-led coalition which came to power in late 1982. The government appointed an administrator to PMPA, and the PMPS bank was brought down with the insurance company.

Joe Moore had close parallels with Ken Bates and Patrick Gallagher. There is no record of any of them having been challenged by their boards. Moore made all investment decisions at PMPA. He fought the government – not only the Fine Gael-led coalition but also the preceding Fianna Fáil government, in particular commerce minister Des O'Malley, who dubbed Moore an 'unstable megalomaniac'. He also fought the administrator.

Moore eventually lost on all fronts, but his recklessness caused mayhem with the public finances. The government decided that PMPA was too big a company to be allowed to fold. In 1984 the state was forced to impose a 2 per cent levy on all non-life-insurance premiums to raise enough money to bridge the deficit which Moore had left. The levy lasted nearly a decade. The cost of Moore's folly was footed by the taxpayer.

Joe Moore died in 1989, aged eighty, still convinced that the government's decision to appoint an administrator to PMPA was motivated by the personal spleen of the minister Des O'Malley against Moore's pal Charlie Haughey. It was not until 2005 that the final repayments were made to PMPS depositors – a twenty-two-year wait for many small savers.

One man, one bank – the fatal formula in the tales of Joe Moore, Patrick Gallagher and Ken Bates – was bad enough. One family, one building society was even more dangerous. Nothing demonstrates the folly of a financial dynasty better than the story of the Farrells.

Ireland's building societies were originally conceived in the nineteenth century as co-operative organizations owned by their 'members' – i.e. their customers. They had no shareholders to satisfy with their demands for dividends or capital growth. Building societies were supposed to benefit their members by prioritizing cheaper mortgages and better savings rates over corporate profits.

A great theory. The practice was different. From their humble beginnings, Ireland's building societies were slowly hijacked. In the 1980s they began to ape the big finance houses. In the nineties they converted into full-blooded banks. As a result, building society chiefs became bankers, and very rich to boot.

The Irish Temperance Permanent Benefit Building Society was founded in 1884. In 1940, when it changed its name to Irish Permanent, Edmund Farrell Snr was the secretary of the company; by the 1950s he had risen to managing director, and he ran the society until his death in 1975. He was an autocrat who was able to dictate the identity of his successor on his deathbed. This, unsurprisingly, turned out to be his son, also Edmund Farrell.

Young Ed took over at the age of twenty-eight. He had qualified as a doctor, but an inner ear infection forced him to look for another job. His father gave him his chance in the Irish Permanent. He grabbed it.

Despite the cuddliness of their stated ethos, by the 1970s building societies – which included the First National, the Irish Nationwide, the Irish Civil Service and the EBS as well as the Irish Permanent – were far from pillars of virtue. All provided happy homes for deposits destined to stay beyond the taxman's scrutiny. They had a clear edge over the banks in that they were not compelled to return the names of their depositors to the taxman. Whereas banks sent on depositors' details to the Revenue, building societies deducted tax from deposits at source and sent a cheque to the taxman. Hoards of hot money – cash on which other tax would be owing if the Revenue knew about it – headed for this more discreet home.

The secrecy of building society deposits made a mighty difference in the war to attract customers: the societies' share of the savings market rocketed from 5 per cent in 1965 to 18 per cent in 1985. They advertised the benefits of 'confidentiality' for those who saved with them. High income tax and capital gains tax in the seventies and eighties had ensured that the black economy ballooned in Ireland; because they were not obliged to identify deposit holders, the building societies were nicely positioned to hoover up much of the hot money floating around at the time. Everybody knew that this was happening: government knew about it; the taxman knew about it; the Central Bank knew about it; the top brass in the building societies knew about it; the customers loved it.

There is no record of any director of these building societies expressing any unhelpful curiosity about the hot-money issue. It appears that these pillars of society, perched on the boards of financial institutions with quasi-bank status, were perfectly content to preside over tax evaders' honeypots – and of course they were under no legal obligation to investigate the source of customer deposits or to seek tax returns before an account was opened. That was financial propriety, Irish-style. The state feared a flight of capital from the country if it demanded the identity of the depositors. Another reason for the lack of scrutiny was that the building societies were providing mortgages to a young population, offering a social service as well as making money for themselves. Too much official probing about the source of their deposits could have prompted a sudden exit of funds – and consequently fewer available mortgages. The black economy was entrenched in the financial system and underpinned the mortgage market.

If there was ever any doubt about the dodginess of many building society deposits, it was dispelled in 1994, when the Irish Permanent was floated on the Stock Exchange. Members of the now-former building society were eligible for free shares, and yet many members declined to claim them. Claiming ownership of the shares would have flushed tax dodgers out of the cupboard of secrecy. Their names would have appeared on a share register. Some preferred to forgo the shares rather than to make their deposits known to the tax authorities.

As a response to the competitive advantage of the building societies, the Bank of Ireland eventually took the 'if you can't beat them, join them' route. In 1985 they bought the Irish Civil Service Building Society, partly as a means of tapping into these hot deposits. Other banks, seeing the Bank of Ireland now sporting both banking and building society hats, cried 'Foul'. In 1986 the government levelled the playing field, putting all financial institutions on the same tax basis. In future all banks and building societies were to pay Deposit Interest Retention Tax (DIRT) at the same rate. Suddenly building societies stood to lose their hot deposits and needed capital to compete in the rapidly deregulating banking world. Ed Farrell Jr was the first of the building society bosses to launch the process of converting his institution into a bank, capitalized via a stock-market flotation – a move that would necessarily involve the forfeit of some of his vast power to run the Irish Permanent as he saw fit.

It was a ground-breaking move. Unfortunately for Farrell it meant that many of his and the society's questionable earlier activities had to be revealed to prospective investors.

Farrell had been the beneficiary of several unusual transactions. His board had agreed a hugely generous one-off restrictive covenant payment of £300,000 to stop him working for any other building society. He was given a twenty-seven-year contract. Most bizarre of all, he had sold his mansion in Dublin's leafy Foxrock to the building society in a deal that gave him a tenancy on ultra-generous terms and the right to buy the house back at the sale price of £275,000 – a right he exercised in 1991. In the meantime the society had spent £437,000 on improvements, and the mansion was now valued at £600,000. Such unorthodox deals might have been the norm for building societies under the thumb of one man, but were not considered acceptable behaviour for public companies.

As Farrell prepared for the flotation in 1994, he recruited lieutenants to serve under him as executive directors of the new bank. These included an ex-AIB boss Roy Douglas, former consultant Peter Fitzpatrick, and Peter Ledbetter, who came from GPA, the aviation leasing company that had gone bust as a result of a botched stock-market flotation in

1992. None of them were heavyweights, but they carried sufficient street cred to satisfy the needs of investors pondering the flotation.

Stock Exchange rules required full disclosure of certain deals made in the two years preceding a flotation. Some of Farrell's deals with Irish Permanent had taken place within the two-year period, and so he wanted to delay the flotation for long enough to avoid the need for disclosure.

Douglas, Fitzpatrick and Ledbetter took the view that it was Farrell or the flotation, and they – together with other directors – forced Farrell out. His transactions with the society had made him an embarrassment to the new arrivals on the board, who regarded him as unsuitable for the head of a publicly quoted company.

Irish Permanent floated on the Stock Exchange without Farrell. The sequel was staggering. Douglas managed to secure a mammoth £201,000 annual salary for himself. Fitzpatrick and Ledbetter pocketed £140,000 each. These were huge salaries for a building society converting into a bank in 1994. Picking at the carcass of the building society, they also helped themselves to a bonanza of share options granted at the flotation price.

Following the flotation the Irish Permanent took Farrell to court. They wanted the Foxrock house back. Farrell countersued for wrongful dismissal. After a day of spectacular charges in the High Court the two sides settled. This was wise: the lid had been lifted on Irish business practices for a day, and too many powerful people had too much to lose. Farrell kept the house and dropped his wrongful-dismissal case.

Soon after Farrell left, it emerged that Irish Permanent had owned a little-known subsidiary, a patent royalty company called Irish Permanent Technology. Farrell had received

£200,000 in tax-free dividends from the company, which exploited a legal tax loophole for patent royalty income. Douglas, widely seen as a crusader for virtue after deposing Farrell, had drawn £100,000 from the same source.

Years later two of the men who had banished Farrell were to meet ends that they would not have chosen. Douglas retired unexpectedly as chairman of Irish Life & Permanent in 2004 just before being linked with an offshore share-dealing operation during his earlier career at AIB. He later made a settlement of €53,000 with the tax authorities. Fitzpatrick resigned as IL&P finance director following revelations in February 2009 that the bancassurer had conspired with Anglo in a deposit swap intended to make Anglo's year-end balance sheet look better. Farrell must have smiled as he saw his protégés-turned-adversaries toppled from their lofty towers.

If Ed Farrell was an old-fashioned autocrat, the men who deposed him turned out to be forerunners of the greed that was to destroy Irish banking in the decade to come, when some of Ireland's biggest bankers enriched themselves to an extent that would set a standard never before experienced on Ireland's corporate boards.

The excesses at the Irish Permanent, and the sharp practices of some small-time financiers and their finance houses, were not a one-off. The two big banks ran their own rackets. Prior to the eighties AIB and Bank of Ireland escaped allegations of scandal, but they quickly learned the ways of some of their smaller rivals. Both pursued unsavoury practices behind a façade of plummy voices, expensive education, smart suits and the cloak of noble histories.

These institutions' pretensions to nobility were skin-deep. What they did have was size. In spades. So big were they that governments buckled at the knee when the banks rattled their sabres.

AIB escaped major controversy or scandal throughout the seventies. It watched as Bates, Gallagher, Moore and finally Farrell bit the dust. It is difficult to explain why AIB so completely lost the run of itself during the eighties and nineties. It was always more of a meritocracy than the Bank of Ireland. AIB had started to poach talent from the civil service in the sixties, while Bank of Ireland continued to recruit through its network of well-connected children of the elite. In 1983, having made a decision to diversify abroad, AIB bought into First Maryland Bancorp in the United States. In the same year it completed the purchase of Insurance Corporation of Ireland (ICI). Despite its name, ICI did most of its business from its London office, underwriting high-risk business. Its UK business was managed by a mover and shaker called John Grace, who gained a reputation as a man who would take risks, underwriting projects others would not touch.

Business was booming – but then in the mid-eighties the insurance market hit a downturn. Reinsurance and underwriting claims started to snowball at exactly the moment when premiums began to drop off. ICI, with its high-risk projects, was the most vulnerable insurance company in London.

AIB had initially taken a laissez-faire approach to Grace's strategy. The home team was happy to see mushrooming premiums in 1983 and early 1984. But by summer 1984 the government's industry minister, John Bruton, had become alarmed at the size of the claims. He was given assurances by AIB that they were pumping in £40 million to strengthen ICI's balance sheet. At the same time AIB sent in a team of investigators to ascertain ICI's real losses. These turned out to be on such a scale as to threaten to bring down not only ICI, but AIB itself.

AIB decided to pull the plug. They left it to the eleventh hour to warn the government of the impending calamity. In a series of meetings between AIB bosses and top politicians, the leaders of Ireland's biggest bank put a gun to the head of the government. They told Taoiseach Garret FitzGerald, finance minister Alan Dukes and Bruton that AIB would go to the wall if the government did not ride to the rescue immediately. The government blinked first, agreeing to underwrite all ICI's debts. That was bad enough. It was worse still that this was a blank cheque. No one knew the extent of the losses at ICI. The Irish government bailed out a bank in distress rather than let it go to the wall.

AIB had pulled a coup in the ICI crisis. Its representatives at the talks with ministers were led by chief executive Gerry Scanlan and his deputy Dermot Egan. Scanlan was the rough diamond of the pair – robust and brash. Egan was a smoother creature, the good cop in the negotiations, an old-style banker who relished membership of the directors' circuit. He was in the mould of many of the later AIB board. He would have fitted in comfortably at the Dublin 4 dinner tables of later chairmen such as Peter Sutherland, Lochlann Quinn, or Dermot Gleeson.

A story is told of Egan which sums up the attitudes of many of his breed. Sometime in the early nineties Egan, recently retired from AIB, met Charlie Haughey, recently retired as Taoiseach. They compared notes on retirement. Charlie, polite as always, asked Dermot what he was doing, now that he was retired. The ex-banker pulled himself up to his full height. Looking down on the little politician, he puffed out his chest: 'Well, I am on the council of the Irish Management Institute; I chair the National Concert Hall;

I am a Companion of the Institute of Personnel Development; I am chairman of the Philately Advisory Council; I am on the board of the Glucksman Gallery and have a host of other interests. Busier than ever. And, Charlie, what are you doing now?'

Charlie looked the silver-tongued ex-AIB chief straight in the eye. 'Same as yourself, Dermot. Shag all.'

Egan was an effective advocate for AIB in 1985. AIB walked away from the ICI debacle, landing the baby in the government's lap. It was not the last time that the banks would hold a government to ransom. The prospect of a collapse of AIB was too catastrophic for ministers to contemplate.

Eventually AIB did grudgingly agree to pay over some money for its part in the fiasco: it consented to pay €5.5 million a year while the other banks were forced to pony up much lesser amounts. But AIB astonished FitzGerald and Dukes by carrying on as if nothing had happened. A few weeks after the rescue was completed the bank announced profits of £85.4 million, plus a dividend, without batting an eyelid. It was two fingers from the bank to the government. The taxpayer picked up the poisonous part of the package while the shareholders walked off with a dividend as though nothing had happened. In the end the taxpayer did not lose out, partly due to a 1992 deal done by commerce minister Des O'Malley, who insisted that AIB should pay more. But the entire affair left a sour taste in the mouths of politicians who felt outplayed and threatened by a bank that had taken advantage of its size.

The sourest taste of all was left by Gerry Scanlan. The man ultimately responsible for the sorry episode was one of the principal beneficiaries. Scanlan bought 50,000 AIB shares at a depressed level during the ICI crisis; not long after the government bailout his purchase was showing a paper profit of more than £80,000. He had received clearance for the purchase from AIB chairman Niall Crowley and the board.

The failure of ICI, together with AIB's need for a government bailout, was due to a bad, but arguably pardonable, commercial decision. The DIRT scandal was worse. Nearly all the banks were caught up in this massive scam, but AIB was the one that blazed the DIRT trail.

It worked like this: depositors were informed that if they used bogus offshore addresses they would not have to pay Deposit Interest Retention Tax (DIRT). Bogus non-resident accounts became the rage. AIB managed to build up a base of 53,000 customers signing declarations that they lived in the US, the UK – anywhere except the Irish Republic. Tax cheating was the business. And it was obviously fine if your local bank manager was promoting it.

Luckily for the nation, not everybody in AIB was happy to co-operate with this organized tax evasion. Internal auditor Tony Spollen blew a whistle that led to the famous Dáil Committee hearings into this institutionalized illegality. At the hearings Spollen fingered many of his former colleagues and clashed with Gerry Scanlan in at least one bitter exchange. AIB unconvincingly claimed that they had done a deal with the Revenue, which had granted them an amnesty. The Revenue strenuously denied this claim. The Committee found against the bank.

At the end of the inquiry it was clear that bankers were not the only players aware of shady activities. Central bankers, politicians, civil servants and other powerful forces must have known what was going on. Bankers were competing against each other to create bogus offshore business. When Liam Collins broke the story in the *Sunday Independent* he revealed that AIB had secured over £600 million in customer deposits for this racket.

When settlements were eventually reached, AIB agreed to hand over £90 million to the state in tax, interest and penalties. Bank of Ireland took the runner-up position, paying £30 million. Even the ACC – a taxpayer-owned bank – had to pay £18 million. In total the state recouped over £225 million.

Not a single member of the staff of any of the banks is known to have paid more than a cursory price. In at least one case the manager of a branch that had been top of the DIRT bogus account league found himself promoted.

The regulator was made a monkey of again in 2004, when AIB made a clean breast of several other breaches. One of these – a tax evasion scheme being run, not for customers, but for top people in the bank – became known as the Faldor scandal.

Faldor was an investment company set up in the Virgin Islands for the benefit of senior AIB executives. The funds in the company were managed by Allied Irish Investment Managers (AIIM) on their behalf. AIB admitted in 2004 that top brass at the bank – Gerry Scanlan, Roy Douglas (formerly of AIB and latterly of Irish Life), the one-time AIB deputy chief executive, Patrick Dowling, and the former director of corporate strategy, Diarmuid Moore – had benefited from this scheme located far away from the prying eyes of the Irish taxman.

Sensationally and simultaneously AIB decided to hang its last chief executive, Tom Mulcahy, out to dry for an unrelated tax offence. An AIB statement revealed that five top executives had 'tax issues'. The first four were the Faldor quartet and the fifth was Mulcahy. Following his retirement from the bank Mulcahy had taken up the prestigious post of chairman of the state-owned Aer Lingus. After a brief conversation about his 'tax issue' with his political boss, transport minister Seamus Brennan, Mulcahy resigned. He also stepped down from the board of the publicly quoted insulation company Kingspan.

Scanlan, Douglas, Moore and Dowling pleaded innocence of any wrongdoing in the Faldor case. They said they had been led to believe by AIB's investment managers that their investments in Faldor were part of a legitimate scheme. They were astonished; they were shocked; they blamed AIB. All four appeared on the tax defaulters list. Gerry Scanlan paid up €206,000 in settlement of his tax liabilities. Roy Douglas forked out €53,000. Moore coughed up €51,000 and Dowling made a settlement of €13,000. They were embarrassed but bit the bullet and brazened it out.

Worse still for AIB was its confession that AIIM had used Faldor for 'misallocating' profits. Favoured clients in Faldor had been allocated artificial profits while ordinary clients had been deprived of those due to them. AIB agreed to pay compensation to any clients who had lost out on the allocation of profits.

It was a devastating admission. It implied that AIB had been playing ducks and drakes with clients' discretionary money. Behind closed doors in the Virgin Islands its investment managers had been allocating profits to their favourite sons in preference to other clients. Trust in the bank's investment arm was shattered.

In admitting the 'tax issues' of the five, AIB seemed to have made a break with the past. Was it dumping on its former employees to draw a line in the sand? Perhaps, but it subsequently emerged that the Faldor investment scheme was only rumbled because Roy Douglas had decided to disclose a tax debt owed from his Faldor exploits. He informed the Revenue Commissioners and AIB. The can of worms would have opened, with everything leaking out eventually. Like all good spinners, AIB took control of the bad news and put it into a single press release. They hoped the latest bombshells would be a one-week wonder.

When AIB was challenged by politicians, the governments bottled it. When confronted by the press, the bankers clammed up, pleading confidentiality. When challenged by the regulator . . . they were never challenged by the regulator. AIB's size was the most obvious explanation for this, but the distinguished make-up of the bank's board over the years may also have been a factor. In the early eighties the board of AIB featured blue-blooded names like Niall Crowley of the famous Dublin accountancy family – the 'Crowley' in Stokes Kennedy Crowley – Sir Peter Froggatt, former Vice Chancellor of Queen's University Belfast, and Maurice Abrahamson, a pillar of the stockbroking community.

Gonzaga-educated Peter Sutherland took over as chairman in 1990. He was succeeded by Jim Culliton, whose distinguished business reputation was destroyed when it was revealed that he had been a secret investor in the illegal Ansbacher investment scheme run by Haughey's bagman, Des Traynor. The same AIB board included former rugby international Ray McLoughlin, who admitted to the Moriarty Tribunal investigating Haughey's finances that he had composed the infamous thirty-six-page memo to John Furze, the man who operated the Ansbacher accounts for banker Des Traynor in the Cayman Islands, outlining a strategy for tax avoidance.

Lochlann Quinn, who succeeded Culliton as chairman, was a Blackrock College boy who went on to UCD. He was

a great friend and near neighbour of Sutherland in Ballsbridge. Quinn's successor in the chair was drawn from the
same pool: Dermot Gleeson, like Sutherland, was a former
Fine Gael Attorney General. Like Quinn, he was educated at
Blackrock and UCD. He too lived in Ballsbridge.

Gleeson had ingratiated himself with Quinn and AIB when
he mounted a sterling legal defence of the indefensible at the
DIRT hearings. Soon afterwards he was parachuted on to
the board and later into the chair.

The difference on the scandal scale between AIB and Bank
of Ireland – the other pillar of the duopoly – was remarkable.
Bank of Ireland were no angels but they did not run amok.

Apologists for the Bank of Ireland sometimes explain its
lower level of offences through its recruitment policy, which
targeted employees from affluent backgrounds; according to
this theory, Bank of Ireland was less hungry. Tom Mulcahy
of AIB was once asked the question about the difference
between the two banks' cultures and answered: 'When chasing a client, Bank of Ireland would politely knock at the front
door and wait for an answer. AIB salesmen would head
straight for a back window with a crowbar.'

Certainly the Bank of Ireland seems more genteel in its
traditions. In the seventies and eighties its board and management was peppered with names like Harvey-Kelly,
Lewis-Crosby and Hely Hutchinson.

Bank of Ireland flaunts its history. In 1802 it bought the
Irish parliament building in College Green, Dublin – redundant after the Act of Union – for £40,000. The building
remained its headquarters until 1970. It has preserved the
House of Lords chamber for display to the public to this
day, and the building remains a flagship for the bank. It was
the banker to the Irish government from the foundation of

the state in 1922 until 1971; as a consequence it was often confused with the Central Bank, a confusion that it probably benefited from.

The Bank of Ireland's traditions were reflected in its governors (i.e. chairmen) and directors. As recently as the 1960s they often sat on the board to represent the bank's biggest customers. Paddy McGrath looked after the multiple interests of his famous family, which included the Irish Sweepstakes and the Irish Glass Bottle Company. Jameson's whiskey propelled Uppingham-educated Alec Crichton into the governorship in the early sixties, while Powers whiskey boss, Ampleforth-educated John Archibald Ryan, was twice governor in this earlier period. Don Carroll of the Carroll's tobacco family also did two turns in the governor's seat, finishing his second term in 1985. Carroll came via Glenstal and later Trinity College Dublin.

The governors plucked from the ranks of the captains of industry were interspersed with academics. Two professors of distinction, Bill Finlay from the UCD law faculty and Louden Ryan from the Trinity economics department, served five-year terms. Two of the last three governors, Howard Kilroy and Laurence Crowley, have been part of an inner circle of Irish businessmen who seem to land on the boards of public companies with uncanny ease. The last governor, Richard Burrows, spent many years as chief executive of Irish Distillers, a stock-market leader before it was taken over by French drinks giant Pernod Ricard. The French company employed Burrows as joint managing director until his retirement. His insider status was confirmed when he was made president of Ireland's insiders' big business club, IBEC, in 1998.

In the mid-eighties the Bank of Ireland was deeply embarrassed by one of its board members. Russell Murphy landed on the board of the Bank of Ireland when it bought Hibernian

Bank, where he had been a director. He was that unusual animal, a colourful accountant. He was generally regarded as eccentric but brilliant. A daily communicant, he was given to fits of generosity, supplying theatre tickets and flowers to friends and acquaintances at the drop of a hat. He regularly took pilgrimages to Lourdes. He was a convincing character when regaling listeners on the topic of money or investments. Several high-profile celebrity figures allowed him to manage their finances.

In 1986 Russell Murphy died. Within days of his funeral it emerged that his affairs were in chaos. Ireland's premier broadcaster of the eighties, Gay Byrne, had entrusted Murphy with his life savings, but Murphy left nothing in the kitty. The late playwright Hugh Leonard lost at least £250,000.

The Bank of Ireland had let a cowboy into the holy of holies. The board was deeply embarrassed. Russell was explained away as the exception to the otherwise untainted integrity of the 'Court', as the bank's board grandly styled itself.

Russell Murphy was not the only board member to upset the apple cart in the eighties. Entrepreneur Tony Ryan, the founder of Guinness Peat Aviation, was then at the height of his powers. Ryan used much of his wealth to buy 5 per cent of the Bank of Ireland's share capital. He caused consternation by forcing his way on to a board that was accustomed to selecting fellow members from among its friends in Dublin's inner circle of favoured businessmen. Ryan was an outsider. Old hands on the board looked on him with deep suspicion, suspecting that he wanted to take over the bank. One contemporary board member told me recently that Ryan was a difficult director: 'He wasn't used to not being in the chair.' Another told me, 'Tony was a hugely divisive influence. He was quite obviously linking up with outsiders whose interest in the Bank of Ireland was questionable. There were multiple leaks to the media about what was happening at the Court during his period there . . . Once Howard Kilroy took over as governor from Louden Ryan in 1991, the game was up for Tony. Howard made it clear that he was in charge and was set for a six- or even nine-year term. Tony left and the leaks ended.'

Ryan left long before the DIRT scandal made the rest of the board blush to their patrician roots. Even to this day the Bank of Ireland finds the issue of DIRT tax evasion difficult to face. The bank that was formed by Royal Charter was up to its eyeballs in defrauding the Revenue Commissioners.

The Bank of Ireland had scored some spectacular own goals in the DIRT affair. The name of Miltown Malbay will be remembered for generations as the star performer in the Irish DIRT championship stakes. The Bank of Ireland's outlaw activity in the sleepy Clare town put it on the map for all the wrong reasons. A former Bank of Ireland director told me: 'The managers in the branches would have known of the disapproval from the top of the bogus non-resident account activity. But [then chief executive] Mark [Hely Hutchinson]'s morality would not have been understood down in Cahirciveen or Miltown Malbay. Dublin is a long way away. Local managers would invariably respond that customers were telling them that unless their deposits had non-resident status they would go across the road to AIB.'

Bank of Ireland chiefs eventually came out with their hands up over DIRT evasion. They paid €30 million over to the taxman, much of it in penalties and interest. They wriggled and squirmed. A spokesman used weasel words to claim that they 'had a lesser scale of issue' than AIB; but they had swallowed their moral scruples and joined the other banks in the scam. They would have been aware that it was highly unlikely that anyone in the bank would have to pay a penalty.

Bank of Ireland's weak defence – the competitive need to break the law – held less water in one of its other rackets. By the mid-nineties they had discovered a more sophisticated way of ducking DIRT. Bank managers identified high-net-worth individuals and persuaded them to move their secret hoards to Jersey to avoid DIRT and to ensure confidentiality.

By the time the taxman got wind of this confidential tax evasion service, about 400 Irish residents had availed them-selves of it. The Revenue approached the Bank of Ireland, which agreed to write to customers saying they'd made an agreement with the Revenue urging them to come out with their hands up. Once the heat was on, the bankers forgot about 'confidentiality'. There was no honour among thieves.

The petty thieves paid the penalty. The chief thief paid nothing. The taxman collected €105 million from the Bank of Ireland's Jersey racket alone. Several of the individual settlements came in at over €1 million. Once again, no banker was punished for this obvious attempt to encourage tax evasion.

The Revenue's success with the Bank of Ireland prompted an investigation into the operations of other Irish banks in Jersey, Guernsey and the Isle of Man, and by March 2005 the authorities had raked in an incredible €812.8 million from Irish residents hiding money in Irish banks overseas. They gathered far more than the earlier collections from DIRT cheats.

Throughout the eighties and nineties the Bank of Ireland continued to stuff its board with the great and the good of Irish business. It replaced an old inner circle with a newer and tighter club of plutocrats. Cross-directorships were legion. At one point in 1998, under Howard Kilroy's governorship, Smurfits and the Bank of Ireland shared three overlapping directors: Kilroy, the glamorous lawyer Mary Redmond, and

former EU commissioner Ray MacSharry shuffled between
board meetings of these two leading quoted companies almost
as if they had birthrights to seats at all the top tables. In 1995
the relationship with CRH, the international building materials group, was equally incestuous: Bank of Ireland director
Tony Barry chaired the CRH board, where he would
welcome Bank of Ireland governor Howard and serial director David Kennedy fresh from the last Bank of Ireland board
meeting. Later on, former Bank of Ireland chief executive
Pat Molloy, already a director of CRH, was to move almost
seamlessly from the Court to double up as chairman of the
building materials company. This close connection still
survives. Today consultant Terry Neill enjoys dual membership of both CRH and Bank of Ireland boards while Tony
Barry still sits on the board of DCC along with former Bank
of Ireland director Maurice Keane. Both Bank of Ireland men
dug in as staunch supporters of DCC executive chairman Jim
Flavin, despite an insider dealing verdict against him in the
Supreme Court. The club is holding firm.

The Bank of Ireland inner circle is almost impregnable. At
times, when certain directors sat around a table, they must
have wondered whether they were at meetings of CRH,
Smurfits or the Bank of Ireland itself.

Meanwhile, the fortunes of the bank were far from pros-
pering. All the DIRT disgraces, the offshore scams and the
rush into excessive directors' pay were beginning to emerge.
The directors were ultimately responsible. If there was any
difference between AIB and themselves, it was only a matter
of degree.

The other banks were not far behind. National Irish Bank
was another to be caught in hot water when it was unmasked
in a massive scam and accused of ripping off its customers.
Once again the malpractices were not discovered by the

regulator, but by journalists, in this case RTÉ's George Lee and Charlie Bird.

For decades Ireland's banks have operated in a world where rules were there to be circumvented; where officialdom turned a blind eye to breaches of codes and laws alike; where customers were cattle; where governments underwrote the activities of cowboys in pinstripe suits. Long before the property bubble and the crisis of 2008–9, Ireland was a land where the bankers were almost untouchable and where the banks were run for the bankers.

2. Seanie

Sean FitzPatrick was a little man with a little bank that became a rather big bank. A one-time colleague at Anglo sums him up coldly: 'He suffered from the "small man" syndrome. And like a lot of small men, he drives a big Merc.' Another portrays him as South Dublin's answer to North Dublin's Charlie Haughey.

Strictly speaking, 'Seanie' was not from South Dublin. Born in 1948, he was brought up in Bray just over the Dublin border in County Wicklow. But his background, determination and drive bear close comparisons with the former Taoiseach. Both men were small in stature. Both were self-made. Both cut corners. Both had strong, pushy mothers. And both became super-rich from humble beginnings. Fitz-Patrick's father was a small farmer. His mother had been a civil servant but devoted her life to the rearing of young Sean and his elder sister, Joyce.

At school Joyce was far brighter than Sean. In 2001 he told Ivor Kenny — author of *Leaders: Conversations with Irish Chief Executives* — that she was 'the apple of my father's eye. It was difficult growing up in her shadow. I used to envy her.' Joyce FitzPatrick was later to become a successful academic at UCD and president of the National College of Ireland in Dublin's International Financial Services Centre; today she chairs the Digital Hub Development Agency. In 2004 she was made a director of CRH, Ireland's blue-chip global leader in building materials.

After a year at the Loreto Convent in Bray, Sean was sent

to Presentation College in his home town. 'Pres' was a rare cocktail, a no-fees rugby-playing school. Sean took more readily to the rugby than to the classroom. Tino Cassoni, a lifelong friend whose family have been in the chip business in Bray since 1949, remembers Sean on the rugby pitch: 'He was small, but an aggressive player. At school I was out-half and he was centre. As a pupil Sean was streetwise rather than academically endowed.'

Sean FitzPatrick's schooldays offer little hint of the success that he was to enjoy later in life. He gives great credit to his mother Johanna, describing her as 'dominant, but she would give up anything for her children'. She encouraged financial prudence. His father Michael was more laid back. He would say, 'If you've got money, spend it now.' His mother was a devout Catholic who took Joyce and Sean to mass. Their father never went with them.

Like others of his age, Sean took jobs during the school holidays. At the age of thirteen he worked in the amusement arcades in Bray and was put in charge of the dodgems. At home he remembers herding the cows with his father, putting the milk into churns and bottles and selling it during the weekend.

FitzPatrick captained the junior and senior Pres rugby teams; he never carried off a Leinster Trophy but reached the semi-final. Maurice Mortell, a former Irish rugby international, coached FitzPatrick in Pres for a while. He remembers him as 'the type of guy you would always like, invariably with a smile on his face. He was a smashing little player. He always had bottle to burn. He was deeply competitive.'

As evidence of this highly competitive instinct a rugby-playing colleague tells a story about FitzPatrick's excessive enthusiasm during his days playing for Bective. Sean, normally a centre or a half-back, was on the substitutes bench one

Saturday. Bective scored a spectacular try. A reporter turned to Sean — the substitute — and asked him the name of the scorer. 'Sean FitzPatrick' was the response.

FitzPatrick was no star at exams. Somewhat surprisingly, in the light of his later dazzling career in Anglo, he merely managed a pass in his Leaving Certificate maths. He picked up only a single honour — in French. Nevertheless he squeezed into University College Dublin and set out to do a Bachelor of Commerce degree. Even before he entered UCD Sean had seen 'big money' being earned by chartered accountants and determined to become an accountant.

UCD seems to have been a happy experience. He played plenty of rugby but, despite his limited academic talents, easily passed his annual exams. He told Ivor Kenny that he had been helped by 'looking hard at the system' and realizing that 'college was quite simple if I got all the lecture notes'. He cutely spotted unlikely allies when he befriended the nuns in his classes. 'The nuns were great at taking notes,' he recalled. 'I was the only one who'd have a cup of coffee with them and I ended up with the best set of notes in college.'

Armed with a BComm, Sean set off in search of the big money. In keeping with his modest roots and barely average exam record, Sean did not hit the dizzy heights of the blue bloods in the accountancy profession. In 1969 he joined Reynolds McCarron & O'Connor, a middle-ranking company. At the time, the Irish tax and audit world was dominated by the Big Two — Stokes Kennedy Crowley and Craig Gardner — plus a few others. The Big Two often provided suitable material for the boards of the banking elite. Sean did not fit the bill. But he was a master at acting the accountant. He was always dapper in his dress, even when in articles. One fellow worker from those days tells of Sean's care with his appearance: 'He was the only one who brought a briefcase to work every day. We often wondered what work or papers he carried in it. One day someone opened it. Inside were ham sandwiches wrapped in yesterday's *Irish Times*.'

FitzPatrick's dream of big money from accountancy suffered an early blow. Of all the trainees in the firm finishing their articles he was the only one to be made redundant. But his self-confidence was unaffected, and he easily found a job in another firm, joining Atkins Chirnside & Co, soon to be part of PricewaterhouseCoopers. One of his colleagues there was Charlie McCreevy, later to become Minister for Finance and a lifelong acquaintance. McCreevy told me about working with the young FitzPatrick: 'We spent a long time debating whether to stay as accountants and apply for one of the new jobs being advertised inside the firm. We both fancied our chances. We dithered for weeks arguing the pros and cons. Suddenly we both met turning points in our careers at the same time. While we were dithering I was offered an accountancy post in Naas which enabled me to pursue my political career. Sean was tempted by the Irish Bank of Commerce because they were offering both a job and a loan at a 3 per cent discount to the market. It was the cheap mortgage, not the job, that convinced Sean. That decisive moment in our lives sent me on the road to become Minister of Finance and Sean on the first step to the top of the Anglo Irish Bank ladder . . . In all the years I have known him, he never lost the run of himself. He wasn't into great big houses, no jets. We used to laugh at him because he always sat at the back of the plane.'

In 1976 Sean landed a job as an accountant at Irish Bank of Commerce, a publicly quoted investment bank with a tiny deposit base and just four employees. Not long afterwards Irish Bank of Commerce was taken over by City of Dublin

Bank. Two years later City of Dublin bought Anglo Irish Bank Corporation, known as 'Little Anglo'. Three small banks with complementary strengths merged. City of Dublin was a finance house, Irish Bank of Commerce an investment bank and Little Anglo a middle-market business bank.

Sean soon became financial controller at Irish Bank of Commerce. And finally, in 1980, with his trademark brazenness, he managed to switch horses from accountant to banker. He had been dispatched to Hay Recruitment consultants to arrange the search for a chief executive for Little Anglo. Instead, he had a brainwave. He demanded the job himself. The board decided to take the chance. Little Anglo had gross assets of less than £500,000 (€625,000).

He gradually established Little Anglo as the most profitable element in the group. He demanded a seat on the group's board and persuaded City of Dublin chief executive Gerry Murphy – the most outspoken banker in Ireland – that their two banks should be merged, trading as Anglo Irish. In 1986 the new Anglo Irish Bank, known in the business as 'Big Anglo', was born. Sean was the chief executive, Gerry Murphy the chairman.

At last, here was Sean's chance for the 'big money'. He grabbed it with both hands.

In his early days as chief executive Sean bought a small finance house, a veritable basket case. A partner from the time recalls, 'I think he bought it for fifty grand. It had five hundred thousand in outstanding loans, all doubtful debts. Sean was in his element. He got into his car and called on every borrower. He knew that once he gathered more than the fifty grand purchase price, he was in the black.'

For a while FitzPatrick was more of a glorified debt collector than a banker. He did deals with all the debtors. 'He sized up the country rogues to a tee. He could have gone to the

Ballinrobe horse show all day,' recalls the former colleague with admiration. The venture showed a profit.

FitzPatrick's ruthless streak was tempered by sporadic outbreaks of humanity. Another associate tells of a day when Sean called at the house of a recently widowed woman. She was in tears, and she was broke. Sean headed back to headquarters, drew up a deed of release and wrote off the widow's debt.

But such tales of compassion are rare. In 2005, speaking to Ivor Kenny for his book *Achievers*, Sean told a tale against himself. He and a long-time colleague, Peter Killen, were on the debt-collection trail. They knocked on the door of a house in Lucan. The owner had borrowed money from Anglo for a car; FitzPatrick was intent on forcing repayments.

The debtor answered the door with no shoes on, and asked them inside, where he was cutting potatoes. According to FitzPatrick, the man told the two bankers that he could not delay because the kids were coming home from school. He had crashed the car and his wife had rung the assessor. When the assessor arrived the wife fell in love with him and scarpered, leaving him with the kids. She and her lover had taken the car and sold it.

FitzPatrick was not impressed. He blew a fuse and demanded the money. Peter Killen took FitzPatrick to one side and told him to calm down. Killen headed back to Dublin, drew £250 out of the bank and sent it to the local St Vincent de Paul to buy presents for the kids at Christmas. FitzPatrick told Kenny, 'I would not have supported that then, but I truly learned from it. That was the decency of Peter Killen.'

Initially FitzPatrick did small things to develop the business. He opened at lunchtime, promoting the move by running a celebrated advertisement promoting the bank as a 'legend in its own lunchtime'. It was a deliberate dig at the other major retail banks, virtually none of which opened at lunchtime. Deeply conservative and under no pressure to change their ways, the established banks continued to dictate terms to their customers rather than vice versa. FitzPatrick was making the point that Anglo was different, new and aggressive.

Working conditions in the traditional banks were the envy of other sectors. Costs were high. Red tape was part of the culture. A job in the bank was a job for life. The new boy on the block was determined to upset the apple cart. The older banks were profoundly unionized and thus presented an easy target for FitzPatrick with his tiny workforce. Offering a foretaste of the later doctrine of Ryanair's Michael O'Leary, he never allowed trade unions inside the door.

He set about building a team. It was not easy: the best brains in the established banks were hardly eager to leave the cosy womb of the cartel to jump into bed with a buccaneer. Competition between the main banks was largely illusory. Their mortgage and savings rates had a comfortable similarity. Profits increased steadily. Security of tenure, pensions and short hours were the order of the day.

FitzPatrick managed to entice Tiarnan O'Mahoney from IIB, Bill Barrett and Peter Killen from AIB, and John Rowan from accountancy. By 1990 Tom Browne, who would later be among those jockeying for FitzPatrick's position, had signed up. Browne was to rise rapidly through the ranks to become Head of Dublin Banking in 1997 and a full board member in 2004.

By his own admission FitzPatrick was ruthless at hiring and firing people. It was part of the new culture. His readiness to sack those who had failed contrasted with the ways of other banks, where it was almost impossible for staff members to lose their jobs unless they were caught with their hands in the till.

The new chief at Anglo had an unorthodox style of interviewing. He had utter contempt for academic achievement: it was almost a minus for a candidate to have excelled in exams. He told Ivor Kenny, 'As an employer, I'm never really interested in what students get academically, nor am I interested in whether they did an arts or a business degree. It's all about their interpersonal skills, how they shape up in an interview.' He would sometimes take candidates for a walk around St Stephen's Green, see how they related to him and award the job on that basis. 'It may not have been the Harvard way. I have a very healthy disrespect for very bright people. What you need are people who are absolutely focused and want to be part of a real team.'

Another former manager at Anglo says that FitzPatrick picked a great team, adding darkly that he 'always had to be in love with someone, but he was dangerous when he fell out of love'.

Once part of his team was in place, FitzPatrick identified a gap in the market – the same gap spotted a few years earlier by the ill-fated Ken Bates. There was an unsatisfied demand for business loans: enterprises with appetites for as much as £150,000 were not being catered for. He knew that medium-sized companies were finding it difficult to secure loans from the other banks, which were traditionally ultra-cautious. He headed for the gap and filled it.

Elsewhere he took his attack on their pedestrian ways deep into their territory. He poached specially selected slices of their business; he didn't want current accounts, credit cards or retail business. An opportunist par excellence, he identified clients with great personal wealth and targeted them. He became the ultimate cherry picker. His team was taught to give quick decisions. Where AIB might take five weeks to give a loan verdict, Anglo delivered a result in five hours. FitzPatrick never promised lower interest rates or even cheaper loans, just speedy replies and less red tape.

Poaching business from the cartel was far from plain sailing. Nor was it a life of big desks, corporate hospitality or golf in the K Club. That came later. In the meantime, in the late eighties, FitzPatrick's team was working hard on building a bigger loan book. Profits from niche banking were climbing. His decision to concentrate on medium-sized businesses was paying off – so much so that Anglo was beginning to attract dark envious mutterings from some of its peers. FitzPatrick was landing a few punches.

In an interview with RTÉ's Aine Lawlor in late 2007, FitzPatrick recalled feeling the disdain of his counterparts at the bigger, better-established banks:

I remember going to dinner parties in Dublin 4 and introducing myself as Sean FitzPatrick from Anglo Irish Bank and they'd look at me, and someone from AIB or Bank of Ireland would sort of snigger . . . and I would say to my own staff coming back, the day will come when you are at a dinner party and you say you work in Anglo Irish Bank. There will be silence around the table. Why?

But the financial establishment sometimes had good reason for denigrating the little upstart bank. In 1992 a skeleton from Anglo's past rose out of the graveyard.

John Clegg had been made a director of Anglo in 1988 at the tender age of thirty. The appointment of this debonair young Englishman had FitzPatrick's blessing. The Clegg family had owned a 17.5 per cent stake in the City of Dublin bank before it merged with Anglo. At one point their stake in the publicly quoted Anglo rose to 20 per cent.

John Clegg became a director in order to nurture the large family shareholding.

In April 1992 a leaked document surfaced in the *Sunday Telegraph*. It told of how a probe had revealed that the Clegg family had been under investigation by the London Stock Exchange for insider dealing. Clegg was the boss of a quoted company, Wace Holdings, alleged to be a vehicle for his subterfuge. It was eventually determined that the Cleggs had personally bought shares in a rival company called Parkway, just before Wace made a bid for it. Later in the year, Wace took over Parkway and the Clegg family made a killing. Fires at a Clegg-owned property destroyed key records.

UK investigators questioned Anglo Irish Bank staff during the probe. They were particularly curious about activity in the Clegg family's bank accounts at Anglo. FitzPatrick was quoted as saying that the investigators 'just wanted to know what we knew about him'.

Not much, or so it seems. Clegg was described as a 'lawyer' in the 1990 Anglo accounts but had actually been removed from the roll of solicitors for non-payment of subscriptions. Around the same time two Clegg family members were made bankrupt in the UK. The Inland Revenue was the petitioning creditor. Somehow, no one in Ireland had known anything about this background. At the very least, Anglo's board had not taken its duty to ascertain the bona fides of one of its directors seriously enough.

Gerry Murphy, who was Anglo chairman during the fiasco, recalls: 'Sean handled the Clegg thing beautifully.' FitzPatrick got on a plane to South Africa with Clegg's Dublin stockbroker for a 'showdown meeting' at which he persuaded Clegg's father to sell the Clegg holding in the bank.

The crisis was defused. The bank survived the scandal. But the whole affair left a sour taste in the mouths of investors.

When the news broke, the damage to the reputation of the bank proved nearly fatal. Any story about the 'cowboys' in Anglo travelled. The top brass at the Irish Banking Federation must have been grinning from ear to ear. Worse still, Anglo had been contemplating raising scarce cash through a rights issue. The Clegg incident put an end to that fund-raising road. No one would invest a further shilling in a bank surrounded by such destabilizing stories.

The damage to the Anglo brand was bad enough, but, worse still, the Clegg stake in Anglo was stuck at an awkwardly chunky 20 per cent. Now there was an ominous block of Anglo shares overhanging the market, depressing the price. As long as the block remained unsold it was a permanent reminder of Clegg's insider dealing.

FitzPatrick was in the mother of all jams. First, he needed to persuade Clegg to resign in order to save the bank's reputation. Second, he had to find a buyer for the wayward director's shares.

The resignation was the easy bit. Clegg reluctantly fell on his sword. Placing the shares with a buyer was harder. It took twelve months in difficult market conditions, but finally the Clegg family's holdings were bought by Investment Bank of Ireland and others for £4 million. The bank was out of the woods; Anglo had survived its first big scandal.

If FitzPatrick had stuck to the knitting of the early years he would have avoided mountains of trouble; but that was not his – or Anglo's – way. During the period 1985 to 1990 he expanded the loan book and deposit base dramatically. In 1987 he dipped his foot in the waters of the Irish Sea by opening an office in the Isle of Man. The decision to head for an offshore tax haven raised eyebrows. The bank insisted that it was to support a growing sterling loan book. There was already a small operation in London. Anglo had operated as an instalment finance house in the eighties, but the opening of an Isle of Man branch had special attractions for depositors. Anglo's profits were on a steady growth path by 1988, when they rose 54 per cent to £2.2 million. At that year's annual meeting, chairman Gerry Murphy boasted that the oldest senior executive was just forty-two.

Still seeking other outlets for his ambitions, in 1988 Fitz-Patrick entered a partnership with a UK car trader. The business bombed, and FitzPatrick closed it down; he had no more fear of cutting losses than he had of cutting staff.

He also eyed the rarefied world of Dublin stockbroking. The 1986 deregulation of financial services in the UK – known as 'Big Bang' – had enabled banks or other outside firms to operate their own stockbroking arms. Ireland followed suit.

Early in 1985 an up-and-coming young businessman named Dermot Desmond had bought 29.9 per cent of a small stock-broking firm, Dillon & Waldron (in which I was a 40 per cent shareholder). When the rules allowed it – in 1987 – Desmond's money brokerage, National City Brokers (NCB), took 100 per cent of Dillon & Waldron's stockbroking business. The entry of this entrepreneur from the north side of Dublin into the tightest of closed shops caused the ageing buffers of Irish stockbroking to choke on their mid-morning gin and bitters in Dublin's Moira Hotel.

All Desmond really wanted, in purchasing Dillon & Waldron, was a broker's licence. He immediately set about challenging all the stick-in-the-mud older firms, revolution-izing the business through the use of white-hot technology.

(After less than a year as a stockbroker, Desmond began to make strong political links. I remember introducing him to Charles Haughey at a lunch set up by government press secretary P. J. Mara and myself in 1986. Desmond and

Haughey were a natural match. As six of us sat around the lunch table in NCB the two north-siders hit it off. Both were self-made men, had little time for red tape, and shared a contempt for the feudal financial chiefs of Dublin in the eighties. Both were chronically impatient for power, progress and influence. Both were strangely patriotic. At that lunch the seed of the International Financial Services Centre was born. Both men's eyes lit up as they visualized Ireland as a hub for new technology and a tax base for overseas operations. The Custom House dock was fingered as the location of a new centre for economic revival.)

Stockbroking had been dominated by a few very rich families and their firms for decades. Names like Davy, Dudgeon and Goodbody held sway. Davy was mostly top-notch Catholic while Dudgeon was mainly Protestant Ascendancy. Goodbody was originally controlled by the Quaker family of that name. The people who ran these firms had attended privileged private schools such as Belvedere, Blackrock, Gonzaga – or even English public schools such as Eton, Rugby, Ampleforth and Downside.

The established brokers may have resented Desmond's invasion but they were quick to realize that the jig was up. They soon started scurrying around in search of a rich banker to buy their declining businesses.

Bankers bought up brokers. They saw savings for themselves and the opportunity to cross-sell multiple products. It was also imperative that they could compete with their rivals overseas, nearly all of which were buying up brokers. In 1988 Bank of Ireland bought 90 per cent of Davy, while AIB followed suit with its purchase of Goodbody.

FitzPatrick took a look around. Like Desmond, he did not want to buy a big broker. He sought a company with a minimum of deadwood to dismiss and compensate. After that, it was up to Anglo to provide the capital for expansion. He bought a tiny firm called Porter and Irvine. He would have been familiar with the personnel, as the recently deposed Anglo director John Clegg had used them for some of his dealings.

FitzPatrick soon bought another firm, Solomons Abrahamson, hoping that the combined entity would give him a platform to rival NCB. It didn't. NCB went from strength to strength while Sean pulled out after less than two years. 'We bought two firms with people of integrity,' he later recalled. 'However, my timing here was impeccably wrong. Within a year of acquisition the business had gone into a cyclical downturn and, while we weren't losing money, we certainly were not making any and there was no light at the end of the tunnel. What was most difficult was the amount of management time that the stockbroking absorbed. It was diverting us from the profitable core business of lending. Once again I had to take the difficult step of closing down a business and letting the staff go.'

He should have waited a little longer. Within months the stock market was booming again. FitzPatrick never made the financial commitment to stockbroking that Desmond had. Desmond had gone for broke, while to Fitzpatrick stockbroking was just another experiment.

Although Anglo boasts that it grew from its own organic efforts, throughout the nineties it made acquisitions to beat the band. In 1995 FitzPatrick bought the Royal Trust Bank in Austria, a subsidiary of Bank of Canada. Tiarnan O'Mahoney described it as a 'cheap source of funding for future lending'.

Gerry Murphy recalls that the Austrian venture 'was a big, big success. The Austrian secrecy laws were hugely attractive, especially for people contemplating divorces or suchlike.

People put their running-away money in the Viennese bank.'
He adds, 'I remember the day Sean decided to buy the
Austrian bank. He was late for our seven o'clock in the morning meeting. I then walked him around the Ringstrasse in
Vienna and he was deeply impressed, constantly remarking
what a wonderful city it was. He would never have bought
the bank if it had been in Hamburg.'

In 1996, at a cost of £13 million, Anglo purchased Ansbacher
bankers (the bank later exposed as the vehicle for Des Traynor's
tax evasion escapades in the eighties and early nineties). In
1999 FitzPatrick picked up Smurfit Paribas, a small bank
jointly owned by the Smurfit Group and the French Paribas
bank, for £30 million cash. It lent mainly to the corporate
sector. In the same year he established a Boston office.

The market's verdict was favourable. By 1999, FitzPatrick
had established a good enough profit record to attract some
seriously grown-up shareholders on to the register. Apart
from the Bank of Ireland, which had bought 7.6 per cent
of Anglo's shares, the traditionally cautious Scottish Provident held 6.2 per cent, Morgan Stanley 5.8 per cent,
Fidelity Investments 3.9 per cent and Prudential Assurance
3.8 per cent. Other public companies would have killed for
such gold-plated supporters. These guys examined the
books with a microscope before investing. Anglo was still
subject to plenty of badmouthing at home, but overseas it
seemed to have overcome the native jibe that it was not the
full shilling.

One ominous paragraph in FitzPatrick's 1999 message to
shareholders should have raised the hair on a few critics'
heads, however.

In addition to our loan book from the traditional sources, we are
very pleased that the new areas of lending initiated in the last two

years – commercial mortgages and invoice discounting – have been favourably received by both existing and new clients.

Anglo had entered the property development market.

Sean should have stuck to the knitting. But he couldn't. He was too often a quick-fix banker. Two further attempts at expansion left Sean with egg all over his face. One of his worst moments during this period was his failed effort to buy the state-owned ICC bank, put on the block in 1999 by finance minister Charlie McCreevy. At a late stage in the negotiations Sean had his eye wiped by former Anglo employee Mark Duffy, of the Bank of Scotland (Ireland).

Duffy was chief executive of the Scots bank, which was eyeing the state sale. Relations between FitzPatrick and Duffy had been bad ever since Duffy, predicting that FitzPatrick would 'last in Anglo for ever and a day', left its employment to run the show at Equity Bank, the vehicle captured by the Bank of Scotland for its entry into Ireland. The battle over ICC – and Duffy's eventual success – is believed to have left relations between the two men frosty.

A second, even higher profile corporate attack also proved a flop. In 1998, First Active – originally the sleepy First National Building Society – was converted into a bank and floated on the stock market. First Active shares soon drifted from the flotation price of €2.80 to a low of €1.85. The bank lacked dynamism and retained the old mutual building society ethos.

First Active was ripe for the taking. Its shareholders were fed up. It had lost John Smyth, its chief executive, after a series of setbacks. It was an ideal target for an opportunist predator like FitzPatrick, who was always at his happiest exploiting the weakness of rivals. After he had run the slide rule over First Active, he decided that it was a good fit. The

acquisition would increase Anglo's size by around 50 per cent
and give it a market capitalization of over €1 billion. Talks
opened in the spring of 2000. An announcement was made
to the Stock Exchange.

Eyebrows were raised at the proposed venture. Anglo's
banking model had been a front runner for so long. It lent
to businesses; its treasury operations were winners; its wealth-
management arm appeared to be adding to profit. But a big
deal to take over First Active would propel it into the residential mortgage market. First Active had more than fifty
retail outlets all over Ireland. The cultures of the two banks
could not have been more different.

On the day that the announcement of talks was released,
shares in Anglo dropped 3 per cent while First Active stock
shed 8 per cent. Investors had given their verdict. The financial details had been agreed with surprising ease, but the deal
broke down over the vanity of the individuals involved. Fitz-
Patrick was the undisputed choice as boss of the new bank,
and other posts were not hard to fill, but the non-executive
directors on the two boards began to kick up. First Active,
although half the size of Anglo, wanted too many former
building society bums on boardroom seats. Both Tony
O'Brien of Anglo and John Callaghan of First Active coveted
the chair. The deal sank in a wave of recriminations.

The proposed merger would have been what analysts today
pompously call a 'transformational' deal. Anglo would have
operated a branch network, chequebooks, credit cards, mortgages – all the products it had hitherto disdained. The little
bank would have begun to compete against the Bank of
Ireland and AIB in their home territory. The attempt to
invade this virgin soil marked a change of tack. The question
began to be asked: Was Sean losing his marbles? Had the little
entrepreneur finally grown too big for his boots?

It was becoming obvious to some colleagues that Fitz-Patrick was changing. He no longer relished the role of an outsider. The boy from Bray wanted to come in from the cold.

It was not a change for the better. One former colleague tells of a more self-centred, almost dictatorial tendency developing as Anglo got bigger. He cites the bank's annual get-togethers for managers at posh venues like the Royal College of Surgeons or five-star hotels. According to his colleague, sceptics nicknamed them the 'Nuremberg rallies'.

FitzPatrick seemed to crave recognition in the circles he had challenged for so long. In 2000 the rebel banker accepted the role of president of the ultra-establishment Irish Banking Federation. He started to make silly, set-piece speeches. In late November of that year he launched the bankers' Code of Ethics. 'The document,' he said sanctimoniously, 'relies on a relatively small number of values and principles. But they are key. The principles of integrity, confidentiality, professionalism and compliance are the most basic of modern banking and we have gone to some pains to ensure that they are at the heart of this Code of Ethics.' He ended with a rousing message: 'Trust is important to us and we are determined to rebuild it.'

FitzPatrick was beginning to sound like all those grandiose old bankers who were running the establishment he had shunned for years. He was going native.

At the same time he became a joiner. He was appointed a council member of the Institute of Chartered Accountants of Ireland. These citizens of middle Ireland were honoured to welcome him into their inner sanctum, and he was equally content that he could place such dull respectability on his CV. He even joined up-market clubs like the Hibernian United Services and became a member of others with cultural pursuits. He remained an enthusiastic member of the Druids Glen golf club, Fitzwilliam Lawn Tennis Club and was often spotted at Michael Smurfit's flashy K Club. He was being seen in all the right places, rubbing shoulders with ministers and captains of industry, including key insiders like Bank of Ireland governor Laurence Crowley, AIB chairman Lochlann Quinn and AIB chief executive Tom Mulcahy.

Golf seemed to feature more in his life. It was good for business. But it also appealed to those competitive instincts. He had a handicap ranging between ten and twelve. One regular opponent says that his golf betrayed his character. 'He hated losing. He wanted to bet on every game. If he was losing he would introduce bets on every hole to compensate. At the end of a game of golf with Sean there could be twenty bets. He had a low boredom threshold, as much in golf as he had in business. He needed the adrenaline rush, the thrill of the holes.'

All the time the bank's loan book was growing. The same colleague who had earlier noted the increasing dictatorial tendency observes: 'But as the business grew, so did Sean's ego. He began to think that he could walk on water. Greed was never far away either.'

The 2003 annual report reveals that in the seventeen years since Sean took over in 1986, there had been an increase in market capitalization from €8 million to €2 billion. Profits had risen from €1 million to €261 million and total assets from €138 million in 1986 to €19.4 billion. In the five years to 2003 pre-tax profits rose on average by 43 per cent annually.

Increasingly, Anglo's big customers were builders and developers. Ireland's construction boom was lifting the bank into a world of fantasy rewards. Anglo had stuck to its tried-and-tested methods: give quick answers and personalize the service. The difference now was that the economy was booming and property was booming most dramatically of all. The rough diamonds of Ireland's building world loved the Anglo style.

The bank's top brass started taking home monopoly money. In the year 2000, for example, total rewards for the six key players – Sean FitzPatrick, Bill Barrett, Peter Killen, Willie McAteer, Tiarnan O'Mahoney and John Rowan – climbed from €3.1 million to €3.9 million, a 26 per cent rise. (It was not yet mandatory to publish individual pay figures in annual reports, so Anglo published block figures.) In 2000 the same sextet were sitting on six million share options between them. The awards of these juicy options had been passed on by a highly co-operative remuneration committee of gentle non-executive directors.

Executive packages continued to skyrocket. In 2003 FitzPatrick took home €2.3 million while Tiarnan O'Mahoney earned €1.5 million. None of their fellow executive directors pocketed less than €1 million. The non-executive directors benefited to the tune of at least a grand a week. By that year Sean held nearly four million shares, worth about €36 million, and he had options pouring out of his ears. Short-term targets for everyone had yielded staggering rewards. The Anglo lads were the best-paid boys in town.

The independent directors of Anglo, many of them friends or business associates of FitzPatrick, were not much of a brake on his ambitions. Sometime around 2000, when Seanie had started to become a joiner, he had begun to play the Dublin directors' game. He was good at it; he knew that he was never going to break into the stuffy boardrooms of the older inner circle, so he started to create his own. His board was full of cronies.

In 1998 Anglo had enlisted Billy McCann as a director. McCann was an old Pres pal of Seanie's, but also a man with a proven record both as managing partner of Price Waterhouse and chairman of the ESB. McCann would have been an asset on any board. Sean got networking; after 2000 hardly a director was appointed to Anglo's board without close business connections to FitzPatrick.

The most controversial of Sean's boardroom capers was undoubtedly his board membership of the Dublin Docklands Development Authority (DDDA), a massive property play. Appointed in 1998, he served for nine years along with the chairman, his pal Lar Bradshaw. Both men were directors of the Authority at a time when massive DDDA developments were being funded by Anglo. Bradshaw joined FitzPatrick on the Anglo board in 2004.

In 2001 Ned Sullivan, chairman of Greencore, was brought on to the Anglo board. Lo and behold, in 2003, Sean was invited to become a director of Greencore. Not surprisingly, he accepted.

It was not a completely clear road to glory. While FitzPatrick was a political appointee to the board of Aer Lingus in 2004, in preparation for the privatization of the airline, the government baulked at appointing him chairman. At the time the Minister for Transport, the late Seamus Brennan, told me privately in Leinster House that 'we cannot risk appointing Sean to the chair. We think he may be too accident-prone. You never know what could jump out of the Anglo cupboard and bite us.'

The minister was on the button – the government could not afford a scandal to wreck the Aer Lingus flotation. Sean had to settle for the post of senior independent director (SID), a vital cog in the Aer Lingus corporate governance wheel. (The SID of a public company is normally a senior director with unimpeachable integrity.)

In 2004 Anglo recruited Gary McGann to its board.

McGann was a close pal of Anglo director Paddy Wright, long-time top dog at Smurfit Group. Three years later, when Smurfit Kappa was seeking a chairman, they opted for Sean. Suddenly he chaired two boards of which Gary was a member.

Other cross-directorships included more evidence of mutual admiration. Director of bookmaker Paddy Power and RTÉ Authority boss Fintan Drury made it to the board of Anglo in 2003. Sean sat on the board of Drury Sports Management in 2001.

Gerry Murphy, now a young seventy-six, is one of the few close colleagues of Sean FitzPatrick who are willing to talk about him openly. Murphy was FitzPatrick's chairman at Anglo for over a decade until 1999, and later served with FitzPatrick on the supervisory board of Anglo's Austrian subsidiary.

'I think he got in with people of a different league, like Dermot Desmond and Denis O'Brien,' Murphy told me. 'He tried to keep up with them and it didn't work.' Both O'Brien and Desmond were clients of Anglo in their early days, before breaking into the big time. 'Denis O'Brien and he [FitzPatrick] were close. I was at the Anglo credit meeting which passed Denis's loan for a radio station in Prague.'

Murphy is right that FitzPatrick was close to O'Brien, who often expressed his admiration for the wizard from Anglo. FitzPatrick was close to Desmond as well, and in 2008 he would propose him as the new chairman of Aer Lingus, but Desmond – the one-time boss at Aer Rianta – turned the job down at the eleventh hour.

According to one notional candidate for the succession, FitzPatrick had muttered about retiring for years. Tiarnan O'Mahoney, Tom Browne and John Rowan, all in their forties by 2003, were no longer in the first flush of youth.

They had itchy feet. No one could push FitzPatrick – he was still only fifty-six – but he had held the post for nearly twenty years.

FitzPatrick worked out a compromise. It was a typical Seanie solution. He would depart from the position of chief executive, but he would succeed Peter Murray as chairman. Such a move was contrary to the Combined Code of Corporate Governance, which FitzPatrick had formerly held so dear. It did not, apparently, apply to him.

The reason for the Combined Code's rule against chief executives becoming chairmen was simple: it might leave a single personality too dominant on the board, and the new chief executive could find his style cramped. In extreme cases he could be a puppet. This principle of corporate governance was tailor-made to prevent people like Sean FitzPatrick from holding too much power.

But, at the end of the day, the code was voluntary. Fitz-Patrick persuaded the board to disregard it. He took the €350,000-a-year part-time job.

The next hurdle was the Irish Association of Investment Managers, the self-appointed group of tame fund managers who ostensibly policed the rules of corporate governance. Having received assurance that Anglo would appoint an independent deputy chairman (an assurance that was never fulfilled), this subsection of the bankers' inner circle gave FitzPatrick the nod, just as they later did to Jim Flavin of DCC when he made the same move (although they were eventually forced to do a U-turn). This was corporate governance Irish-style.

FitzPatrick's apologists insist that it was not the prospect of a loss of money that kept him on the board. He simply could not bear to miss the buzz. The property market was in full frenzy when he pulled out of the front line at the January

2005 AGM. A year earlier he had raised €27.6 million in cash by selling half his Anglo shares, and it is widely speculated that he used the proceeds as a basis for personal property plays. More importantly, he was massively indebted to the bank. Later events gave rise to suspicions that he needed to stay on the board in order to keep the lid on his huge loans from Anglo.

If his decision to grab the chair of Anglo was not his finest hour, then his handling of the succession was truly shabby. He had managed to keep the three pretenders to the throne (Tiarnan O'Mahoney, John Rowan and Tom Browne) on board for a decade by frequently hinting at his retirement.

Tiarnan O'Mahoney was the natural successor. He had been in charge of Treasury operations for two decades and was generally regarded as a genius around the money markets. He had his differences with FitzPatrick from time to time, but on the whole he had gone with the flow. He was a numbers man and would have been a safe choice.

Tom Browne and John Rowan were high fliers, more in the FitzPatrick mould than O'Mahoney. Browne had been on the board since 2004 and was described as 'Head of Lending Ireland' in annual reports. Press speculation that Browne was the heir apparent kept surfacing as the race hotted up. Rowan, talented and ambitious, suffered from having been slightly out of the loop as chief executive in the UK when the jockeying for pole position went on.

The eventual choice staggered the banking fraternity. A complete outsider in the succession stakes was selected. But if the general public had never heard of him, he had been a quiet force in the bank ever since his return from the United States in 2003.

David Drumm was parachuted into the top post.

He was only thirty-eight. Having joined Anglo in 1993, he

had left Ireland to set up its operation in Boston in 1998 and returned to take over the Irish lending division in 2003. He was not a director. He had been on the bank's strategic management board, but that tier was solidly second division.

Even to this day, the contenders are reluctant to speak of the reason for Drumm's selection. One says that he was 'on the lending side that produced most of the profit. He was a property man. He was very much in the Seanie mould.'

Another insists that Tiarnan O'Mahoney was never a live prospect. 'Tiarnan was incapable of ingratiating himself with anyone. He never went to charm school or read *How to Win Friends and Influence People*. He was on the Treasury side, which produced less than 25 per cent of the profits. The lending boys didn't like him.'

All three of the disappointed front runners left the bank within months of Drumm's elevation. Although FitzPatrick was not on the committee that selected his successor, it was unthinkable that he did not exert influence on the directors making the recommendation. Seanie may have got the general he wanted, but he lost all his lieutenants. Anglo was never to be the same again.

(A feature of the selection process that is sensational in retrospect was the identity of one of the external advisers on the succession: Donal O'Connor. In June 2008, four years after Drumm's selection in 2004, FitzPatrick asked O'Connor to join Anglo's board. In December 2008 he became chairman of Anglo upon FitzPatrick's resignation. In June 2009 he told me that Drumm had been selected as chief executive on the basis of his interview.)

David Drumm was a bad choice. He was not quite a clone of Seanie but he was close enough. Like FitzPatrick, he had started his career as an accountant. Like FitzPatrick, he had got itchy feet and headed for more profitable pastures.

Like FitzPatrick, he took the top Anglo job at the age of thirty-eight. Like FitzPatrick, he was a lender. When he was receiving Sean's benediction for the job, the chairman described Drumm as 'soaked in the ethos of the bank'.

The new man's competence was not in question – he had done a reasonable job setting up the Boston division. A former employee of Anglo told me that the main amber light against Drumm, in the eyes of those who chose him, was his inability to stand up to his mentor. 'Sean was very pro-David Drumm,' Gerry Murphy recalls. 'Tiarnan O'Mahoney was the cleverest of the prospective successors but he was not good with staff.'

Supporters of Drumm point to the profits record in his early days: Drumm kept reporting figures that stunned the market. But critics saw the profits as a bubble, based on careless lending in an overheated property market. For three years under Drumm, Anglo denied that it was taking undue risk. The bank stood behind its highly optimistic provisions regarding bad debts for losses on property. So did its auditors, Ernst & Young.

While the bad debt numbers (or 'impaired loans' as they loved to call them – because nobody really understood what this meant) remained minuscule, the figures for lending were becoming sensational. In 1998 the bank had lent €3.5 billion in advances to customers. By 2008 it had reached €73 billion. In the first year of Drumm's stewardship lending increased by 41 per cent. In his second year it soared by another 45 per cent.

Anglo was brazen about its worship of the new deity of property. The annual reports, while coy about using the 'property' word, were shameless. Flashy pictures of some of the projects the bank had supported took garish pride of place in the reports, which began to look more like auctioneers' brochures than bankers' tomes. By 2006 Anglo's display of the properties it had funded verged on the vulgar. Harvey Nichols in the fashionable Dundrum shopping centre sat alongside a massive project in London's Earls Court and Olympia. The front of the 2007 annual report was a full-page, in-your-face picture of the five-star Ritz Carlton Hotel in Enniskerry, Co. Wicklow. Inside were more full-page pictures, accompanied by boasts about how the bank had provided finance for the Thistle Hotels in the UK. Hotels all over the US were featured with similar pride. The subliminal message was clear: 'Come over to Anglo. We are the property developers' bank.' Anglo was going for broke on property.

During these frenzied days a strange anomaly was emerging. Out in the marketplace during 2007, as the property bubble started to deflate and the global credit crunch kicked in, Anglo's shares fell by nearly 50 per cent. Yet in the same year, under Drumm's leadership, profits were reported as rising. All the time, Anglo was increasing its lending to property developers. The stock market began to think the bank was barmy, and some observers believed that Anglo was releasing fantasy figures. The shares peaked at €17.53 in June 2007. By December they had plunged to €10.94. In May of that year Anglo reported first-half profits of €462 million, up from €289 million a year earlier. Many of those buying the shares had been punting in the deadly 'contracts for difference'. One of the investors was the first major global bank to collapse, Bear Stearns.

But wiser counsels, like investment house Merrill Lynch, put Anglo on their 'least preferred' list because of its exposure to property. The shares fell as investors regarded the figures as failing to reflect the dangers inherent in a bank so dominated by property lending. By December Anglo reported that its profits were just short of a billion euros

(€998 million, up from €657 million the previous year). Anglo was defying gravity.

An insider suggests that the departure of all the disappointed pretenders to the throne, the front-line talent, was fatal. 'Tiarnan had certainly curtailed Sean's excesses,' he says. 'When Tiarnan went so suddenly, there was no fireguard around the fire.'

The fire was blazing out of control in every corner of Anglo. Pay for the bosses kept going up; by 2008 FitzPatrick's own pay as chairman had shot up to €539,000, a 48 per cent increase in two years. David Drumm had his snout buried deep in the trough. Revised figures show that in 2007 Drumm received a 'performance bonus' of €2 million and a total package of €4.656 million – not a bad reward for a boss whose bank would face nationalization or liquidation barely a year later. The three disappointed contenders for FitzPatrick's job took obscene amounts of money with them as they left: O'Mahoney bagged €3.65 million, Tom Browne trousered €3.75 million and John Rowan had to be satisfied with a mere €1.1 million, all 'in recognition of their substantial contribution to the Group' – not to mention any pension arrangements they had quietly organized.

The parting pay-offs were stunning. The three had already been lavishly rewarded over the years; no one had forced them to leave; Anglo had gone completely over the top. It is hard to find a more extreme example of corporate gluttony.

Drumm was not judged strong enough to stand firm against the FitzPatrick doctrine that had controlled Anglo for so long. No one expected him to challenge the supremo. Some suspected that FitzPatrick had been unwilling to support any of the three leading contenders for his post precisely because of their abilities, their record and their capacity to stand up to him. Worse still, they might steal his limelight. Sean was being fêted as a banking hero in the media, in political circles and even among some of the old establishment. He was winning gongs, such as the 'Business & Finance Business Person of the Year' award in 2002. He was sitting on judging panels. He was 'Mr Anglo'. David Drumm was never going to seize that title from him; other contenders might have done.

Anglo was in big trouble long before anyone had heard of Sean Quinn and the 'Golden Circle', or of Seanie's hidden loans or even of the sham deal with Irish Life & Permanent to boost Anglo's balance sheet artificially. It was a powerful bank in the grip of one man. It was making property loans that were 'secured' by other property plays. Its loan book was dominated by a handful of favoured clients. It ignored many of the principles of corporate governance. It was paying obscene money to its current employees, its former employees, and to its directors. It was a property junkie – or, in the words of a London investment house in early 2008, 'A Building Society on Crack'.

The story of the boy from Bray ended in his resignation in disgrace on 18 December 2008. Just a year and a day earlier, RTÉ's Aine Lawlor had asked him a telling question.

Lawlor: This is what the other guys were running around saying about you guys: 'They're nothing but buccaneers, nothing but pirates. You know they take far too many risks and it's all going to come and topple one day.'

FitzPatrick: 'Will they last? Will they, they're a fine bank but will they last?' That has been said about us in the seventies, the eighties, the nineties, and indeed even in recent years, but we have arrived, and we ain't going anywhere. We are now the fourth largest company in the Irish Stock Exchange, we've got a market capital of over ten billion, we've got lending now, loan books that would be bigger than either AIB or Bank of Ireland of five years ago. So we've arrived and we're going to stay and we're going to continue to progress . . . because of the culture within the bank and within the people.

A year later – almost to the day – Seanie was gone.

3. The Regulators

Eugene McErlean walked through the door of my Senate office on 18 June 2008. Not often does a former internal auditor of AIB arrange to meet a critic of the banks – something I had been for years. I confidently expected that this was to be my Tony Spollen moment.

Tony Spollen, who had preceded McErlean as an AIB internal auditor by eight years, became Ireland's first celebrity whistleblower. Spollen left in 1991, but in 1998 Liam Collins of the *Sunday Independent* published Spollen's top-secret report to the board about DIRT tax dodging at AIB. McErlean was one of Spollen's successors as internal auditor in the same bank. He had parted company with AIB in 2002. He knew where the bodies were buried.

McErlean had a good CV. He had been a lawyer with British Airways before returning to Northern Ireland with his wife Niamh and family in 1991. Over the next eleven years he gradually worked his way up the AIB ladder, to the key post of internal auditor. He was the second internal auditor to know too much, throw down the gauntlet to his employers and decide that the only honourable road was to leave.

McErlean carried a promising-looking briefcase, stuffed with documents. He had a slightly haunted look about him – not surprisingly, as he had bottled up a galaxy of banking secrets for six years.

I sensed a scoop.

Our conversation started off stiffly. The fifty-year-old Roman Catholic from Belfast, educated at St Malachy's and with a law degree from Queen's University, was not a natural soulmate for a TCD Prod; but his whole demeanour, while reserved, was profoundly impressive and engaging.

McErlean had made life awkward for the banking establishment back in 2001 when he had reported to his bosses at AIB that the culture of overcharging at AIB was endemic. We know now that his report also revealed sharp – and possibly illegal – practices in other areas of AIB. The report had gone to the Central Bank.

Liam O'Reilly was assistant director general at the Central Bank at the time. (Two years later, in 2003, he would take over the top job at the Financial Regulator when it assumed the regulatory powers of the Central Bank.) In early 2002 O'Reilly met McErlean to discuss the allegations contained in his internal audit report. The Central Banker promised to consider all McErlean had said and to take appropriate action. AIB had already committed itself to addressing McErlean's report and to restoring money to those who had been overcharged.

Soon after his first meeting with Liam O'Reilly in 2002, McErlean found himself in the departure lounge at AIB. Within a few months he was an ex-employee. He remains convinced to this day that his pursuit of these thorny topics is the reason why AIB wanted to see the back of him.

After McErlean's departure, O'Reilly asked to meet him again, and the two sat down in October of that year. According to McErlean, at this meeting O'Reilly asked him to withdraw all his allegations against AIB, but he refused. According to the Central Bank, however, he withdrew them. Not much common ground there.

In May 2004 RTÉ broke a fresh overcharging scandal at AIB. Another whistleblower within the bank had tipped off the regulator several weeks earlier; fed up with waiting for action, the whistleblower had then spilled the beans to the RTÉ newsroom. The Financial Regulator, not for the first time bounced into action by a whistleblower, launched a clever public relations offensive, vowing remedies for consumers and insisting that it had already been probing the issue when RTÉ went big on the story. Perhaps, but was it ever going to tell anyone? McErlean, meanwhile, was indignant: he felt that the new revelations had striking echoes of the contents of his internal audit report in 2001, and that the impression had nevertheless been given that this was the first time the regulator had ever heard these allegations. His withdrawal of his case against AIB had, he believed, given the regulator a chance to lose interest in a scandal at Ireland's biggest bank. He wondered if the Central Bank and AIB were tick-tacking each other.

McErlean had delivered quite a big fish for me to fry. His conflict with AIB was over, but the credibility of the Financial Regulator was at stake. McErlean felt he could not feebly let the regulators duck the issue just because he had settled his battle with AIB. He had spent two years in search of minutes of his 2002 meetings with Liam O'Reilly. The Financial Regulator refused to release them; the Data Protection Commissioner released some documents but withheld bits that McErlean required. That day in my office he wanted advice on how to secure the key documents from O'Reilly – now head of the Financial Regulator – that would resolve the dispute about whether McErlean had really withdrawn his allegations of overcharging.

That Wednesday morning in June 2008, I was frustrated by McErlean's refusal to blow the lid on AIB. He insisted that he had a 'confidentiality' agreement with them, agreed as part of the terms of his departure from the bank. The prospect of breaching it, either clandestinely or up front, horrified him. My subversive reassurance that these behind-closed-doors agreements were regularly honoured in the breach cut no ice with him.

McErlean bore no grudge against AIB. Ireland's biggest bank, for all its wrongdoings, was not his target. He even spoke in complimentary terms of its chief executive Eugene Sheehy. This gritty Northerner was keen to tackle an arguably even more formidable foe, Ireland's Financial Regulator, and he suggested that he should give evidence to the Oireachtas Committee on Economic and Regulatory Affairs.

I introduced him to my fellow committee members – Fine Gael TD Fergus O'Dowd and the chairman, Michael Moynihan of Fianna Fáil. They too were impressed by his story. We all knew that McErlean's unhappy experience had the capacity to chip further into the watchdog's diminishing credibility.

We encountered delays in finding a slot for a hearing. Constantly unfolding banking scandals were occupying a lot of the committee's time. McErlean himself was not the easiest to bring to the committee. The first time he was due to appear he suddenly developed a health problem, possibly brought on by stress. Michael Moynihan, a man of great humanity, had doubts about calling him again if the ordeal threatened his well-being. But McErlean recovered and insisted that he was fit to appear.

He was equally insistent that he could not give detailed evidence about AIB, because he had sworn confidentiality. We decided that such a restriction left little to talk about and stopped pressing for a hearing. Eventually McErlean agreed to contact AIB to request release from the gagging clause, but we held out little hope.

Out of the blue McErlean received a reply from AIB. He was released from the confidentiality condition for the purposes of the Oireachtas committee. It was an unexpected gesture from a bank that had a lot to lose. We were back on course.

On 24 March 2009, nine months after he had first walked into my office with his strange tale, McErlean gave evidence. It was worth the wait. His credibility was enhanced. He told of how he had warned the Central Bank about overcharging in 2001 and how it had failed to act. The newspapers bought into the story, and Pat Kenny gave McErlean a full half-hour on his RTÉ radio show.

The Financial Regulator was stung into a reply. Its acting chief executive, Mary O'Dea, fired with ambition to be appointed to the position on a permanent basis, sprang to its defence. A statement was issued suggesting that McErlean was confusing his complaint about overcharging of 'management' time with other more wide-ranging overcharging; that the complaint had been referred to the Office of the Director of Consumer Affairs, which had found an overcharge of €255,000 (and not the tens of millions that McErlean had audited); that McErlean was comparing chalk and cheese; that it was all a terrible misunderstanding.

The regulator's response was careful not to question McErlean's bona fides. All neutral observers had formed the opinion that he was telling the truth. The 'misunderstanding' route was one of the few avenues left open to the retreating watchdog.

Apart from his testimony about overcharging, McErlean had also dropped a bombshell at the committee. Suddenly released from his seven-year oath of confidentiality, he testified that AIB's subsidiary Goodbody Stockbrokers had, back in 2000 and 2001, been dealing in AIB shares while hiding behind the anonymity of secret accounts based in exotic offshore tax havens, most notably the Pacific Island of Vanuatu and the red-hot Caribbean island of Nevis. Nevis was blacklisted by many reputable brokers. According to

McErlean, his internal audit team reported these activities to the regulator at the time. The trades ran into multi-millions. McErlean believed the dealings were illegal. Goodbody maintained the opposite.

The Financial Regulator did not deny McErlean's assertions. A spokesman claimed that the regulator had fulfilled its duties and boasted that 'significant personnel and operational changes took place at Goodbody' following McErlean's warnings.

Once again the Financial Regulator was under scrutiny. In the overcharging case it had discovered nothing. In the Goodbody case it had discovered nothing. Discovery had been left to someone else. Only when confronted with the problem had the watchdog begun to bark. It had been noticeably reluctant to inform the public of the goings-on at one of Ireland's top stockbrokers, a company that enjoyed a reputation for straight dealing. The lid had been kept on this volcanic story for eight years, right up to the day that McErlean surfaced before the committee. McErlean had been acting in the interests of the consumer when he warned the regulator of AIB's overcharging and the malpractices at Goodbody. Perhaps that was why he was banished into the wilderness for six years.

A couple of decades ago McErlean's challenge might have been dismissed as a hopeless attempt to fell a colossus; but in the Ireland of 2009, awareness was growing that the financial policeman had a flawed pedigree. Volumes of evidence that it had a history of being a servant of the banks, not a master, helped to explain its behaviour during the deepening banking crisis. Eugene McErlean arrived in Leinster House bang in the middle of this awakening.

The wake-up call had taken a long time. Ireland's Central Bank had carefully cultivated a forbidding profile. For most

members of the public, the Central Bank was a dull institution, but probably beyond reproach. A retired Central Bank
director told me that when architect Sam Stephenson was
given his brief for the design of its headquarters in Dame
Street, he was told to make the building 'a statement of
power'. In political circles it was sometimes considered
dangerous, if not downright disloyal, to challenge the Central
Bank's methods or question its integrity.

No longer. Ordinary citizens of Ireland were beginning
to realize that banks had run amok because they had been
allowed to do so. Anglo Irish, AIB and Bank of Ireland had
been competing suicidally for high-risk lending business
and had not been pulled up. Overcharging was chronic in
the retail banks. AIB was not the only culprit. Statistics
from Belfast bank auditing firm Bankcheck confirm that the
Bank of Ireland, Ulster Bank, National Irish Bank and Irish
Nationwide were all guilty of numerous overcharging
offences.

The regulator never caught them in the act, but would
move against them if they were unmasked by a nosey third
party, such as RTÉ in the overcharging scandal or the *Sunday
Independent*'s Liam Collins in the DIRT swindle. Once caught
by someone else, the guilty bank was likely to be forced to
repay the money it had stolen from customers or the state,
but banks were never fined.

The Central Bank and its successors had a long tradition
of being protectors and allies of the banks, a tradition that
included some noble names in the annals of Irish banking.
Central Bank directors had often moved comfortably on to
the boards of commercial banks once their terms of office in
the service of the state were over. Professor James Meenan,
an early Central Bank director, moved to the Bank of Ireland.
So did legendary and distinguished bankers like Dr Ken

Whitaker and Professor Louden Ryan. At one point the relationship between the regulator and the regulated was so close that there were instances of AIB and Bank of Ireland directors sitting simultaneously on the board of the Central Bank. The Bank of Ireland's Donal Carroll and Ian Morrison pulled off the double. AIB managed to place Liam St John Devlin and Joseph McGlinn on both boards at the same time. In the eighties retired Central Bank secretary Bernard Breen was spirited on to the board of the Bank of Ireland. And in 1998 accountant Billy McCann moved from a stint on the Central Bank's board to become a director of Sean FitzPatrick's Anglo Irish Bank. Finally, McErlean's nemesis, Liam O'Reilly, saw his talents recognized in his retirement as chief executive of the Financial Regulator by an appointment to the board of Irish Life & Permanent.

Given the existence of such a well-oiled revolving door between regulator and regulated, it is not surprising that the two often found time to socialize together. Golf, as ever, was the glue. AIB regularly held a lavish golf outing at Portmarnock, Dublin's most exclusive golf club, specifically to butter up central bankers. One AIB source told me that they gave away free balls with the AIB logo and that it was 'customers' golf, meaning that they always let the regulators win.

Eugene McErlean told me that his bank used to wine and dine regulators from the Central Bank in the 1990s and later: 'AIB would roll out a five-star lunch with all the bells and whistles' to satisfy the palates of the watchdog's head honchos. The hospitality was never returned by the regulators. It was all one-way traffic.

McErlean also said, 'From my experience [as AIB's head of compliance in the UK], no one from the Bank of England, or the UK's Financial Services Authority would ever accept such opulent hospitality. In the UK, regulators had a code about accepting hospitality from banks, ensuring there was no appearance of being compromised.'

But things were done differently in Ireland.

The occasion when Ken Bates slipped through a very lax Central Bank vetting procedure to become the kingpin of Irish Trust Bank was embarrassing enough. The failure to spot DIRT, overcharging and other abuses was incomprehensible, and Sean FitzPatrick's ability to doctor the Anglo books without coming to the notice of the Financial Regulator is deeply disturbing. But by far the most alarming example of the Central Bank's craven behaviour in the face of bankers' skulduggery was the regulator's capitulation to one of Ireland's most cunning white-collar crooks, banker Des Traynor.

Des Traynor was chairman of Guinness & Mahon Bank. He was also Charlie Haughey's accountant – that relationship should have been a warning sign in itself. Yet in the late 1990s High Court inspectors were appointed on the application of the government to probe into Traynor's Ansbacher accounts in the Cayman Islands. Irish customers of the bank had deposited money beyond the reach of Irish law and the taxman. The inspectors discovered that the Central Bank had known about the accounts since 1976.

The list of Ansbacher account holders was a who's who of the great and the good in Irish business. Several of them were associates of Charlie Haughey, who was Minister for Health at the time. Among them was none other than Sam Stephenson, designer of the Central Bank building in Dublin's Dame Street. Another Ansbacher account holder was Liam McGonagle, a well-known solicitor. But the name that must have devastated the Central Bank's investigator, Adrian Byrne, struck closer to home.

Ken O'Reilly-Hyland was not a household name in Ireland in 1978. He was chairman of the oil company Burmah (Ireland). A cigar-smoking plutocrat, he lived in one of Dublin's finest residences, in Ballsbridge. He had made a fortune in property deals in the sixties and seventies and was a leading light in the glory days of Taca, the collection of businessmen who forked out for Fianna Fáil. More significantly, he was originally one of Haughey's magic circle when the ambitious young Fianna Fáil leader-in-waiting was Minister for Finance in the late sixties. At the time of the Arms Trial – Haughey's lowest ebb, in 1970 – O'Reilly-Hyland switched allegiance to Jack Lynch. He was rewarded for his volte-face by Haughey's arch-enemy, Lynch loyalist George Colley, who was Minister for Finance in 1973. Colley gave O'Reilly-Hyland a plum appointment to the board of the Central Bank.

Despite falling out with Haughey, O'Reilly-Hyland continued to share business interests with Traynor and McGonagle.

In 1976 an on-site inspection of Guinness & Mahon by Central Bank official Adrian Byrne hit upon some unsavoury activities designed to evade tax. Byrne must have frozen when he spotted O'Reilly-Hyland's name on the Ansbacher list. He passed the details up the line. O'Reilly-Hyland had a £400,000 loan from Guinness & Mahon secured by a deposit of £230,000 in the Caymans. Byrne reported to his Central Bank bosses that 'the fact that the bank [Guinness & Mahon] takes such extreme precautions to keep the existence of the deposits secret from the Revenue Commissioners indicates that the bank might well be a party to a tax evasion scheme'.

Byrne's charge was staggering. It challenged the Central Bank, as regulator, to take action immediately. The Central Bank responded all right, but the response was dumbfounding.

An official deleted the word 'evasion' from Byrne's report and substituted the word 'avoidance'. The difference is vital. Evasion is illegal. Avoidance is above board. With the stroke of a Central Banker's pen, Traynor was in the clear, on the right side of the law. He promised to run the Ansbacher accounts down, but he did nothing of the sort. The tax dodge continued until 1997.

In 2000 the Central Bank's then deputy general, Tim O'Grady-Walshe, tried to explain the bank's failure to act against the Ansbacher scam, pleading that they feared a run on Guinness & Mahon that would have caused the collapse of the bank. He also told the tribunal that Des Traynor was 'a very clever and very skilful man' and that he was convinced that Traynor would not break the law. Adrian Byrne spoke to Mr Justice Moriarty of the high esteem in which Traynor was held in banking and accountancy circles, adding: 'We thought he would work his way out of this.' He went on somewhat smugly: 'The fact is the bank didn't collapse and depositors didn't lose money; that was our prime objective.'

It was not the Central Bank's finest hour.

Ken O'Reilly-Hyland's appearance before the Moriarty Tribunal lasted five minutes. He claimed that he had told Minister for Finance George Colley of his need to protect his family assets with the Cayman offshore trusts. Mr Colley was dead, so unable to corroborate the story. Similarly, O'Grady-Walshe testified that he was sure that O'Reilly-Hyland would have declared his offshore trust to the Central Bank governor of the day, Charlie Murray.

O'Reilly-Hyland is now eighty-three, living much of his life abroad. According to Maureen Cairnduff, a society hostess of the eighties and author of *Who's Who in Ireland*, he and his wife are 'beautifully preserved and still exude charm'. Professor Dermot McAleese, a fellow director of the Central

Bank with O'Reilly-Hyland, confirms that he was a 'delight-
ful person'.

The High Court inspectors refused to mince their words
in their report on the Ansbacher deposits. They blamed the
Central Bank for failing to follow its own nose in pursuit of
the accounts. They condemned the Central Bank for accepting Traynor's promise to run down the scam. They even
suggested that the Central Bank should have known on the
evidence available that Traynor was lying.

Ansbacher and other banking scandals at last prompted moves
to reform bank regulation. These moves commenced against
the backdrop of Ireland's adoption of the euro between 1999
and 2002. We no longer had our own currency, with the
power to devalue or revalue; nor did we have the right to set
our own interest rates. Questions began to be asked about
what the governor of the Central Bank, his army of economists and the currency gurus down in Dame Street were
going to do for a living. A re-examination of the Central
Bank was long overdue.

Meanwhile, a turf war was brewing between the Department of Finance and the Department of Industry and
Commerce. While the need for a single regulator for all financial services was now agreed upon, there was no consensus
about which arm of the state was going to pull the strings.
Two political heavyweights, Minister for Finance Charlie
McCreevy and Minister for Industry and Commerce Mary
Harney, good friends in private life, went to war over who
should regulate Ireland's banks, insurance companies and
lesser outfits.

McCreevy, an instinctive sympathizer with the cause of
the banks, favoured the Department of Finance's line that
little change was required. Harney, a consumer champion,

wanted a new financial regulatory body to be independent of the Central Bank, in order to protect punters from the worst excesses of the banking vultures. Harney was supported from the sidelines by Michael McDowell, temporarily out of the Dáil but serving as chairman of the Progressive Democrats, who wrote the definitive report on how to make a new regulatory body work.

McCreevy was the eventual winner, securing a hybrid model which left the balance of influence with the old Central Bank. A new Financial Regulator was given limited autonomy. The membership of its board overlapped with that of the Central Bank. The result was a fudge, well illustrated in the gobbledygook posted on the Financial Regulator's website to explain what the two outfits do.

The roles are complementary and we enjoy the closest cooperation with our colleagues in the Central Bank. Indeed the recent and ongoing market turbulence has reinforced our view that prudential supervision, financial stability and consumer protection are inextricably linked so as to merit the combined approach to supervision that our structure demands.

There was no break with the old mindset.

Nowhere was that more apparent than in the appointment of the Financial Regulator's first chief executive, Eugene McErlean's Central Bank nemesis Liam O'Reilly, who took the helm of the new body at its inception on 1 May 2003. O'Reilly jumped straight out of the old Central Bank stable. Deeply imbued with the Dame Street headquarters ethos, he was appointed after what Financial Regulator chairman Brian Patterson called a thorough search of the 'private and public sectors'. Patterson insisted that there was 'extensive interest from both Ireland and overseas' in the position. Perhaps there was, but the interview board decided to look no further than the next-door office. The Central Bank's number two was given the role as the new regulator's number one.

O'Reilly's pedigree was predictably dreary. He had been assistant director general of the Central Bank since 1998 with responsibility for its supervision functions, precisely the area that had not covered itself in recent glory. Before that he had held all the dullest jobs imaginable in the Central Bank. In short, he was a man hardly likely to bring radical thinking to his new post.

In an ominous response to his appointment, O'Reilly declared: 'I know we already possess within our existing regulators a team of young, talented and dedicated staff.' Far from a new outfit sprouting up, many Central Bank staff merely found themselves re-employed under a new flag. O'Reilly did not see the need to look any further. Although the structure was about to change, the same regulators with the same approach were set to move offices, just down the corridor. The culture was undisturbed.

Down at AIB headquarters in Ballsbridge they should have been cheering. Bank of Ireland and Anglo Irish Bank must have been equally euphoric. Here they had a man whom they all knew well, sliding comfortably into the hot seat. No danger of any of those free-thinking foreigners, who would not understand how regulation works Irish-style.

The creation of the new Financial Regulator did bring one substantive change: a far sharper consumer profile. Mary O'Dea was appointed to front the budding division, with the title of Consumer Director. Addressing this appointment, Brian Patterson insisted that the board had surveyed 'a field of very impressive candidates for this position and the selection panel was unanimous in its view that Mary O'Dea was the best person for this job'.

O'Dea had worked in the Central Bank for sixteen years, since her early twenties. The press release announcing the appointment noted that O'Dea came hotfoot from the Regulatory Enforcement and Development Department of the Central Bank, where she had been responsible for policy across all its supervision departments. More sensitive employers would have kept quieter about this aspect of O'Dea's past, as supervision had never been the bank's strongest suit.

Once again the interview panel had opted for an insider. Consumer champions without a Central Bank pedigree were rejected.

The scene was set for a new era in the supervision of Ireland's banks. Never has so much been promised and so little delivered. The delivery on the consumer side was strong on the optics. A website was set up with price comparisons, consumer advice, helpline numbers, surveys, fact sheets, an information centre and a range of services designed to give the impression that the Financial Regulator was the consumer's friend. Mary O'Dea tried to turn the belated 2004 discovery of the overcharging scam at AIB to her advantage, promising to pursue the bank for every last penny. Here was the punter's pal, handed an opportunity to restore money to bank customers who had been robbed. But behind the bluster the awkward question still lurked: where were the regulator's hit squads when the whistleblower was warning them? Why did it take RTÉ to reveal the scandal?

Behind the scenes the Central Bank and the Financial Regulator still shared the same press officers. They shared board members; they shared a building; they shared staff; they shared secrets.

While Mary O'Dea gave the consumer division a vocal and visible start, in the background her boss, Liam O'Reilly, rarely surfaced. He was a participant in Oireachtas committee hearings, when summoned. Unlike O'Dea he was camera-shy. He briefed the media in one-to-one interviews on appropriate occasions, but generally he kept to the twilight zone. O'Dea's mission was to tell the public how much the Financial Regulator cared about them. She must have hoped that her love would be requited.

Initially it was – partly because the public had no idea that the Financial Regulator had another duty, to ensure that the banks were solvent. To do that it had chosen a 'principles-based approach' to regulation. According to Liam O'Reilly's successor Patrick Neary, speaking in 2007, the principles-based approach 'places responsibility for the proper management and control of a financial service provider, and the integrity of its systems, on the board of directors and its senior management'.

Decoded: 'We leave it to the banks.'

The bankers loved it. It was regulation without rules.

Imagine the reaction of Sean FitzPatrick, Brian Goggin, Eugene Sheehy, Denis Casey and Michael Fingleton when they first took their jobs and read the rules, only to discover that there were none. Just long-established 'principles', which they were expected to respect. Poor Pat Neary spelled them out ad nauseam at an IFSC conference in 2007: banks should be transparent and accountable; act with prudence and integrity; maintain sufficient financial resources; have sound corporate governance procedures; have clear oversight systems; have adequate internal controls; maintain sufficient financial controls and risk policies; comply with solvency needs; produce accurate information when required.

It was a list so banal that only an eighteen-carat crook could argue with it. And in an alarmingly consistent reference to what banks should do about their own liquidity and funding requirements, Neary stated: 'Banks must assess the most appropriate stress tests and scenario analysis to be applied to their own exposures and operations. This approach is in line with best practice and ensures that proper risk assessment is conducted rather than a tick-box approach.' If they were worried about their liquidity risk or funding requirements they could decide what to do themselves. This was self-regulation by another name.

In the same speech Neary emphasized that the whole principles-based method of regulation was founded on trust. So trusting was the regulator of the banks that he kept on-site inspections of their books down to a minimum, and gave prior notice in advance of such inspections.

In Liam O'Reilly's last full year in office, 2005, the Financial Regulator – which was responsible for forty-eight financial institutions – carried out just eight on-site inspections. This fell short of even the watchdog's own lamentably modest target of inspecting 25 per cent of regulated institutions every year – it had set itself a low bar and then failed to clear it. Worse still, it did not make a single unscheduled inspection of a bank during 2005. All eight banks were given advance warning when the inspectors were coming to call.

Insurance companies had an even easier ride. Only 9 per cent of them were subjected to the rigours of regulatory scrutiny in 2005, and there were no unannounced inspections.

The Comptroller & Auditor General was critical of the number of inspections carried out in 2005, when Neary was prudential director, and he marginally stepped up the numbers when he became chief executive: in 2006 there were thirteen inspections and in 2007 there were fifteen. In neither year was the regime of trust threatened enough for a dawn raid to be instigated. All the big bankers must have slept easy. If the watchdog's boys were going to drop in, they could expect a tinkle to alert them.

Independent assessments of the Financial Regulator's performance were hard to find. It did not benchmark itself against global counterparts – many of which have rules to govern their banking sectors, not merely principles.

Until 7 October 2008 not a single Irish bank or banker had been fined as a result of inspection; banks that were found to have overcharged their customers had merely been compelled to restore the money. In response the Financial Regulator justly pleads that it did not have powers to fine until 2006; but even then, it failed to use them. In the UK – proud home of 'light-touch' regulation – the Financial Services Authority levied an average of £14 million in fines on banks and building societies between the years 2002 and 2007, and more than £27 million in the eighteen months from January 2008 to June 2009. While Ireland's bankers had been spared any punishment at all for their sins, during that period the Financial Regulator had fined the *Irish Times* €10,000 and *Phoenix* magazine €5,000 for minor offences.

Eventually, taunted by jibes that he had never fined a bank or building society, Neary slapped a penalty of €50,000 on Michael Fingleton's Irish Nationwide. In the context of the large-scale malfeasance and mismanagement that had plagued Irish banking for years, the offence was petty. Fingleton's son, also Michael, a salesman for the building society, had emailed clients following the government's guarantee of bank deposits, advising them that the Irish Nationwide was now far safer than non-Irish competitors. The government was furious, as any move to use the guarantee for competitive advantage might have offended the already raw nerves of European Commission competition officials. Neary overreacted, seizing the opportunity to fine a financial institution for the first time. His response could have been interpreted as more a nod in the direction of the anger of his political masters than a sudden conversion to regulatory vigilance. It was in any case the beginning and the end of Neary's appetite for fining the banks.

The nub of the issue had been coldly addressed by the Financial Regulator's own consumer panel chairman, Brendan Burgess, in 2005. Burgess noted that 'producing leaflets and codes of conduct' was the easy part. And then, with lethal precision, Burgess stuck the knife in:

We have seen very little evidence in the year under review that the Financial Regulator had the resolve to stand up to some institutions and individuals who were misbehaving. It appears that this lack of resolve is due to fear of having its decision challenged in the courts and losing. It seems that when challenged by misbehaving institutions the Financial Regulator simply backed down.

The so-called independent regulator – just two years in existence – was a paper tiger, frightened of the banks, and its own consumer panel had said so.

Patrick Neary's appointment in early 2006 to succeed Liam O'Reilly came as no surprise. Neary's main competitor for the €260,000 job was the ambitious Mary O'Dea; but the regulatory body's board was in no mood for its thrusting consumer arm to win a victory over the old guard. Neary had been in the Central Bank since 1971. He wasted no time putting his stamp on the office, baldly stating at the 2006 Regulation 360 Conference that, 'Our regulatory approach is good for business . . . We will seek to implement rules to the minimum extent necessary.'

Neary was as good as his word throughout his short tenure in the job. In his first annual report, covering 2006, he stated: 'I am satisfied that the majority of financial service providers operate to a high standard.'

He had come to the post at a time of economic boom. Bank

shares were heading for fresh highs and the housing spurt was still in full flow. Nothing would stand in the way of eternal growth and bankers' exuberance. Certainly not the Financial Regulator. But Neary's honeymoon was short. In late 2006 the tide began to turn.

Ireland's stock market – dominated by financials – topped out in February 2007 after years of outperforming most global markets. Now foreign investors started dumping Irish bank shares because of the banks' heavy exposure to a property sector that had all the hallmarks of a bubble. Meanwhile, in the United States, sub-prime borrowers were missing repayments on their mortgages, which in many cases had been bundled into 'securities' that were held by financial institutions all over the world. The uncertainty created by the sub-prime contagion caused banks to become nervous of lending to one another, and this brought about a global credit crunch, starting in the summer of 2007.

As early as 2005 the *New York Times* had branded Ireland the 'Wild West of European Finance'. We had shrugged that off, but consistent criticisms of our regulation in the UK press were beginning to hit home in the minds of foreign investors.

A few minor measures were taken to dress the darkening windows. Neary responded to the market turmoil by requiring the banks to give weekly, not quarterly, liquidity reports, though it's not clear if anyone ever read them; and the banks were forced to set aside additional capital to cover increasingly risky mortgage and commercial property lending. One or two other gestures were made, including setting the bar higher for stress-testing mortgages.

Meanwhile, the plunging prices of Irish bank shares were blamed on derivatives markets, short selling, hedge funds and vague global forces. We were asked to believe that while neither the banks nor the economy could be completely sheltered from outside influences, Irish banks were robust. Similar reassurances were voiced by Brian Goggin of the Bank of Ireland and Eugene Sheehy of AIB, always emphasizing that Ireland had no exposure to the dreaded American sub-prime mortgages.

Bankers and regulators alike were in denial. Ireland's trouble was not caused mainly by external forces. It was self-inflicted. We were not exposed to US sub-prime mortgages – that much was true – but we were fuelling a ruinous property inferno of our own. The banks, almost unchecked by the Financial Regulator, had embarked on a competitive frenzy of lending. Anglo Irish Bank led the way and all the others followed. Mike Soden, Bank of Ireland chief executive until 2004, admits that he used to ring Sean FitzPatrick after sensational sets of annual figures and congratulate him. Then Soden and his board of directors sat down and wondered how on earth they were going to compete. If Seanie was defying gravity, so would they. AIB, Bank of Scotland, Ulster Bank and the others joined the stampede. Even the two mutual building societies, Irish Nationwide and, eventually, the traditionally cautious EBS, gatecrashed the party. They all competed for the business of property developers, now on the rampage. Neary watched from the sidelines. His beloved 'principles-based' system would see them through.

Neary's self-congratulation in the 2007 annual report is breathtaking. As Ireland's banks faced into their worst year ever, he wrote:

I believe our actions and increased vigilance and monitoring have provided useful supports to a strong system of supervision which has enabled the industry in Ireland, which had no sub-prime exposure to any degree, to withstand this prolonged period of serious turmoil in international markets.

Just over a year later, he was out of a job.

The failure was not Neary's – or Liam O'Reilly's – alone. The annual stability reports from Central Bank governor John Hurley during the years in which Ireland's property bubble inflated hardly predicted the doomsday that was approaching. Hurley was the inheritor of a long tradition. He came to the Central Bank governor's job through a time-honoured route. For decades the secretary of the Department of Finance had – almost without exception – a personal right of automatic succession to the plum job as governor. Consequently, the deeply conservative outlook of the Finance Department was, over time, transferred to the Central Bank. One of the best gigs in the entire state sector was inherited by an insider rather than subjected to competition. One consequence of this was that these two arms of the state often moved in lockstep, and change was not easy to effect.

Hurley's November 2004 Financial Stability Report did, almost alone in the entire sector, sound alarm bells about the dangers lurking in the property boom. He did not mince his words:

The risk of an unanticipated and sudden fall in residential property prices, accompanied by an increase in the default rate among mortgage holders . . . is the risk that poses the greatest threat to the health of the banking system.

By November 2005 a slowdown in house-price increases had reassured the governor. In that year's report he anticipated a soft landing but was still on alert in case property showed signs of a resurgence.

Hurley's 2006 Financial Stability Report was again wary of the dangers of renewed property rises and warned of indebtedness as a result, but crucially the report gave the banks a clean bill of health: 'The banking system is well placed to withstand the impact of any major adverse developments in the short to medium term.' In November 2007 Hurley was more circumspect, acknowledging the difficulties faced by banks wishing to borrow in the tightening interbank markets. He also recognized the hostility of overseas investors towards Irish banking shares. But he concluded that the 'current situation and outlook for Irish banks, based on an assessment of developments so far, is positive'. And in a final flourish he claimed that 'Irish banks are solidly profitable and well-capitalized. In this context it is worth noting that they have one of the lowest rates of non-performing loans in Europe.' The problem was that the figures on non-performing loans were unchallenged figments of bankers' imaginations.

This was November 2007. By the end of 2008 profits from Irish banks had tanked. Dividends had been cancelled. Anglo Irish was probably insolvent. Far from being 'well-capitalized', Bank of Ireland and AIB were on the point of receiving a capital injection of €3.5 billion each.

Property developers were strangely a low priority in Hurley's analysis and in Neary's commentaries. Even the dogs in the street were worrying about the big-ticket property boys. Their huge bank borrowings were making headlines by the day. But the builders and developers hardly seemed to feature in the vision of the regulators.

The regulatory body's earlier measures had simply bounced off the intended targets. Its limited attempts to restrict the banks' scope to lend to house buyers were easily circumvented by the canny lenders. The watchdog failed to recognize the root of the problem: property, property, property. Ireland's bankers had gone bonkers on one commodity. The amounts lent and the actual size of property loans as a proportion of the banks' overall lending book was ballooning. This infatuation with property ensured that if there was ever a turndown in the sector, let alone a deep slump, Ireland's banks would be out on a limb. The Financial Regulator failed to instruct them to bring property loans back to prudent levels, to reduce them as a proportion of their overall book. Unchecked, the banks heaped fuel on the inferno.

Not only did the Financial Regulator baulk at restricting the proportion that banks could lend to property, it put no ceiling on bonuses or bankers' pay. Their staggering incentives pushed them towards bigger and bigger property loans and instant personal gratification. They steered the banks into 2008 on a wing and a prayer.

Neary's first public appearance in 2008 was an attempt to reassure the Oireachtas Public Service and Finance Committee that the nation's banks were in good shape and under prudent supervisors. He appeared with Hurley. Both men sang from the same hymn sheet. Hurley was the senior partner in a united front.

Neary again made much of the 2006 measures he had taken to compel the banks to set aside more capital to counteract the dangers of higher-risk property lending. He repeated the same defence that he had ordered precautionary measures. The committee chairman, Michael Finneran, thanked Neary and Hurley for their 'reassuring reports'.

It was too late. They had been whistling past the graveyard.

Even more market turmoil was to follow in the next six weeks, culminating in the St Patrick's Day massacre of Anglo Irish Bank's shares in London. The price of its stock fell by 23 per cent in a single session. As a result Anglo's top brass complained to the Financial Regulator that some Dublin stockbrokers were not playing ball. They particularly deplored the bearish noises of Davy and Merrion Capital towards their shares. They believed that brokers were spreading damaging rumours. Anglo even sent a solicitor's letter to Merrion Capital threatening to sue. Merrion responded with a robust denial of any culpability, pointing out that the stock-market view of Anglo reflected their own. No legal action ever materialized.

Neary's response to this spat was the instinctive reaction of a tame Central Banker, not an independent regulator: he launched an inquiry. Davy and Merrion received letters asking detailed questions about their dealings in Anglo's shares. Nothing untoward was found, but Neary had stood up for Anglo.

When Neary next appeared before an Oireachtas committee, in April 2008, he faced a few tougher questions. Deputy Seán Ardagh of Fianna Fáil asked him about the probe into dealings in Anglo (though nobody named the bank). His reply betrayed an instinctive Central Banker's attitude to markets.

On St Patrick's Day we commenced an investigation. We spoke yesterday of the rumours in the market then, which reached a crescendo on that particular weekend. We felt there were unjustified stories about a leading financial institution in circulation and we were extremely concerned that well-capitalized, strong, profitable financial institutions could be severely and negatively impacted by unfounded and groundless rumours emanating from unknown sources.

Hostages to fortune were being scattered around like snuff at a wake. Anglo was neither well capitalized, nor strong, nor profitable. Nor were the other Irish banks. As it turned out, the rumours about Anglo were bang on.

Michael Casey, a former Central Bank chief economist, told me that there was plenty that could have been done: 'They could have brought in the banks and offered to act as ringmaster. There was a race to the bottom in progress. The banks would have appreciated that.'

The banks needed a cool, independent and authoritative hand to guide them collectively out of the morass. Perhaps they would have welcomed an outsider telling them all together to reduce the levels of risk they were exposed to. The banks were on an uncontrolled roll, far beyond rescuing themselves, and the Financial Regulator did nothing about it.

On 18 September, after the markets closed, Neary followed the UK Financial Services Authority's lead and banned short selling of financial stocks. It was a blatant attempt to protect Anglo's and the other banks' tumbling share prices. The market rally that followed was short-lived. Within days, even with short sellers off the pitch, bank shares began to slide again.

On 29 September Neary and Hurley were holed up in the Taoiseach's office at the famous late-night emergency summit called to save the Irish banks. The government's bank guarantee – agreed that night – was a tacit admission that at least one bank was on the point of collapse. Reports of the crisis meeting describe Neary as cool as a cucumber. Like Ireland's bankers, he calmly blamed the outside world, the credit crunch, anything but domestic factors.

Within a week of the historic crisis meeting, Neary appeared before an Oireachtas committee for the last time. He saw it as his duty to reassure the nation that the banking system was secure. His rhetoric was suddenly more urgent, but his personal demeanour seemed strangely aloof. As a member of the committee, I called for his head, but received scant support.

Neary took the orthodox government/banker/regulator line. Ireland faced an unprecedented international financial crisis. Wholesale funding in the interbank market had dried up. Lehman Brothers was hauled into the Irish mix. So were

Northern Rock, Bear Stearns, Freddie Mac and Fannie Mae. The kitchen sink was not far behind.

Neary had a point. All of those factors had played a part in the Irish banking crisis. But until that day the elephant in the room had been virtually ignored.

Suddenly the elephant became visible.

'There will be losses,' Neary admitted, 'on property-related loans, and increased provisions and write-offs will be necessary. The potential difficulties in this regard are linked to how the economy unfolds.' The game was up. Figures began to come spilling out. 'Speculative lending to construction and property development in Ireland amounts to €39.1 billion,' Neary revealed, 'of which €24 billion is supported by additional collateral . . .'

Even hardened sceptics gasped.

After these words it was probably only a matter of time before Neary departed from his post. The international reputation of Ireland as a regulated financial centre was in tatters.

But Neary had a last hurrah. A few days later, still fancying his ability to calm the nation's nerves, this strangely unconvincing figure headed for RTÉ's *Prime Time* programme to cross swords with interviewer Mark Little.

That night, my telephone at home rang. At the other end of the line was the broadcaster Eamon Dunphy. There was fear in his voice, which may have reflected the mood of the entire population. 'I have just seen Pat Neary, the financial regulator, on *Prime Time*,' he whispered. 'I am terrified. I am going to emigrate.'

Neary had sealed his own fate. Asked by Little about Irish banking's exposure to property, he tried to fudge. Eventually, when Little challenged him with a direct question about the weakness of Irish banks being their exposure to property, he said that he 'did not accept that at all'. He grudgingly admitted that there would be 'certain levels of impairments'. He spoke of how well capitalized the banks were and how there was enough liquidity in the system. It was the denial of the bottomless pit facing Ireland's banks because of their exposure to property that petrified Dunphy and the rest of the nation.

Neary was pictured at the end of the interview smiling happily, like everyone's lovable old grandfather. It was a bizarre performance.

Neary limped on for a couple of months. Then, on 18 December, Sean FitzPatrick announced that he was resigning. He had doctored the year-end books at Anglo.

It was one undetected scam too many. Questions were asked of the auditors, the directors and the Financial Regulator about how Sean had managed to pull such a stunt without any of the watchdogs twigging. None answered satisfactorily. Nearly all Anglo's non-executive directors departed within weeks. The auditors, Ernst & Young, clung on.

Minister for Finance Brian Lenihan was reputed to be furious with Neary. His lukewarm endorsement of Neary in the Dáil as early as October had made it clear that he wanted the chief bank regulator to fall on his sword.

It was confidently expected that Neary would resign after a meeting of the board of the Financial Regulator just before Christmas. But Neary was mounting a sturdy defence. He insisted that he knew nothing of FitzPatrick's loans. No one had told him. Mary Burke, a senior staff member, was equally insistent that he had been informed verbally. There was a direct conflict of evidence.

An inquiry was set up by the board of the Financial Regulator. Politicians made it clear to the board that there was only one acceptable outcome. The inquiry carried out by Dermot Quigley, a former Revenue commissioner, and John

Dunne, chairman of the IDA, failed to resolve the conflict of evidence, but the end was inevitable. Neary agreed to retire early with a golden handshake of €630,000 and a full pension. On 31 January 2009 he stepped down after a crowded farewell office party.

Patrick Neary was a failure as a regulator, but he was also a victim of a terrible system that he did not invent. The Central Bank and Irish commercial banks had been joined at the hip from their beginnings. Cross-directorships fuelled a culture of common purpose. 'Principles-based' regulation ensured the continuation of this warm, and ultimately destructive, relationship. The bankers accepted the laissez-faire camaraderie of the Financial Regulator. Anglo seized on it as an invitation to lend dangerously and excessively. Fired by fear and greed, the rest followed. They abused the opportunity offered in the sure knowledge that they had nothing to fear from the watchdog. And they found co-conspirators in Ireland's rapidly rising band of property developers.

4. The Building Societies

One day in September 2000, Ethna Tinney was browsing through the *Irish Times* in her Limerick home. The 42-year-old horse lover, who had just landed a job as a producer at RTÉ Lyric FM, was happy with her lot. The last thing on her mind was another job. Suddenly she spotted an interesting advertisement.

The EBS building society had decided to embark on a great experiment: it had placed a newspaper advertisement seeking directors. Ordinary EBS members were encouraged to apply to sit on the Society's board. Ethna Tinney was one of 300 EBS members who decided to go for it. In a matter of weeks she was among seven candidates shortlisted by the recruitment agency.

Tinney's final interview took place in Dublin's Jurys Hotel. Today she describes the encounter as a real 'grilling' from EBS chairman Brian Joyce, board member and TCD professor Yvonne Scannell, chief executive Ted McGovern and vice-chairman Ron Bolger.

Joyce was a taciturn type who had served as chairman of CIE and other state bodies. A graduate of University College Galway with a BComm, he became a management accountant. He worked in RTÉ from 1967 to 1969 and then moved to the Dairy Board, where he served as managing director from 1979 to 1989. After that he took to the boardrooms full-time, and made plenty of money, but never landed the plum positions – such as a director's seat at the major banks or CRH.

His vice-chairman, Ron Bolger, was a former managing partner at the accountancy firm KPMG. Bolger had served on the board of Eircom when it was in state ownership but, like Joyce, had never quite made it as a director of one of the big prizes. He was always hovering around somewhere near the top of the second division.

Joyce and Bolger did not see eye to eye, but back in 2000 they agreed about Tinney. She was the outstanding candidate among the shortlisted applicants. She was given the job.

For the next two years there was relative harmony at the EBS. The building society lived on its reputation as being less cut-throat than its rivals, more humane in its methods and a genuine nurturer of its members.

But in the Ireland of 2005 there was little room left for the small building society in a mortgage market infested by banking sharks. In the early years of the millennium the EBS began to lose its edge. Its mortgages and deposit rates were not the most attractive in the market. The high moral tone of mutuality had worked wonders for decades, but the shine was rapidly coming off the society's halo. Loyalty was wearing a bit thin as depositors tended to be old, and choosy young borrowers were shopping around for the best deal. EBS, a high-cost operation, found it hard to compete.

The chief executive, Ted McGovern, was fiercely ambitious. A solemn Scot, he hoped to attach the EBS to a foreign institution with size and muscle, and in 2004 he began merger talks with the giant Dutch co-operative Rabobank. Some board members backed McGovern's plans; others saw them as a vainglorious attempt at expansion. Eventually the proposed merger fizzled out.

It was suspected that McGovern was jealously eyeing the huge profits earned by Michael Fingleton at the rival Irish Nationwide Building Society. Fingleton also took home a pay packet of more than double McGovern's healthy €760,000. There was only one way to compete with the buccaneering

Nationwide chief – form an alliance with a big partner or follow him into the danger zone: commercial property.

While Fingleton never had any trouble from his board, Ted McGovern's was beginning to splinter under the strain of the new, but compelling, commercial demands. Chairman Joyce and his faction supported McGovern in most of his expansionary moves. Ron Bolger, Cathal Magee (a director of Eircom and the VHI) and Tinney were sceptical.

The growing tensions reached boiling point when in 2005 McGovern recruited PricewaterhouseCoopers accountant Alan Merriman to the post of finance director at a salary so high for a mutual that it shocked some of the independent board members. In his first full year (2006) Merriman's total package fell just short of €700,000, more than twice that of his predecessor. EBS had not been one of the biggest sinners in the pay stakes, but the arrival of Merriman at a high salary was seen as having the potential to lift others, including McGovern himself, into the salary superleague.

Members of the remuneration committee, most vociferously Cathal Magee and Ron Bolger, were irate that the appointment had happened without their approval. Civil war broke out on the EBS board. Bypassing the remuneration committee was not the only cause of battle. A €5m payment into the senior managers' pension fund without board approval sent Magee into anger orbit, while Bolger was constantly agitated by corporate governance issues. Bolger, Magee and Tinney frequently challenged Joyce. At one board meeting in the summer of 2006 heated words were exchanged when Joyce turned on both Magee and Bolger. Magee resisted McGovern's hopes of a tie-up with Rabobank. Bolger demanded an audit of corporate governance at the society, a thinly veiled criticism of the way the board was run by Joyce and McGovern. The gloves were off.

Insiders now agree that the EBS had reached a crisis point, and not just at board level. The booming mortgage market of 2005–6 masked fundamental problems at the small building society. Its high costs and lax attitude to them were in contrast to the Irish Nationwide's tight discipline: EBS's cost-to-income ratio was running at three times the level of Fingleton's. EBS was no longer the cheapest mortgage in the market. Its competitors in the banks, with lower cost bases, were able to undercut it.

Bolger had been tipped to succeed Joyce; but he was not Joyce's choice. After months of squabbling the two adversaries eventually reached a devil's pact. They would leave simultaneously. They could not trust each other enough to be sure that any staggered deal would be honoured, so they jumped together.

Joyce had the last laugh when he was succeeded by Mark Moran, who had floated on to the EBS board in 2002 while chief executive of the Mater Private Hospital; Joyce himself had already done the double as chairman of the Mater and the EBS for seven years until 2006. A champion bridge player who twice captained the Irish team, Moran had made himself very rich by leading a management buyout of the Mater Private from the Sisters of Mercy for around €42 million in 2000; five years later he and his fellow shareholders sold the business for €350 million to CapVest, a UK-based private equity firm. Cruelly known by his enemies as 'The Claw' because he is missing a finger on one hand, Moran was a controversial choice, widely referred to as 'son of Brian'. Joyce's patronage of Moran and another director from the Mater Private, Jim Ruane, caused eyebrows to be raised, as few could see how – despite Ruane's earlier career in banking – the Mater Private made a natural recruiting ground for directors of a building society.

Moran had no banking background. He left UCD with a degree in chemical engineering before heading for Smith-Kline Beecham in Cork. He followed SKB with a stint as a finance director at biopharma company Centocor and as managing director of a company reclaiming VAT for US and Japanese companies in Europe. In 1997 he applied for the job of managing director of the Mater Private.

Ethna Tinney was none too pleased by Joyce's manoeuvring to land Moran in the chair, but eventually she reluctantly agreed not to oppose his accession to Joyce's post and the outgoing chairman achieved a unanimous vote for his protégé. However, the experiment in corporate democracy had backfired on the old guard: Tinney had not toed the line. The process of trying to remove her had already begun under Joyce. Two years earlier he had told her that her 'performance' on the board was below par.

Boards often practise internal self-evaluations. Once a year each director awards marks to the others in certain defined categories. They are totted up. If any board member does not cut the mustard, his or her colleagues sometimes suggest that the director stand down. In theory, this keeps directors on their toes. In practice, it usually allows cabals to congratulate each other or cliques to gang up against their opponents.

Tinney was singled out.

In February 2007 Mark Moran arranged a meeting with Tinney in the Castletroy Hotel in Limerick. Moran told her that the board wanted her head. Tinney refused to bow to the pressure.

A few weeks later, Tinney received a letter from Yvonne Scannell of the EBS nomination committee telling her that her 'skills' were no longer needed and that she would not receive EBS board support for her re-election that year.

There were two months between February and the

members' vote at the annual meeting. Tinney decided not to go quietly, but to stand and fight. The board was against her, but a few weapons were available to her: the media, the EBS members and her own gritty personality.

Battle was joined. Suddenly leaks about civil war at the EBS started to hit the press. Highly sensitive boardroom documents surfaced, revealing that the warring factions had been lining up for months. As the battle raged, I contacted Tinney. When I met her it became obvious within minutes that she had been a confounded nuisance to the troika of Joyce, Moran and McGovern. The last thing they wanted was an inquisitive woman challenging their business strategies. I urged her to take on the board and immediately began to seek postal votes for the annual general meeting in April 2007. We were going to appeal to the membership to vote for her over the heads of the directors. It was time to see how they felt about the treatment of Ethna Tinney.

The EBS board, led by Moran, employed public relations consultants Q4 at great expense to make their case. The campaign against Tinney was based on the whispered word that she was not 'up to the job'.

In the *Sunday Independent* the day before the vote I anticipated a crushing defeat. One woman against an awesome machine was no contest. Yet we nurtured a faint hope of a good showing.

Building society elections are the most democratic in the corporate world. Each member has one vote, regardless of the size of their savings or borrowings in the society. The widow with a thousand euros has the same influence on the result as the rich man with half a million euros on deposit. (In public companies, by contrast, one share equals one vote, giving total dominance to the big shareholders.) Members of building societies can vote in person at the AGM or send in postal votes mandating a member attending the meeting to act as their proxy and vote on their behalf.

There was palpable tension at Dublin's Burlington Hotel when over a thousand members gathered. Tinney was undoubtedly the star of the day. She carried the members in the hall with her by a distance. Journalist Sarah Carey, then of the *Sunday Times*, spoke eloquently about the society's problems. Linda O'Shea Farren made a thinly disguised bid for a board place in the future, while I tried to make the best possible case for Tinney.

The platform looked sullen – none more so than the dour chief executive, Ted McGovern. The plump plutocrat with the €760,000 pay package fiddled with his moustache as speaker after speaker devoured him. Chairman Mark Moran sat beside him. Tinney was perched on the podium awaiting execution. Cathal Magee, who had finally sided with the board against Tinney, looked as though he would rather be in Siberia. McGovern loyalists, including Jim Ruane, the battle-hardened Barbara Patton, TCD law professor Yvonne Scannell and the tough, but attractive, company secretary Emer Finnan were in a clear majority. All afternoon the board was under siege from the membership in the hall. Tinney had the masses behind her, but far fewer votes in the ballot boxes.

Suddenly a well-groomed woman at the back of the hall stood up and began to speak. Ted McGovern beamed down on her from the platform.

This prosperous-looking, perfectly tailored member, who identified herself as Mary Caffrey, was no friend of Tinney's. She supported the board and above all she admired McGovern.

'Shane Ross,' she thundered (apropos of nothing), 'is a self-serving, publicity-seeking individual both as a journalist and a politician.' I had no problem with that, but wondered who she was.

'He is,' she continued with venom, 'campaign manager for Ms Tinney.'

But who was *she*?

She then dubbed me 'a fantasist, an opponent of mutuality, a manipulator'. Quite a bit more bile followed from this seemingly ordinary EBS member. Ted McGovern's smile widened further; the board nodded approvingly; chairman Mark Moran indulged Mary Caffrey's rhetoric, where he had cut others short. The PR guys lurked in the background and smirked.

No one should blame Mark Moran for permitting this polemic. He had been given stick for a couple of hours; he was momentarily enjoying himself. Ted McGovern too was entitled to his surprise moment in the sun. But who was the well-manicured lady? EBS employees were conspicuous by their presence at the AGM, cheerleaders for the board in a room overwhelmingly opposed to it; perhaps she was one of their number, though she didn't say so. The chairman allowed her to rabbit on.

When Mary Caffrey had finished, the ranks of the EBS employees at the back of the Burlington clapped. Ted McGovern grinned back benignly at the lady and his loyal staff.

I headed for the Gents. As I entered I felt a heavy hand thrusting a note into my pocket. The note was not signed. 'The lady who insulted you personally,' it read, 'is the wife of EBS managing director Ted McGovern.'

EBS member Mary Caffrey was Mrs Ted McGovern, wife of Tinney's arch-enemy. By the time this was made known to me she had presumably retreated to her upmarket Dalkey homestead. No wonder the employees at the back clapped as Ted eyed them from the platform. They were applauding the boss's missus.

When challenged, Mark Moran maintained that he had no

idea that the speaker was Ted McGovern's wife. So the EBS chairman did not recognize the EBS chief executive's spouse. An unusual, but not wholly implausible, state of affairs.

Later, very helpfully, Ted McGovern confirmed that Mary Caffrey was his wife. The serious Scot told me he saw no reason why she should identify herself as such. She was a woman and an EBS member in her own right. She just happened to be married to the man living off the members' €760,000 a year. No need to tell the members.

Ted's own AGM performance was true to form. The boss said less than his missus. When a member asked chairman Mark Moran the cost of the failed effort to negotiate a merger with Rabobank, Mark hadn't a clue. Ted himself did not have the figures 'available at his fingertips'. 'My best guess,' he added pathetically, 'it was €3.5 million.'

Tinney intervened. 'Ted, it was €6 million.' Bullseye for Ethna.

When the vote was taken the board came home by a whisker. Tinney was defeated by 10,252 to 9,417, a margin of 835 votes.

Mark Moran soon set about repairing the rift. He hoped to mend fences, make changes and repair the damage done to the building society. Less than three months later Mary Caffrey's husband, Ted McGovern, was on the way out. He received an exit package of nearly €1.9 million that would have made even Michael Fingleton blush.

Moran set out in search of a new chief executive and board. He managed to recruit Liam Mulvihill, fresh from his spell as director general of the GAA, Pat McCann, just out of Jurys, and Philip Williamson, ex-CEO of the UK Nationwide Building Society. Moran was beefing up the board as a buffer against another assault from Tinney. His biggest fear was that the narrowly defeated Tinney would run a campaign among the membership to reverse the 2007 vote. Would she expose the board as out of touch with the membership by defeating their plans in a revenge putsch?

Meanwhile, EBS headquarters in Burlington Road was leaking like a sieve. Insiders there were ringing journalists to inform us of every move. Stories broke at various intervals in the *Sunday Independent*, where we were able to tell readers about McGovern's enormous pay-off and to monitor the feverish but failed attempts to find a successor. Appetizing reports of internal witch-hunts and culls of key staff reached those hungry for news about the troubled outfit.

The executives were running around like headless chickens. Eventually in 2007 – after the departure of McGovern but before the appointment of a new chief executive, and with Moran acting as executive chairman – they decided to go further down the Fingleton road and expand their lending in the commercial property market. A lucky escape happened when the EBS bosses tried to link up in a joint mortgage venture with Britannia in the UK. EBS even flirted with the tempting sub-prime market.

Moran's six-month tenure as temporary chief executive was calamitous. Not only did the society dig far too deep into commercial property at the peak of the market, but it also had a high-profile disaster when it lent to rogue solicitor Thomas Byrne and was forced to take a €15 million hit as a result; it was caught in the Icelandic bank meltdown after lending to the bankrupt, but later nationalized, Kaupthing bank; the EBS Haven Mortgages subsidiary, which separated out the society's mortgage-broker business from mortgage lending (for no obvious reason and at huge set-up costs), failed to meet its targets. Almost everything Moran's EBS touched turned to dust.

When I met Ethna Tinney in October 2007, she was

indifferent to an attempt at a comeback. Moran had now slotted credible people on to the board. Liam Mulvihill's GAA credentials were impeccable and Pat McCann had a good business record. But as December approached, she decided to run. Her nomination was lodged. Sources at the Burlington bunker reported that the board was preparing to man the ramparts. There were eight candidates for seven seats. Someone had to lose out.

This time it was not simply a vote of 'Yes' or 'No' to Tinney. She was pitched against other candidates. Predictably, after her speech at the previous AGM, outside candidate Linda O'Shea Farren was in the field. Board members offering themselves for re-election were secretary Emer Finnan, Philip Williamson, Cathal Magee, Liam Mulvihill, Pat McCann and Jim Ruane.

The tension carried all the way to the AGM. Anyone could have lost.

Ethna Tinney topped the poll. Jim Ruane of the Mater nearly lost his seat. O'Shea Farren lost out. The entire slate of sitting directors who had been put up for re-election, with the support of the board, came trotting in thousands of votes behind Tinney. It was sweet revenge for one who had been so cruelly humiliated just a year earlier. It was a sour rebuff to Mark Moran.

Meanwhile, Moran had recruited a new chief executive. Fergus Murphy was a former boss of Rabobank subsidiary ACC. He accepted Moran's offer of the job and set about putting an end to commercial property lending. Murphy wanted to bury the past, to bite the bullet on the bad debts. And he wanted a new chairman.

He set about his task just as Irish banking entered its biggest-ever crisis. Unlike many of his peers, he insisted on making realistic write-offs of bad debts: in 2008 the EBS wrote off €110 million. It declared a loss of €38 million for that year, a far more realistic acknowledgement of the state of its business than was forthcoming from the big banks.

Fergus Murphy was the sole chief executive to survive the cull of bosses that followed the state's guarantee of the six Irish banks and building societies. Moran was not so lucky. At the AGM of 2009 he resigned, admitting that he should be accountable for the mistakes made in his time as interim boss. His tenure had been a failure. He was accompanied into the wilderness by his able, but less lucky, finance director, Alan Merriman.

At the same AGM former assistant garda commissioner Martin Donnellan charged on to the board with 7,819 votes. He toppled long-time Ted McGovern loyalist Tony Moroney, the chief executive of Haven Mortgages. In the same vote O'Shea Farren finally made it on to the board.

The most significant result in 2009 was a ringing endorsement for Fergus Murphy, the new managing director, who had distanced himself from the old regime. Murphy topped the poll, well ahead of the field.

The McGovern legacy was obliterated within two years of his departure – the board had been turned inside out by the Tinney revolution.

I first met Michael Fingleton back in the eighties in Scruffy Murphy's pub, just off Lower Mount Street in Dublin. At the time it was a watering hole for financiers, politicians, artists and journalists; among its regular denizens were Charlie Haughey's closest adviser, P. J. Mara, and journalist Eamon Dunphy. Dermot Desmond and his NCB gang were regulars, as they had moved into offices next door. Fine Gael 'national handlers' Pat Heneghan, Enda Marren and Bill O'Herlihy (also a television football pundit) were good customers of the pub. Many of them were also good customers of Fingers.

Fingleton liked journalists and they liked him. He saw politicians as a means of getting things done. So Scruffy Murphy's provided a useful network for him. Fingleton became a provider of mortgages to politicians, journalists and artistic types. He rarely gave them preferential terms, but he often arranged speedy loans for those with good political or journalistic connections. These relationships gave him access to the corridors of power and to the media.

In those days the mortgage provider was considered to be doing a favour for the customer. All sorts of conditions were imposed by lenders. They frequently forced hopeful borrowers to save specified sums with them for a set period before even considering them for a house loan. Fingleton was prepared to waive these niceties, helping him to multiply the mortgage business at the Irish Nationwide.

The novelist and ex-journalist Colm Tóibín is typical of customers given mortgages by Fingleton in those days. In April 2009 Tóibín told the *Irish Times*: 'I was in the Conrad Hotel earlier this year and Michael Fingleton came in, alone. I was proud to stand up and shake his hand. He gave me my first mortgage when he mightn't have, when I wasn't the most solvent person in Ireland.'

Fingleton's strategy of cultivating politicians and journalists worked. He secured wide media coverage, much of it identifying his personality with the building society. The two were inseparable. Both Fingleton and the Nationwide became household names. He was given publicity that no amount of advertising spend could buy.

At the same time he became a familiar figure in Leinster House. He had access to politicians at the drop of a hat. He knew many of the top TDs, especially those in Fianna Fáil, on familiar terms. Later, the huge leap in his profits was partly due to his close connections with both Fianna Fáil and its builder friends. He was one of the initial beneficiaries of the property bubble.

Such high-flying connections were also to be his downfall.

Fingers had started from small beginnings. In the early seventies, when he took the reins of the Irish Industrial Building Society (renamed the Irish Nationwide in 1975), it had a staff of five and assets of just €2 million. By 2004 it had assets of €8.5 billion and profits of €135 million. In 2007 profits reached €391 million.

Fingleton travelled an unlikely route into Ireland's financial world. The son of a garda from Tubercurry, Co. Sligo, he attended a seminary but eventually baulked at taking the vows. He then spent two years working for Concern, the Irish aid agency. A story is told that he was once stopped at customs in the Nigerian breakaway region of Biafra carrying £100,000 cash in his suitcase as bail for Irish priests who were being rounded up and imprisoned. Somehow he talked his way out of trouble.

When his two-year spell with Concern ended, he faced a choice between God and mammon. He was good at God but better at mammon, so mammon won. He had already done a spell at Allied Irish Finance in the early sixties and a commerce degree at UCD. He answered an advertisement to become general manager of the tiny Irish Industrial Building Society and was hired. In 1975 he qualified as a barrister. Among his classmates at the King's Inns were future Attorney General Michael McDowell, future Supreme Court Judge Adrian Hardiman and future Labour Party leader Dick Spring. He recalls that he 'sat at the back with Dick Spring; McDowell and Hardiman sat at the front'.

Fingleton cultivated an image as a personality banker. He

was a willing sponsor of media events and, as his society went
from strength to strength, he was paid back with plenty of free
media coverage. At the same time he continued to keep close
to politicians and the press. For over a decade the Irish Nationwide sponsored the annual golf outing between teams from
the Oireachtas, the press, the army and the Gardaí. It was often
held in Woodbrook Golf Club where he was a member. He
took a delight in being photographed with the winning team.

The Fine Gael party saw him as a Fianna Fáil sympathizer.
A story is told that his access to Leinster House was stopped
after a spat one evening with Fine Gael TD Sean Barrett and
a party colleague. Fingleton is supposed to have been striding
down the main corridor towards the restaurant when he spotted the two Blueshirts just in front of him. Apparently he
made a cutting remark – a reference to their loss of the 1987
general election – with the result that Leinster House became
a Fingleton-free zone for three months.

He enjoyed the high life and the company of high livers.
He golfed at the K Club. He was a regular guest at Michael
Smurfit's annual bash, joining a collection of the great and
the good who paid homage at the packaging millionaire's
court. Politicians Michael Lowry, Albert Reynolds and the
late Jim Mitchell were regulars. Others to attend included
businessman Denis O'Brien, beef baron Larry Goodman and
builder Sean Mulryan. It was a lavish affair often held in one
of Dublin's five-star hotels.

Fingers was part of the Smurfit inner circle that made the
cut for the great man's seventieth birthday party cruise in the
Mediterranean in 2006. It was the party to beat all parties.
One hundred and twenty of Smurfit's closest friends were
there, including Gary McGann of Smurfits and Anglo, former
Smurfit boss and Bank of Ireland governor Howard Kilroy,
and Michael Smurfit's one-time right-hand man, the late

Paddy Wright. Dermot Desmond, auctioneers Padraig Hassett and Arthur French, solicitor James O'Dwyer and entrepreneur Gerry Purcell and his wife Aisling also relaxed on the luxury yacht.

Fingers's socializing in such elevated circles meant that he met plenty of property developers. The Irish Nationwide had a corporate box at Croke Park, and Fingleton used it to host big clients including developers Sean Mulryan and Sean Dunne and supermarket king Ben Dunne.

Such corporate massaging badly backfired in one case, as Ben Dunne told me. The former supermarket mogul used to receive tickets from his friend for all the big GAA matches. He had come to look forward to them. He was doubly pleased when the GAA finally lifted the ban on foreign games and the date of the highly charged Ireland versus England rugby match approached in the spring of 2007. It was billed as a historic event, with all the memories of the original Bloody Sunday at the GAA ground due to be exorcized. Dunne waited for his tickets. A few days before the game, they had still not arrived. Fearing some mistake, he rang Fingers.

Fingers played for time. He asked Dunne to 'leave it with him'. He rang Dunne back the next day.

'Ben,' he said, 'those tickets are as scarce as hen's teeth but I have tickets for you for Hill 16.'

Ben bristled: 'You know what you can do with your Hill 16 tickets.'

Dunne is convinced that the goateed building society boss was holding on to the better seats for his Dublin 4 pals. A few weeks later, when his fixed-term deposit came up for renewal, Dunne removed several millions from the Irish Nationwide. Still angry two years later, Dunne told me, 'I am not good enough for those Dublin 4 snobs. Since that day the only man with a beard I ever trusted was Santa Claus.'

While Fingleton's style ensured that he received far more media attention than any of his rivals, his operation had substance and he ran a tight ship. After the Irish Permanent (in 1994) and First National (in 1998) had embarked on public flotations, their members received windfall gains. Hungry investors immediately sought the next building society on the block. The Nationwide became the clear favourite, and members of the building society began to anticipate the windfall that would come with a sale. Deposits poured in as hopes rose of a distribution approaching €15,000 for each qualifying member. Building societies were not obliged to disclose the number of depositors on the books, but Fingers was rumoured to have built up some 125,000 savers, giving him a strong capital base. To deter carpetbaggers he introduced a minimum level of savings – at least €20,000 for over two years – for those who would ultimately benefit if the society was ever sold. Members with home loans would also qualify.

Expectations among members were unrealistically high. Along with those expectations came impatience. Year after year Fingleton was frustrated in his efforts to sell the society outright: a change in the law was needed in order for him to take his preferred route of selling the society in a single transaction to a bank. As the law stood, no such sale could take place until five years after the society dispensed with its mutual status.

At successive AGMs he pleaded with angry members that legislation was just round the corner. The meetings attracted increasing numbers of rebels seeking to depose the boss. Despite Fingleton's political clout the legislation was delayed for several years as the government wavered between the competing demands of the Irish Nationwide and its rival society, the EBS. Eventually, in the spring of 2006, the two building societies agreed a compromise which would allow both to take whichever course they wanted. The Building Societies Bill was passed in a late-night Dáil debate just before the summer recess. Fingleton was at last free to sell the society.

Fingers, now sixty-eight years of age, was in a hurry. He quickly headed for the market in search of a suitor. But the clouds were beginning to gather over the global banking system. By the time he was ready to talk turkey, it was autumn 2007; Northern Rock had gone bust and the credit crunch had begun. In October he appointed Goldman Sachs as advisers on the sale, but by then banks were faltering worldwide. None of the big Irish banks showed much interest. Members had hoped for a bidding war between a blue-chip foreigner and Irish Life & Permanent, but none materialized. The quality of possible bidders was second-division. Interest had been expressed by Landsbanki of Iceland, and also by Irish financier Derek Quinlan's vehicle, Quinlan Private, in a joint bid with the Bank of Scotland. The optimistic number of €1.5 billion was put on the value of the society, but the valuation diminished by the month and the suitors began to vanish. First Quinlan Private, furious that its name had appeared in the press, and next Landsbanki, under intense pressure on the home front in Iceland, pulled out. A few months later Landsbanki was rescued by the Icelandic government.

Fingleton was a year too late. There was no one left in the field.

On one flank there was an irate membership seeing its windfall evaporating by the day. On the other Fingers suddenly faced a group of property developers with debts to the Irish Nationwide that looked increasingly menacing. For years the same developers had been the source of a spike in his profit figures. They had made Fingers into a magician. Now he was facing a horrific figure for bad debts.

Fingleton was more personally vulnerable than other

bankers. Two fundamental questions were suddenly being asked. How was a building society ever allowed to become a developers' bank? And how did Fingleton himself manage to be paid millions while his society was facing possible doomsday?

For years Irish Nationwide members were happy for the maestro to walk away with a huge pay packet as long as he performed miracles for them and as long as the prospect of €15,000 or €20,000 landing in their pockets remained alive. Fingers was given the credit for building up this comfort zone for their rainy day. But once the prospect of a big payday for the members drifted, they began to question whether he was the magician they had once believed. Admiration turned into disillusion.

When the property market was booming, members and managers alike were gung-ho; but when the manure hit the fan, everyone started to play the blame game. In a matter of months Fingleton turned from hero to villain.

5. A Deadly Triumvirate

Ireland's bankers could not have destroyed the economy on their own. They did it in league with the property developers, who borrowed recklessly on the apparent assumption that the good times would never stop rolling, and with the Fianna Fáil-led government, which provided a tasty menu of tax breaks for its developer friends.

In early 2007 all three elements of the triumvirate – banks, developers and Fianna Fáil – seemed to be unstoppable. The government, awash with revenue from property taxes, was on the verge of winning a hat-trick of general elections; hugely enriched bankers had announced record profits; and the builders were billionaires.

The Tent

It was Tuesday 15 May 2007. The general election campaign was in full swing, and Bertie Ahern's old friend Tony Blair had set up a 'spectacular' to help him out. The Taoiseach was to be honoured for his role in the peace process, and would deliver a historic oration. Back in Ireland the live television coverage was designed to portray him as a great statesman – in the dying days of his faltering election campaign.

Tickets were like gold dust. Irish TDs and senators had been turned away. Staff at the Irish Embassy in London were relegated to the waiting list. Even one of the architects of the peace process, Albert Reynolds, was excluded. Albert was no friend of Bertie's.

Assembling in the Royal Gallery of the Palace of Westminster were Blair, his predecessor John Major and Chancellor Gordon Brown, who would succeed him as prime minister the following month. Former Labour Party leader Neil Kinnock, General John de Chastelain, former Secretary of State for Northern Ireland Lord Peter Brooke and the incumbent Peter Hain took their seats.

Suddenly, down the Royal Gallery strode a couple in full plumage. They were unrecognized by the British VIPs, but familiar to the very few Irish politicians who had made the cut. One told me that he gasped with shock at the sight of them. He asked himself, 'What in the name of God are they doing here?'

Ireland's most controversial property developer, Sean Dunne, and his beautiful young wife, journalist Gayle Killilea, strutted into the Royal Gallery as though they had single-handedly brought peace to the warring communities in Northern Ireland. The glamorous duo were there by special invitation of Bertie Ahern. Apparently the builder from Carlow had asked for two tickets and the Taoiseach had delivered. Tongues in Ireland instantly began to wag. Many asked how a rough diamond like Dunne, a property developer to boot, had such clout that he could command a seat at the table of the mighty.

It was a fair question.

And it was not the last time that Dunne surfaced surprisingly in Bertie's party at international events of historic importance. A year later, in April 2008, he pulled off the double when he was included in the Irish delegation visiting the US Congress for Bertie's farewell address.

Dunne was a uniquely conspicuous example of his breed.

In July 2005 he had shocked his fellow developers – who are not easily shocked – when he paid €260 million for the five-acre Jurys site in Ballsbridge, a transaction that set a spectacular new Irish record of €53.7 million an acre. A few months later Dunne bought the adjacent Berkeley Court Hotel site for another €119 million, this time clocking up a new record of €57.5 million an acre. He was soon to reveal ambitious plans to develop the site into 'Dublin's Knightsbridge', with 500 apartments and a 37-storey tower. In April 2006 Dunne paid €200 million for a piece of the AIB Bank-centre site, just down the road from the hotel sites. And in August 2006 Dunne's love affair with Ballsbridge climaxed: he bought Hume House, on a 65-acre site, in a swap deal with Irish Life. In their book *The Builders*, Frank McDonald and Kathy Sheridan calculate that Dunne paid the equivalent of €195 million an acre for the site.

Dunne is a Fianna Fáil groupie who cultivates the party top brass assiduously. He invited both Ahern and Finance Minister Charlie McCreevy to his wedding to Killilea in 2004, but the two had more pressing engagements. By all accounts they missed a good bash on Aristotle Onassis's yacht, *Christina O*, in the Mediterranean, a celebration reputed to have cost the developer €1.5 million.

Dunne's personal assistant Anto Kelly is a prominent member of Ógra Fianna Fáil and was a one-time election agent for the former Fianna Fáil minister and current Dáil Ceann Comhairle, John O'Donoghue.

Dunne may have relished the elevated atmosphere at Westminster and Washington, but he could also mix it with the other side of life. As a Fianna Fáil groupie he was a frequent visitor to another, but more humble, Bertie gig: the infamous Fianna Fáil fund-raising tent at the Galway Races.

He has happy memories of the Galway tent. One day, as

the racing ended, Bertie Ahern was holding court at his table. His usual gang of Des Richardson, Attorney General Rory Brady, the late senator Tony Kett and Dunne himself were shooting the breeze. A young reporter from the *Sunday Independent* approached the Taoiseach's table to interview Richardson for the paper. Before she could reach her quarry, Dunne was on his feet. He hijacked the young Gayle Killilea and began the wooing process that ended in the high-society marriage. Killilea never did the interview with Richardson.

Dunne was only one of many developers to frequent the Fianna Fáil tent in Galway. The tent was established in 1994, when Albert Reynolds was in his last months as leader, and it grew to flourish under Bertie. Other key personalities there included the most colourful of all Ireland's builders, Mick Bailey.

The Bailey brothers, Mick and Tom, were the original villains of the Flood Tribunal. After giving evidence to the tribunal in 2000 about corrupt payments to politicians and council officials in North Dublin, they were savaged in Justice Fergus Flood's 2002 interim report. He threw the book at them, condemning the brothers for lying, making false allegations, obstruction and leaking to the media. Unperturbed by the tribunal's dressing down, the Bailey brothers surpassed themselves when, four years later, they made an all-time record settlement with the Revenue for €22.17 million.

The Baileys were quintessential Fianna Fáil. The quieter of the brothers, Tom, had taken time off work in 2002 to canvass for the party in Roscommon. Both men remained loyalists to the last. In turn they were never cold-shouldered by the party hierarchy, despite their transgressions. They remained welcome guests in the Galway tent.

The news of Mick's record tax settlement broke in June 2006 – the same day as Charles Haughey's state funeral. Mick, a pal of the former Taoiseach, was greeted at the funeral mass by the party faithful as an honoured guest.

Mick Bailey, a fanatical racegoer and also joint Master of the Ward Hunt in his native Co. Meath, was invariably the life and soul of the Galway tent. He would regularly take a table for three days at the Galway Races – two days for himself and one for his wife on Ladies Day.

At the end of the meeting he would often render 'The West's Awake' to a well-lubricated audience. It was Mick who, in a moment of exuberance at Cheltenham Races, was reported to have given the Queen Mother a big hug, planted a kiss on her cheek, told her she was 'a great woman' and invited her to Ireland.

Less colourful builders and businessmen who made frequent trips to the Galway tent included Bernard McNamara of Michael McNamara & Co, Paddy McKillen of Clarendon Properties, Sean Mulryan of Ballymore Properties, Johnny Ronan of Treasury Holdings, Seamus Ross of Menolly Homes and Padraig Rhatigan, a top Galway builder.

The tent became an annual flashpoint of controversy. When asked, Bertie Ahern insisted that Fianna Fáil only raised €150,000 each year at the races; but it was widely seen as an occasion where developers could rub shoulders with cabinet ministers in a well-oiled atmosphere. It gave the builders access to power and it provided funds for the Fianna Fáil party. A table of ten on the most popular days, Wednesday and Thursday, cost €4,000 in 2007, its final year. For that, supporters could chew the ear off Bertie and his cabinet colleagues. After they had enjoyed the Galway tent hospitality, some of the guests appeared on the list of those giving generously to Fianna Fáil candidates standing for election.

Paschal Taggart, property investor and former chairman of Bord na gCon, the semi-state greyhound racing organization, was a regular guest at the tent. He enjoyed it and did not see anything sinister in it. 'I never saw any business done in the tent,' he says. 'It was real end-of-term stuff for everyone. It was the end of July, the Dáil was in recess, the school exams were over and it was the beginning of the builders' holidays. It was fun, fun, fun with a few glasses of wine drunk, meaning that everyone was in the best of form.'

Bang in the centre of it all was Bertie. The Taoiseach would move from table to table, greeting his wealthy guests with his standard, 'How are all the hard-working men?' Then he would pose for the mandatory photograph with a builder's wife or two and move on. 'We can't run the party without it,' he insisted in 2005, when the propriety of the tent was questioned once again. He said it was not a rich builders' bash, contrary to media claims: 'The people in my constituency who come are ordinary Joe Soaps who put their hands in their pocket and have a great week in Galway.'

His successor Brian Cowen, although a frequenter of the tent, took a less benign view. Cowen believed that the image of builders and politicians scratching each other's backs, at a time when the excesses of property developers had brought about a national crisis, was doing damage to the party. In the words of Fianna Fáil Senate leader Donie Cassidy, the Galway tent 'was making us a holy show'. Cowen killed off his predecessor's baby within three weeks of gaining power.

So the tent folded – just in time for the builders, who had run out of cash by the time Brian Cowen judged it a liability.

The Tribe

The connections between Fianna Fáil and the property developers stretched far beyond a gig in Galway. They shared

social, cultural and tribal occasions. Builders turned up in
force at Fianna Fáil weddings and vice versa. They liked each
other's company and shared a common outlook. Builders
became part of the Fianna Fáil family. Galway was merely
an annual tribal war dance.

The warriors included Bernard McNamara, a former
Fianna Fáil councillor and 1981 general election candidate;
Sean Dunne, a close neighbour of Bertie's moneybags, Des
Richardson, before Dunne moved to his Shrewsbury Road
pile; and Seamus Ross, the biggest house-builder in Ireland,
who had crossed paths with the late Fianna Fáil TD Liam
Lawlor over housing deals. Ross told the Mahon Tribunal
that he had paid Lawlor over £40,000 to change the postal
address of one of his estates from 'Clondalkin' to 'Lucan'. As
a result he was able to charge £5,000 extra for each house.
He was reported in Frank McDonald and Kathy Sheridan's
book *The Builders* to have the ear of Finance Minister Brian
Lenihan, Ross's local TD in Castleknock.

Johnny Ronan of Treasury Holdings has multiple ties to
Fianna Fáil. Ronan's Treasury Building in Dublin's Grand
Canal Street was used as the Fianna Fáil party's campaign
headquarters in the 2002 and 2007 general elections. It was
nicknamed 'Tora Bora' by P. J. Mara, likening Fianna Fáil's
zealots to the fanatics holed up in Osama bin Laden's cave.

Ronan also employed Paddy Teahon, the former secretary
general of the Department of the Taoiseach, as a director and
a consultant. Teahon was forced to stand down as head of
the Campus Stadium Ireland project – aka the 'Bertie Bowl'
– in 2002 in a row over the award of contracts. Unsurprisingly, Teahon moved into banking and property development
after leaving the Taoiseach's department, joining former
financial regulator Liam O'Reilly on the board of Merrill
Lynch International Bank. At the Leopardstown Races in

2007 he told Michael O'Regan of the *Irish Times*, 'I must be the most occupied non-executive director of all time.'

One of the curious features of the property boom was the extraordinary ability of the internal Fianna Fáil magazine, *The Nation*, to attract advertising. *The Nation* included the sort of dull articles you'd expect in such a publication – 'A day in the life of a Taoiseach', notices about party matters, functions and fund-raisers. Few niche magazines of this sort achieve much advertising, but *The Nation* was an exception. It was overflowing with advertisements. Launched in November 2003, it was edited by Conor Lenihan, later to become a junior minister under Bertie Ahern. In its second edition, thirty out of sixty advertisements were from builders and developers. The familiar old names were there – Mick Bailey's Bovale, Paddy Kelly's Redquartz, Johnny Ronan's Treasury Holdings, Sean Mulryan's Ballymore, Gerry Whelan's Maplewood and Jim Mansfield's Citywest Hotel. The two building societies, Michael Fingleton's Irish Nationwide and the Fianna Fáil-leaning EBS, also took space. Some developers advertised in *The Nation*; some gave donations; some headed for the Galway tent. But all roads led to Fianna Fáil.

The Club

The K Club in Straffan, Co. Kildare, competed with the Galway tent as a playground for Ireland's rich builders. Here a wider set of developers could be found networking at the Smurfit-owned hotel and golf club. A number of them were so close-knit that they opted to live together – for part of the time at least – as neighbours, buying multimillion-euro second homes in the K Club complex.

Michael Smurfit himself led the way with a magnificent

mansion built in the grounds of the Smurfit 'Village'. K Club part-owner and property tycoon Gerry Gannon followed suit. Gannon, who owns vast swathes of land in north and south Dublin, is a Fianna Fáil supporter. In early 2009 he was named by the *Sunday Times* as one of the ten members of the 'Golden Circle' who were lent money by Anglo Irish Bank in order to buy the troubled bank's shares after Sean Quinn's vast shareholding was unwound.

Purchasing houses within the K Club complex became a status symbol, almost a rite of passage among the Smurfit set. One owner told me that, 'If you didn't have one you were not really on the inside track.'

A second member of the Anglo ten named by the *Sunday Independent*, Paddy McKillen, also bought a K Club trophy house and numbers among a growing group of residents who do not even play golf. McKillen, like so many builders and developers, left school in his teens. After working in the family business, DC Exhausts, he became wealthy in property and established good Fianna Fáil connections, being appointed in 1989 by Minister for the Environment Pádraig Flynn to the board of the Construction Industry Development Board at the age of just thirty-four.

His first really big property break was his purchase of Dublin's Jervis Hospital site in 1992 for €5.7 million. He built a shopping centre on the location, greatly assisted by the grant of urban renewal status in 1994 by a Fianna Fáil administration. The incentives attached to the status allowed McKillen to write off the capital he spent on construction against income he received from rents. He coined it when the new shopping centre took off and rents rocketed. In September 2008 the *Irish Times* valued his investment at €400 million.

McKillen's property interests are global. He has quietly bought up properties in Japan, Vietnam and France. He is believed to own a vineyard in France and several buildings in Paris. In 2008 he paid €38 million for a prime investment site on Oxford Street. He is part-owner of the Clarence Hotel on Dublin's quays along with Bono, the Edge and Derek Quinlan, and lives in a massive modern house in Dublin's Foxrock. He is a non-drinker with huge energy for work, but is no puritan. He drives a Mercedes and is married to a glamorous former model, Maura McMenamin.

Seamus Ross, a third member of the Anglo Golden Circle named by the *Sunday Times* and a K Club neighbour of Gannon and McKillen, was yet another to leave school in his teens. He finished his formal education in Ballinamuck, Co. Longford, and went to work as a carpenter. Like McKillen, he is not known for his golfing prowess – but he knew the value of tickets to the Ryder Cup when the event was held at the K Club in 2006, offering tickets to every member of South Dublin County Council. All the councillors, bar one Fianna Fáil member (who later had a change of heart), turned them down, sensing they might be compromised by accepting a gift from a property developer.

After Tiarnan O'Mahoney lost the battle to succeed Sean FitzPatrick as Anglo's chief executive, he set up a specialist lending outfit called ISTC and sought investors. According to the *Sunday Times*, Ross entrusted €10 million to O'Mahoney, who promptly lost the lot.

Seamus Ross was not alone in putting his faith in O'Mahoney's new venture. Other high-profile clients of Anglo backed the bank's former Treasury chief with minimum investments of €2 million. These included Sean FitzPatrick himself, billionaire businessman Sean Quinn, telecoms king Denis O'Brien, Smurfits' Gary McGann, and builder Paddy Kelly. O'Mahoney's enterprise borrowed money in the international debt markets, invested in complex credit products and lent the money on as capital to banks. It also brokered and managed debt transactions for financial institutions. In 2007 it was caught in the credit crunch when it was forced to sell some of its loans at deep discounts. Barely two years old, ISTC fell into examinership, losing €850 million – the largest cash loss in Irish corporate history.

Sean Mulryan, another Fianna Fáil supporter with a K Club home, plays a good game of golf and, in a rare corporate coup, managed to persuade its owner Michael Smurfit to sit on the board of Ballymore. Trained as a stonemason in Roscommon, Mulryan moved to Dublin in his early twenties and funded his first project with the sale of his own house. He has since gone on to develop a seriously international profile as a developer, with major projects in London's docklands and Eastern Europe. He has a genuine interest in horses, owning the 350-acre Ardenode Stud in Ballymore Eustace, Co. Kildare, where he is reputed to hold lavish parties. Numbered among the guests are many of the great and the good in Ireland's political and banking world, including Michael Fingleton and Sean FitzPatrick. He counts Brian Cowen among his friends.

In the 2009 *Sunday Times* Irish Rich List, Mulryan was ranked in 18th place with a personal wealth of €363 million despite a loss of over €230 million in just one year; he and his wife Bernardine suddenly sold off half of their fifty racehorses.

Other property developers with K Club houses include Noel Smyth and Bernard McNamara. Sean FitzPatrick is among the most prominent members of the K Club who have resisted any pressure to buy one of the plush residences. FitzPatrick's Anglo lent money to McNamara, Gannon, Mulryan, McKillen, Ross and Smyth. He knew them all. He preferred the golf course at Druid's Glen in his home county of Wicklow but he kept Anglo's profile high in Straffan –

where both of his major competitors, Bank of Ireland and AIB, had taken out corporate memberships. Anglo needed a watchful presence there.

The Incentives

Why were the developers so keen to support Fianna Fáil?

Naturally enough, they wanted access to the party that seemed to be permanently in power. They needed influence at the top to grease the skids on their speculative activities. Starting in the late 1990s, Fianna Fáil brought in a number of measures – many relating to the tax code – that encouraged a frenzy of development and debt.

Early in his tenure as Finance Minister, Charlie McCreevy, a true believer in the ideology of the free market, halved capital gains tax, reduced capital acquisitions tax, brought corporate taxes lower and introduced a series of income tax cuts which meant that every citizen began to see more in his or her weekly pay packet. Spending power increased, including the ability to pay more for houses and repay more on mortgages. McCreevy's reduction of capital gains tax from 40 per cent to 20 per cent in 1997 released assets that had been paralysed for decades. Perhaps most significantly, the taxes on profits from residential development and on development land were both halved to 20 per cent, in 1998 and 1999 respectively.

In addition – and far more controversially – Bertie's government created a number of tax breaks that built a Utopia for the construction boys. Some of them were extremely grateful – none more so than Bernard McNamara, who told Ivor Kenny in his book *Leaders* that his move into property 'largely came about from the capacity to use tax breaks'.

McNamara may have moved beyond his Fianna Fáil electoral ambitions, but he always maintained his political
contacts. He is a close friend of Tony Killeen, the Fianna Fáil
junior minister from his native Clare, and he employed Fianna
Fáil follower Jim Nugent – one of six pals of Bertie Ahern
who gave the soon-to-be-Taoiseach a 'dig-out' in 1993 – as
an industrial relations adviser. McNamara told Ivor Kenny
that confronted with a five-week bricklayers' strike, Nugent
advised him to send the brickies' last ten payslips to their
wives; shocked to learn how much they were earning, the
brickies' wives had them back on site within ten days.

McNamara's good standing within Fianna Fáil was reflected
by his appointment to numerous state boards, including the
Great Southern Hotels Group (before it was privatized) and
the National Roads Authority. John O'Donoghue, then Arts
Minister, made McNamara a director of the National Gallery
in 2003, two years after McNamara built the gallery's €25
million Millennium Wing.

Tax breaks sprouted up everywhere in the Fianna Fáil
years. Capital allowances were on offer for hotels, holiday
camps and holiday cottages, sports injury clinics, third-level
education buildings, student accommodation, multi-storey
car parks, park and ride facilities, crèches, private hospitals
and nursing homes. Running parallel with these tax breaks
were rural, urban and town renewal designations, which
targeted certain specific areas as suitable for development and
allowed for up to 100 per cent of the costs of construction of
a building to be deducted from the owner's tax bill over a
number of years.

These measures gave an early lift-off to the ambitions of
developers, and had the effect of tilting the entire national
economy: by 2006, 24 per cent of gross national product was
accounted for by the construction industry.

McNamara was typical of his breed. He saw all the angles. Borrowing money from indulgent banks, he built hotels, hospitals, car parks and student accommodation. McNamara borrowed from Bank of Ireland, Ulster Bank, IIB, AIB, HBOS and, above all, Anglo. They were all screaming for McNamara's business; they would have stabbed each other for it.

McNamara seized the opportunity to build an empire. Flagship buildings included Dublin's redeveloped Shelbourne Hotel, the Donnybrook Burlington (financed with a €288 million debt from HBOS), the Radisson in Galway, and Bertie's favourite hotel, the Parknasilla in Co. Kerry. He had also constructed a string of private hospitals, including the Galway Clinic and the Hermitage in Lucan.

McNamara was only one of many with a sharp eye for the tax breaks. Another was Derek Quinlan, McNamara's partner in the old Glass Bottle site in Dublin's Ringsend. Along with the controversial Dublin Docks Development Authority (DDDA), the two bought the site for €411 million.

Quinlan, a tax expert turned property developer, was ideally placed to take advantage of all the incentives provided by Fianna Fáil. He had been educated at UCD, taken a BComm and qualified as an accountant with Coopers & Lybrand before joining the investigation branch of the Revenue. Quinlan was a skilful gamekeeper turned poacher. He formed Quinlan Private in 1989 as a humble tax consultancy before converting it into a go-go property investment company. He enlisted some of the richest people in Ireland on to his books as clients, building his assets under management up to over €1 billion. In 2000 he led a consortium of big business names into a project funding Dublin's Four Seasons Hotel. He used his expertise from his Revenue days to exploit many of the government's tax incentives, particularly the break for car parks.

Unlike most of the other developers, he would not have
been seen dead in the Galway tent. Quinlan was the son of
an army officer from Kerry. He attended Blackrock College,
where he formed a lifelong friendship with Dermot Gleeson,
later to become AIB chairman; today the two are neighbours
in Shrewsbury Road, Dublin's most expensive avenue. When
Quinlan assembled the consortium to bring the Four Seasons
Hotel to Dublin's Ballsbridge, he enlisted Gleeson as an
investor.

Quinlan may have exploited the openings offered at home,
but his most sensational deal was undoubtedly his 2004
purchase of the Savoy group of hotels, which includes the
Savoy, the Berkeley, the Connaught and Claridge's, for £750
million. The deal caught the Irish public's imagination as it
represented a sensational success for an Irish property mogul
in England. He managed a quick turn from the deal, selling
the Savoy alone to a Saudi prince for over £200 million
within a few months.

While the tax breaks were giving a boost to the construction industry, political criticism was intensifying. Stories
were emerging in the media about how many of Ireland's
richest men were not paying a cent in taxes. In September
2004 Brian Cowen took over from Charlie McCreevy as
Minister for Finance. In his December Budget he announced
a review of tax incentives. Indecon Consultants, a consultancy group, was commissioned by the Fianna Fáil government
to conduct the review.

The choice of Indecon was important. Indecon was not
one of those consultancies whose arm could be twisted to
reach a conclusion convenient to the clients. They were in
no one's pocket. Their conclusions would be independent
and might not suit the government or its builder friends.
They were thorough. They had an international reputation.

At the same time Goodbody Economic Consultants was appointed to report on urban and rural renewal schemes.

Was Cowen suddenly serious? Had he realized that the balloon might go up? Did he want cover for necessary measures certain to alienate party supporters? Perhaps he wanted a robust analysis? There was a crying need for it. Incredibly, no one in the Department of Finance knew how much the property-related tax breaks had cost the Exchequer. Nor was there any data on what impact the tax breaks had had on property or land prices. Indecon found that they had increased both. Perhaps more alarming was Indecon's finding that all financial institutions agreed this to be the case. They had done nothing about it – except lend more money, further inflaming the market.

Political opponents regarded Cowen's decision to seek a consultant's opinion as a delaying tactic. The extra time needed to report would give the builders further breathing space. And more profits. In a Dáil exchange on 7 February 2006 Labour leader Pat Rabbitte clashed with Taoiseach Bertie Ahern over the tax breaks. Rabbitte predicted that 'the property-based schemes will not finish until after the general election, when we will have a whole new situation'. The Labour leader saw property breaks as a purely party issue for Fianna Fáil: they would keep Fianna Fáil's building buddies featherbedded in exchange for political funding.

Bertie replied by insisting that the tax breaks had been introduced for the good of the nation, maintaining that if there had been no incentives for property developers 'this country would still be a basket case'. Fianna Fáil had put the incentives in place for the good of the state, to bring jobs and prosperity to Ireland.

Rabbitte was right in at least one respect. It took until after the general election of 2007 for anything concrete to be done about the property tax breaks. They were terminated in July 2008. By then, of course, it was far too late. The economy had overheated, and then it had turned. The property market was heading over the precipice. Builders were being badly stung. The bankers had been rumbled.

But by that time it didn't matter to Fianna Fáil. They had won the general election, with a little help from their builder friends.

The car-park tax incentive had stirred calm thoughtful Brian Carey, business editor of the *Sunday Tribune*, into uncharacteristic anger. As early as January 2003 he wrote that:

Quinlan's meteoric rise is one of the most tangible manifestations of the government's Faustian pact with the country's high rollers. When funds were scarce and tax breaks were plentiful, government was happy to allow generous reliefs to high-net-worth individuals in return for a flood of investments in car parks, hotels and urban regeneration projects.

John FitzGerald of the Economic and Social Research Institute had given early warnings of the fundamental dangers inherent in the tax breaks. Despite being the son of former Taoiseach Garret and the husband of former Labour minister Eithne, John FitzGerald did not bang on about a few Fianna Fáil cowboys becoming billionaires. Instead, he made the more telling point that the incentives for property developers threatened the whole economy. At the time of the Indecon report, he told the *Sunday Times* that the tax reliefs had made 'a hard landing more likely. Even if tax incentives were not behind the building of your house or the one next door, they have driven the construction boom and allowed builders to put up prices.'

He was right. The artificial nature of the boom ensured a matching collapse when the worm turned.

It is not as if Fianna Fáil did not see the danger. As early as 2002 Charlie McCreevy had signalled that most of the property incentives – including urban, rural and town renewal and tax breaks on car parks – were set to be terminated by 31 December 2004. One year later, however, he extended the termination date by another eighteen months, to July 2006. The property bubble was well inflated by then. Politicians were reluctant to burst it before a general election due by May 2007. And all the time the builders had been lobbying the government frantically for a delay.

It took until February 2006 for the full Indecon and Goodbody reports to be published, more than three years after McCreevy had first announced the beginning of the end for property reliefs. The delay had bought valuable time for the builders.

Indecon's report was brave and decisive. There was no ambiguity. It gave the thumbs down to nearly all the property breaks. The incentives did not stand any serious scrutiny. Indecon's words – 'the tax incentives are an extremely high-cost and wasteful mechanism to achieve objectives' – could not have been comforting for Cowen or Ahern.

The figures cited in the report were devastating. The total cost to the Exchequer of all the property-based tax breaks granted came to €6.8 billion. The net figures were even more revealing. The consultants reported that even after all the stamp duty, the VAT and the employment spin-offs, the Exchequer – and hence the taxpayer – was a net loser.

Indecon recommended an immediate end to tax incentives for hotels, student accommodation and multi-storey car parks. Indecon asserted that it saw 'no cause of market failure which would justify government subsidies for multi-storey car parks'.

The Goodbody Economic Consultants report revealed that

the urban and rural renewal schemes had been even costlier to the state. Goodbody asserted that the rural renewal scheme, aimed at reviving counties Leitrim, Longford and certain electoral areas of Cavan, Roscommon and Sligo, had merely resulted in excess supply of housing – with a state subsidy of €59,300 per house. Surprisingly, it claimed that the urban renewal scheme had been 'extremely valuable' with positive impacts on dereliction and urban design, and had kick-started developments in a number of areas. It said that there had been benefits in the areas of commercial development, but the scheme had been less successful in delivering social benefits.

Goodbody then confirmed the worst fears of the government's critics. The tax benefits had gone to a small group of high-income individuals; they had brought about 'significant property price inflation'; and the beneficiaries had been not the ordinary people of urban and rural Ireland, but 'land-owners and property developers'.

Neither Indecon nor Goodbody asked the sixty-four thousand dollar question. Were specific political decisions on urban and rural renewal designations capable of enriching individuals at the stroke of a ministerial pen? That was beyond the consultants' brief but it remained the elephant in the room. The power to designate whole areas as fit for urban or rural renewal lay with the Minister for the Environment. Allegations of abuse of this power have been made against Fianna Fáil in the tribunals of inquiry.

Taoiseach Bertie Ahern was at the centre of one such allegation that remained unresolved for several years. Whatever the merits of the case – which led indirectly to the discovery of the peculiar transactions that brought about Bertie's resignation – it demonstrated the unhealthy scope for corruption in legislation that gave such power to ministers to alter the value of a potential site.

Bertie Ahern has denied a claim that he was given £80,000 by builder Owen O'Callaghan to block a rival businessman's bid for a tax break. Tom Gilmartin, a celebrated but erratic witness in the Mahon Tribunal, claimed that he had been told by O'Callaghan that he gave Bertie the money to stop Green Property from developing the Blanchardstown Centre. Green Property was seeking to gain urban renewal status for Blanchardstown.

Blanchardstown failed to get the renewal status even though local politicians had engaged in a serious lobbying effort. Gilmartin claimed that O'Callaghan had boasted that his £80,000 bung to Ahern had ensured that Green Property failed to get the tax break. O'Callaghan denied the claim.

Numerous other cases in the tribunals showed what a political minefield the renewal designations were. Another Fianna Fáil minister, Pádraig Flynn, came under serious scrutiny from the Mahon Tribunal for his decision to designate land in Tallaght for urban renewal benefits.

Monarch Properties, well-known supporters of Fianna Fáil, had been sitting on the land in Tallaght until Flynn used his powers as minister to designate it as eligible for urban renewal. These included mouth-watering 100 per cent capital allowances for investors, double rent allowances and rates remission. The anchor tenants, including Dunnes stores, were entitled to write off their capital costs against tax over five years.

When Flynn appeared before the tribunal in 2006 he insisted that three meetings he held around that time with Phil Monahan of Monarch Properties were only courtesy visits. When asked how he reconciled this claim with the detailed preparation of land rezoning material for these meetings by his staff, he replied that he had no recollection of discussing rezoning.

Phil Monahan had made a £25,000 contribution to Fianna

Fáil in 1991 and other individual contributions to Fianna Fáil candidates' campaigns.

Goodbodys and Indecon found that the net tax forgone by the Exchequer in relation to the various incentive schemes was €2.8 billion. Combined, the property tax breaks, the urban renewal schemes and the rural renewal schemes had been a drain on the taxpayer; but they had been a bonanza for the builders, an election-winning formula for the government and a godsend for the bankers.

In June 2006 Cowen signed an order to phase out urban and rural renewal together with many of the more controversial tax breaks. Most would end by December 2006, but transitional arrangements remained in place until June 2008. It took Fianna Fáil politicians five and a half years to phase out the main legislative measures that had blown up the property bubble.

Despite the tribal relationship between Fianna Fáil and the builders, many of the property developers proclaim no party allegiance, pleading that they are practical people and must deal with those in power. 'Fianna Fáil is always in power. Politicians are a channel for getting things done. So we deal with Fianna Fáil,' says one of them. It worked.

It also rings true. When Fine Gael last came to power for a brief period in 1994 their debt was almost instantly cleared by their main fund-raiser, Michael Lowry. The scent of power brought a flood of money. A multimillion-pound party debt was cleared in a matter of months. Some of the subscribers were the same builders who had supported Fianna Fáil a few months previously.

But one Fine Gael insider remembers that it was the bankers, not the builders, who gave the party a dig-out once they enjoyed their period in power, however brief. She recalls that

Bank of Ireland suddenly gave Fine Gael much better terms, writing off interest once they were in office. 'AIB under Tom Mulcahy changed its attitude to us too. We saw money from the banks. At the time the builders were nothing like as flush as they were to be ten years later.'

She remembers that Richard Burrows, then chief executive of Irish Distillers, was particularly sympathetic at the time. Ten years later, Burrows was to become governor of the Bank of Ireland.

Burrows seems to have been a political neutral. In 2002 Irish Distillers' name cropped up as a supporter of Fianna Fáil. The drinks company, where Burrows was chairman, held a fund-raiser for Fianna Fáil. They sent the party €750 from the fund-raiser followed by a €5,078 donation.

Richard Burrows's name surfaced again in support of another Fianna Fáil campaign, this time as a banker in 2004. Mary McAleese was soliciting funds for her re-election. Eyebrows were raised when directors of the Bank of Ireland flocked to the Fianna Fáil candidate's flag. Burrows personally ponied up €2,500 for McAleese. A diplomatic move, as he was next in line for the governorship and McAleese's re-election fund-raising committee was chaired by none other than the governor at the time, Laurence Crowley. Two other directors of the bank, Terry Neill and chief executive Brian Goggin, sent McAleese a €2,500 personal donation towards her campaign. Their decision looked like a three-line whip imposed on the top brass. Goggin was never – before or since – known to have as much as a hint of a party-political preference.

Crowley told me that, 'I personally asked them for the contributions. I was chairman of President McAleese's re-election fund-raising committee. I think she is a fine person and I knew her husband Martin from our Stokes Kennedy Crowley accountancy days. I admire their efforts to bring the communities in Northern Ireland together. At the end of the day all the money was returned as she was elected unopposed.'

Another bank director to back the Fianna Fáil presidential candidate was Kieran McGowan, a board member of Irish Life & Permanent. No such enthusiasm was shown by AIB, where former Fine Gael Attorney General Dermot Gleeson held the chair.

Some of the usual suspects sent in similar cheques for McAleese, including four from the Durkan builders' stable (all for €2,500) and one from Mark Kavanagh's development company, Hardwicke.

Apart from the presidential campaign, financial payments from banks to politicians have been scarce in recent years. Local golf classics have sometimes been supported by branches, but the head offices have shunned the bigger picture, fearful of controversy or being accused of political bias.

There is a mixture of evidence that bankers kowtowed to powerful politicians, but only on a one-off basis. They buckled at the knee in front of threats from Charlie Haughey that he could be 'a dangerous adversary'. AIB and Ansbacher banks absolved Garret FitzGerald of almost £200,000 when he lost a mint on GPA shares. (FitzGerald said in 1999 that he believed his former Attorney General Peter Sutherland, who was chairman of AIB at the time, was unaware of the deal.)

The failure of the banks to cough up large sums of money to political parties is, on the surface, a puzzle. How do they exercise huge political influence without playing the normal political game?

They are good at the game, but they play it a different way. First of all, they fund two lobby groups, not one. They have a stranglehold over both.

Bankers have been the main moneybags of the employers'

The author with Sean FitzPatrick, chief executive and latterly chairman of Anglo Irish Bank, in happier times.

Phil Flynn, the former vice-president of Sinn Féin who became chairman of Bank of Scotland (Ireland). The bank's dramatic cut in mortgage rates in 1999 helped to bring about the lending practices – 100 per cent mortgages, looser lending criteria – that did so much to inflate the property bubble.

John Hurley, long-time governor of the Central Bank, who sounded alarm bells about the property bubble but did little to rein in the banks.

Patrick Neary, the chief executive of the Financial Regulator, whose 'principles-based' regulatory approach proved inadequate.

Sean Dunne, the developer whose land purchases in Ballsbridge constituted perhaps the single biggest property gamble of the boom years, at Croke Park with Irish Nationwide supremo Michael Fingleton.

Fingleton photographed with the Oireachtas golf team that competed in the Army/ Garda/Press/Oireachtas Challenge Cup, sponsored by Irish Nationwide, in 1987. *Back row*: Austin Deasy TD, Senator Denis Cregan, Cathal O'Laoighaire, Hugh Byrne TD, Denis Reid, Senator Donie Cassidy; *front row*: Tom Enright TD, Robert Molloy TD, Michael Fingleton, Colm Hilliard TD.

The Taoiseach and the developers at the races: Bertie Ahern with Bernard McNamara (*upper left, at Galway Races*), Sean Mulryan (*upper right, at Punchestown*), and Sean Dunne (*below, with his wife Gayle Killilea, at Punchestown*).

Businessman and racehorse owner J.P. McManus with Dermot Desmond, who has had a sometimes tempestuous relationship with Ireland's banking and financial services establishments; most recently, in his capacity as a major Bank of Ireland shareholder, he has criticized the appointment of Richie Boucher as the bank's chief executive.

Mick Bailey: property developer, Flood Tribunal villain, tax defaulter, Galway tent regular, and joint master of the Ward Hunt in Co. Meath.

The summer 2004 edition of *The Nation* – the internal Fianna Fáil magazine that was packed with ads bought by property developers and construction firms.

Sean Quinn, Ireland's biggest businessman, whose massive indirect shareholding in the ruined Anglo Irish Bank was unwound with the help of the 'Golden Circle', ten Anglo customers who bought up the shares using money loaned by Anglo itself.

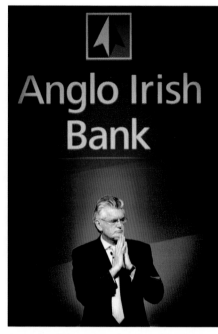

David Drumm, Sean FitzPatrick's successor as chief executive of Anglo Irish Bank, who presided over the bank's most spectacular profit figures – and then over its collapse.

Donal O'Connor, the new Anglo chairman who has various old connections to the bank, at the EGM held immediately after the bank was nationalized.

The author makes a point at the Anglo EGM as Eamon Dunphy (*to author's right*) and other shareholders look on.

Eugene McErlean, former internal auditor of AIB, with the author on his way to testify before an Oireachtas committee regarding the handling by the Central Bank and the Financial Regulator of his allegations about the bank's practices.

Richie Boucher, the Bank of Ireland insider who succeeded Brian Goggin as chief executive.

Gillian Bowler, chairman of Irish Life & Permanent, who survived the fallout from the revelation of the bancassurer's deposit-swap deal with Anglo.

Dermot Gleeson, chairman of AIB, after being hit by an egg hurled by an irate shareholder at the bank's AGM.

When it rains . . . Minister for Finance Brian Lenihan.

Colm McCarthy, the economist whose 'Bord Snip' recommended swingeing cuts in public spending in order to control deficits created by the collapse of government tax revenue and the recapitalization of the banks.

Liam Carroll, arguably Ireland's biggest property developer, photographed outside his home after he was forced to seek court protection for some of his companies against one of his creditors, ACCBank; the other banks supported Carroll's application.

group IBEC for many decades. In 2008 AIB (€194,000), the Bank of Ireland (€200,000), Irish Life (€133,000), National Irish Bank (€64,000), Ulster Bank (€194,000), the Irish Nationwide (€14,000) and EBS (€58,000) were IBEC's biggest contributors.

IBEC was bought long ago – and IBEC has stayed bought. The lobbying body makes representations on behalf of its paymasters to the government. It has suited all governments to keep IBEC and its most important component, the banks, onside over the entire period of social partnership. IBEC has invariably played ball with the government and the social partnership powerhouses in the Department of Finance. IBEC's stance would have pleased its funders in the banks, anxious to keep on the right side of their traditional allies among the mandarins in Merrion Street. Successive administrations (nearly all Fianna Fáil-led) have had reason to be grateful to the banker-led employers group.

Recent returns from IBEC reveal that the influence of bankers on the employers' ruling council is massive. Richard Burrows was IBEC president before he became Bank of Ireland governor. In 2004 IBEC's president was Gary McGann, then a director of Anglo Irish Bank. The treasurer was Tony O'Brien, chairman of Anglo until 2002. Of the four trustees, two were bankers. Maurice Pratt, later to become chairman of the Bank of Scotland, and David Dilger, already on the Bank of Ireland board, ensured that the bankers' ethos was well represented.

Even Eugene Sheehy, the boss at AIB, joined the happy band of bankers and ex-bankers sitting on the IBEC council. Apart from their key leverage with IBEC the banks operate their own Irish Banking Federation to lobby solely for the banking sector. Five years ago the outfit was taken over by Pat Farrell, a former general secretary of Fianna Fáil, an ex-senator and a friend of most of those in power. Farrell is able to pick up the telephone to Finance Minister Brian Lenihan at the drop of a hat. The banks have their social partnership angle sewn up at national level. They are shadow social partners. Their political lines of communication to Fianna Fáil are second to none.

But above all the banks have seen little need for direct access to politicians. In many ways they have deliberately kept their distance. Life has been good for them. As long as they remained below the radar, they were undisturbed. Opposition politicians railed against their overcharging, their monopolistic practices and their downright dishonesty, but governments mainly left them alone. They were the province of the Financial Regulator and the Department of Finance. They were there to be policed by people who supposedly understood the mystery of banking. Politicians were happy to leave oversight of the bankers to others.

The politicians looked after the mandarins. The mandarins looked after the Central Bankers and the regulators. (The governor of the Central Bank was paid more in 2008 than the chairman of the US Federal Reserve, as was the chief executive of the Financial Regulator.) The Central Bankers looked after the bankers. The bankers looked after IBEC. And IBEC looked after the government. The circle of oligarchs was watertight.

The builders and developers were temporary visitors to the oligarchs' table. They were natural outsiders, but they were welcome to the table as long as they provided the vital vehicle to outrageous riches for the insiders. Once the bankers had identified the builders as a vehicle, the regulators turned a blind eye to the orgy of lending, the Department of Finance collected the property taxes and the government used the windfall to win elections. Such a loose, almost anarchic, financial order was a gift to any rogue banker plotting a quick road to riches. Anglo Irish Bank was an inevitable child of such a chaotic system championed by so many powerful vested interests. Provided they all looked after each other, no one would call 'Halt'. Huge pay rewards, not just to the banking elite, ensured co-operation between all the participants in this largesse. Other bankers, eyeing Anglo's easy pickings, set out in hot pursuit of the developers. It was dead easy. Every oligarch was a winner.

The banks did not need to fund the parties. In their hands they always held the ultimate weapon, the destruction of an entire financial system with its unthinkable economic and social consequences. It was not a gauntlet that any government could ever afford to pick up.

6. The Mortgage War

One day in March 1996 the telephone rang in Phil Flynn's office. On the other line was Greg Sparks, a powerful chef de cabinet in the Irish government. Sparks was acting on the orders of the Minister for Finance, Labour's Ruairi Quinn.

Flynn, a former vice-president of Sinn Féin, had been a trade union official for decades. Many, including Ruairi Quinn, believed he had put his republican past behind him. Quinn recalls that as Minister for Labour in the mid-eighties he had hosted a lunch in Leinster House at a time when Flynn was being ostracized by various ministers, including Quinn's Labour Party colleagues Barry Desmond and Liam Kavanagh. But at the lunch Flynn made a speech about how he 'no longer believed in the armed struggle'. Quinn regarded the statement as a watershed.

By March 1996 Flynn had been general secretary of two powerful public service unions, so it was not unusual for him to receive calls from Labour ministers or their fixers, like Greg Sparks, on mundane matters of business.

This call was different. Sparks had an idea to run past Flynn. He wanted the old republican to join the board of the state-owned ICC Bank.

Flynn accepted immediately. Later he met Quinn, told him he did not know much about banking, and was astonished to hear that the minister wanted him not merely as a director, but as chairman.

It was an act of faith by Ruairi Quinn. He believed in Flynn's conversion. Not everyone did, but Flynn became an effective chairman of ICC, working happily with Quinn and his successor as Minister for Finance, Charlie McCreevy. Perhaps his most memorable legacy as chairman was the sale of the ICC to Bank of Scotland in 2001. So skilled did he prove as a negotiator on the ICC side of the table that a hugely impressed Bank of Scotland team asked him to stay on as chairman.

Flynn had worked wonders for himself. A former supporter of the armed struggle, a trade union chief, had become chairman of the Irish subsidiary of a British bastion of capitalism.

The appointment suited the Scottish bank. After their expansion into Ireland the Scots needed some Irish faces to front the operation. None could be better than the nationalist with trade-union street cred.

By the time Flynn took the chair in 2001, the Bank of Scotland had already made a huge impression on Irish banking. Two years earlier it had announced that it would be the first foreign bank to challenge the comfortable club in the Irish mortgage market. It did so by slashing mortgage interest rates to 3.99 per cent, a high-profile reduction to below the psychological Rubicon of 4 per cent. Other banks had been charging on average 1.25 per cent higher for variable rate mortgages.

By any standards the move was groundbreaking. A cut of a full 1 per cent in variable mortgages by a single bank in one swoop was unprecedented. The Bank of Scotland's invasion was greeted with waves of welcome in the media. The bank won the *Sunday Independent* 'Business of the Year' award, narrowly pipping rising entrepreneur Denis O'Brien for the prize.

The Irish business was run from Bank of Scotland's Edinburgh base. As the Bank of Scotland had no retail outlets in Ireland, all mortgages and accounts were put through mortgage brokers.

Some of the shell-shocked bankers of Ireland were initially slow to respond. John Smyth, the boss of First Active, smugly asserted that he was not going to 'lose any sleep' over the dramatic 3.99 per cent rate. Ten days later he reduced introductory rates for first-time buyers to 3.99 per cent. But he kept his variable at 5.25 per cent.

Others were not as sanguine. Within two weeks both AIB and Bank of Ireland took fright. They saw the invader as a real threat. AIB matched the Bank of Scotland's variable rate of 3.99 per cent while Bank of Ireland cut its own to 3.95 per cent.

A full-scale mortgage war had broken out, and the effect on the banks' share prices was dramatic. On the day that their profits were threatened by the rate cuts, a billion pounds was wiped off the value of AIB and Bank of Ireland on the stock market. Bank of Scotland had upset the settled lives of Ireland's bankers.

As the price war raged all the lenders were forced to cut out the fat. Margins on their mortgages (the difference between the borrowing and lending rates) dropped from 2.4 per cent to just 0.5 per cent.

The banks reacted in different ways to the narrowing of their margins on home loans. Tracker mortgages took off. All the lenders shovelled money at potential customers, making up in volume what they were losing in margins.

Lower rates meant that borrowers could afford to borrow more – as they now had to pay back less each month on their mortgages. At the same time, standards began to slip. Lending criteria were quietly relaxed. Where buyers might previously have been allowed to borrow about two and a half times their annual income, bankers began to make loans of

three or four times income. Sometimes applicants for mortgages were encouraged by bank salesmen to state on their
applications that they would take paying guests in their houses
to top up their incomes, even if they had no plans to do so.
Mortgage terms were extended from the normal 20 or 25
years to 35- or even 40-year terms. Buyers could now afford
to borrow even more, because the longer term of the loan
meant that monthly repayments would again be reduced.

All of this was widely seen as great news for consumers.
Cheaper mortgages meant more disposable income. That was
true in the short term, but the longer-term reality was that
bigger loans and looser lending criteria meant higher house
prices and a greater debt burden on borrowers. By 2006, 70
per cent of first-time buyers in Dublin were taking out mortgages with a term of over 30 years. Some borrowers saddled
themselves with debt stretching well into their seventies.

The final, but most inflammable can of petrol thrown on
the raging property furnace was the 100 per cent mortgage:
a loan for the entire selling price of the house. First Active
led the way in introducing these lethal loans in 2005. Others
followed suit, including Bank of Ireland, EBS, Permanent
TSB and Irish Civil Service Building Society.

A few held back from the madness of the 100 per cent loan,
including AIB, Irish Nationwide and National Irish Bank.
But elsewhere 100 per cent mortgages took off. In 2006, 36
per cent of first-time buyers took them out.

Bank of Scotland (Ireland) was also hell-bent on competing
with Ireland's major banks in products other than mortgages.
It rapidly became just like them. In 2005 it bought fifty-four
ESB shops to form a branch network and began offering
deposit and current accounts. The next year it changed its
name to Halifax and began to sponsor *The Late Late Show*.

Its product range expanded to include personal loans, buy-to-let mortgages and Ireland's cheapest credit card.

Above all, it entered commercial property.

After losing its position as the market leader in the mortgage market, Bank of Scotland (Ireland) launched a crafty public relations campaign to distance itself from the other banks: it promised product after product to suit the Irish punter, in keeping with its supposed pioneer spirit. Chief executive Mark Duffy railed against the banking establishment, demanding changes to the prohibitive cost of switching banks and positioning himself as the retail banking customers' champion. 'The dynamics of the Irish banking market are undergoing a sea change at the moment . . . the cosy club will finally be laid to rest,' he claimed in September 2004. That year the Bank of Scotland walked away with more awards, including 'Company of the Year' from the *Sunday Times* and Enterprise Ireland. It also won predictable plaudits from mortgage brokers – predictable because the Bank of Scotland was using the mortgage broking channel to market its mortgages.

In February 2005 Phil Flynn was outed as a director of another company, an outfit without quite the same kudos as the Bank of Scotland. Chesterton Finance, an unregulated moneylending service based in Ballincollig, Co. Cork, was being investigated by the Criminal Assets Bureau. Flynn was on Chesterton's board. Its boss, Ted Cunningham, was arrested and charged with laundering more than £3 million sterling stolen in the £27 million theft from the Northern Bank in Belfast the previous December. (In April 2009 Cunningham was sentenced to ten years' imprisonment for money laundering.)

Flynn resigned as chairman of Bank of Scotland (Ireland) immediately. It would hardly be appropriate for the chairman of a division of a publicly quoted bank to be linked to the armed robbery of £27 million from one of its rivals. The Bank of Scotland moved to distance itself from Flynn, but it later transpired that they gave him €240,000 in compensation for loss of office.

Flynn was not charged in relation to Chesterton or the Northern Bank robbery. 'I have no involvement, good, bad or indifferent, in money laundering, full stop, for the republican[s] or for anybody else. And if I'm proven wrong, I'll run up and down the street naked for you,' he said at the time. In what appeared to be a fit of petulance by the Gardaí, he was brought to court for possession of a pen gun. Technically, possession was illegal. Flynn agreed to donate €5,000 to charity.

Following Flynn's resignation, the bank appointed Maurice Pratt as chairman. Pratt had been a successful marketing director of the supermarket chain Quinnsworth, but since then his marketing edge had been blunted. He had become the ultimate insider, appearing on boards galore, including those of IBEC, Eircom and Brown Thomas.

Pratt looked on as Duffy steered Bank of Scotland in a strange direction for self-proclaimed champions of the small customer. The bank caught the Irish disease. It rapidly pursued commercial property interests like a stag left behind by the herd. In 2006, when nearly every Bank of Scotland (Ireland) press release was trumpeting new consumer products and branch openings, in the background the invaders were quietly going bananas, lending to property developers.

Duffy's decision to chase Anglo into the property jungle was hardly a surprise, as Duffy had originally sprung from the Anglo stable. Furthermore his bank's parent, HBOS, was by far the worst offender in the binge of property speculation in the UK.

Duffy's bank funded much of the €288 million Burlington Hotel deal with Bernard McNamara. It tied up a €1 billion securitization agreement with Liam Carroll on the Cherrywood site on the south side of Dublin. Other prominent clients included Pat Doherty's Harcourt Developments, Joe Moran's Manor Park Homes and an assortment of key property magnates. Duffy had arrived as a player in the most dangerous game in town.

Astonishingly for a bank that had entered Ireland to disrupt the mortgage mafia, mortgages accounted for only 24 per cent of the Bank of Scotland (Ireland) loan book; fully 21 per cent (and rising) was in construction and property development loans. By the end of 2007 the numbers had reached staggering levels. Mark Duffy had bet more than half the bank – 56 per cent of all loans – on the crumbling property market. Bank of Scotland's property lending now stood at over €16 billion, nearly eleven times its exposure in 2001. More than half of this was lent to developers. Duffy was a long way from being the punter's champion.

The Bank of Scotland had gone native. Worse still, it was late into the game. It bought at the top of the market. Bank of Scotland's whirlwind intervention in the Irish market had shown that competition in the banking sector is a double-edged sword. It had brought cheaper financial products to consumers but, combined with chronically weak regulation, it led to irresponsible lending that would eventually create a national crisis.

Duffy retired with an undisclosed golden handshake in February 2009. The bank had recorded a €250 million loss. The price tag associated with the loosening of standards in the Irish mortgage market – a loosening that had been partly provoked by Bank of Scotland's bold entry into the market – would be much, much higher.

7. Poodles and Spoofers

Bankers had seized unchallenged power in the Ireland of early 2007. Their influence had mushroomed in parallel with the growth in Ireland's prosperity. Their tentacles were everywhere, not just in fuelling the construction frenzy or in their life-or-death power over small businesses. They were also by far the biggest ingredient on the Dublin Stock Exchange, accounting for 47 per cent of the ISEQ index of Irish shares. Construction-related companies such as CRH, Kingspan, McInerney, Abbey and Grafton – who thrived on the credit the banks fed to developers – also comprised a massive share of the index, which peaked on 21 February 2007 at 10,041. The property bubble achieved maximum inflation at almost exactly the same moment, with the price of the average home reaching an all-time high of €311,078 in February.

Just as they had peaked in tandem, Irish property and Irish shares fell together. By Christmas of 2007 the ISEQ had plummeted by 44 per cent. House prices were down 8 per cent, and would fall a lot further.

Ireland's stock market had been one of the best performers in the world in 2006, rising 28 per cent and beating major indices like the Eurostoxx 50, London's FTSE, New York's NASDAQ and the Dow Jones Industrial Average. Such stardom reflected the outside world's view of Ireland as a magic economy. Foreign investors piled into Irish shares as a way of grabbing a slice of the Celtic Tiger action. When investors bought Irish shares they generally bought banks; and when they bought banks they bought property.

Bankers obligingly supplied the market with bullish comments about Ireland, the economy and their own shares. The same bankers also kept two house-trained poodles in their kennels. The first poodle, Ireland's sycophantic stock-brokers, indulged in the most shameless puffing of bank shares imaginable.

Since the eighties, Ireland's two biggest banks had owned Ireland's two biggest stockbrokers: Bank of Ireland owned Davy and AIB owned Goodbody. In November 2006 Davy's management engineered a buyout of the company. They were now theoretically free of the Bank of Ireland monkey on their back, but they remained brokers to the same bank, enjoying all the accompanying lucrative corporate spin-offs. Nobody in the broking world recalls anything but a favour-able circular by Davy about Bank of Ireland when Davy was a fully owned agent.

Davy was the most powerful broker in Ireland with an unbeatable portfolio of global clients. External investors will have read constant glowing reports about Bank of Ireland shares from them, in which their 'price target' for the bank's shares – ostensibly the price the brokers see the share reach-ing – was nearly always pitched above the market level. Some clients will have taken the reports seriously.

Two weeks after the buyout, Bank of Ireland shares stood at €16.00. Davy upped their price target to €18.25. Even as late as February 2008, after Bank of Ireland stock had tumbled to €9.59, Davy wrote: 'A low-risk balance sheet and cheap valu-ation provide a safe place to hide . . . This is a low-risk bank.'

They remained strong supporters all the way down, setting price targets above market levels in every report. Even as the shares hit 89 cents at the start of 2009, Davy launched another lifeboat, saying they were worth €1.50. On 5 March 2009, Bank of Ireland hit a new low of 12 cents.

An identical pattern played out with AIB. Its agreeable stockbroking subsidiary, Goodbody, was never found wanting when writing a circular about its parent. They recommended the shares as a 'Buy' in August 2006 at €19.94, again in November 2006 at €21.81 and in December at €21.50. In 2007 both their reports were 'Buy' recommendations. The message was repeated in 2008 when their four reports all emerged with a 'Buy' tag. In February 2009, when the shares had tumbled to just 52 cents, Goodbody's analysts finally lost their nerve and changed the designation from a 'Buy' to a weaker 'Add'. The simple word 'Sell' was not in their vocabulary. It would have been the right word to use in nearly all instances. When their analyst, Eamonn Hughes, was asked if Goodbody had ever issued a sell notice on AIB he said, 'I don't know if we even keep records going back that far.'

Goodbody's proud motto is 'independent and international'.

Any investors who took Goodbody's advice about AIB would have lost their shirts. Many did. The same applied to Davy's advice on the Bank of Ireland.

Both brokers were part of the hype surrounding the Irish economy, the banks and property. It was nearly impossible to unearth any home-grown, objective views on bank stocks. Potential investors received a drip-drip of highly subjective, often compromised information, all of it boosting the banks.

Brokers were constantly seeking corporate business from the same public companies on whom they were writing investment circulars. A bearish circular would not enhance their chances of the spin-offs.

Even shares in Anglo Irish Bank earned plaudits from Irish brokers, right up till their delisting from the market. Davy, as broker to Anglo, remained believers to the last. They were believers in 2005, when they set a price target of €11, nearly two euros above the price on the day. They were believers in 2007 when the shares stood at €16.88 and they targeted a level of €18.50. And they were believers in late 2008 when the shares languished at 85 cents as they set a deathbed target of €3.00. A few weeks later the shares were delisted as the price hit the deck at 22 cents.

Foreign brokers were slow to detect the rot in Irish banking, but at least they were not so one-eyed as the big Irish brokerages. As early as November 2006 the French investment bank Société Générale sounded a warning. In a research note headed 'Going, Going . . .' SocGen pointed out the disproportionate dependence of Irish banks on property, warned of 'clouds gathering' over AIB and reduced Ireland's premier bank's rating to 'Hold' (often regarded as brokerspeak for 'Sell'). Worse still, it downgraded Bank of Ireland to a blunt 'Sell'. At precisely the same time, Davy and Goodbody were advising punters to pile in.

The bankers' second pack of house-trained poodles barked even louder than the stockbrokers. Every bank and brokerage worth its salt employs a chief economist whose main purpose is to comment on the economic outlook through the mass media. The chief economists came into their own as opinion formers during the boom, when there was a hunger everywhere for news of the Celtic Tiger. The bankers' hired guns were more than happy to satisfy the appetite. Their analysis of the Irish economy was mostly, but not in all cases, upbeat. The media eagerly sought their opinions, often presenting them without a health warning.

The career of Jim Power demonstrates the dangers. As chief economist at Bank of Ireland until 2001, Power told me that he became 'increasingly fed up with the lack of independence allowed in my work. I was under constant pressure to deliver the bank's line. They wanted me to voice a consistent politically correct message. They were intent on not upsetting the government. It really angers me, looking back. In my last two years I was constantly getting into difficulty.'

Power recalls giving a paper at a weekend conference in which he suggested that 'social partnership was becoming a mere vehicle for the public-service unions'.

'On Monday morning,' he continued, 'I was called up to the top floor in Baggot Street headquarters and slapped across the wrist by the then chief executive of Corporate and Treasury, Brian Goggin.'

Power landed in trouble again after he addressed the economic and financial affairs subcommittee of the House of Lords on 17 October 2000 about the European single currency. At the committee Power expressed his view that the euro was creating an inflationary bubble in the Irish economy. He says, 'I did not believe that the Irish government was capable of managing an economy within the single currency.'

He was to be proved right.

Power's independence from his banking employers did not go as far as permitting him to predict a property crash, but it did land him in hot water when he attacked social partnership, so beloved of the banking hierarchy. He handed in his resignation the day after his address to their lordships.

Power's replacement, Dan McLaughlin, was an inveterate bull, known for the unusual intensity of his economic optimism even in the days when almost everyone was optimistic. His optimism was unaffected by the evidence of a housing bubble.

In March 2007, when the property market had just peaked, the Bank of Ireland line on property was made clear. In a statement the bank coolly asserted that 'the Irish housing market is cooling off in the "soft" manner as predicted'. Wishful thinking from a bank with an abundance of mortgages.

McLaughlin – who earned a PhD in economics from Queen Mary College in London, and who carries the prefix 'Dr' in his public appearances – was still happy about the prospects for the Irish economy as late as November 2007. At the launch of the Bank of Ireland's quarterly review he insisted that, 'The government's fiscal position is not one to prompt concern. The Minister for Finance has announced a spending total for 2008 which is virtually identical to that signalled twelve months earlier, and tax revenue is forecast to exceed day-to-day spending by €6.0 billion, which hardly suggests the need for revenue-raising measures.'

Far from there being a surplus of tax over expenditure, the opposite occurred in 2008. Day-to-day spending outpaced revenues by nearly €4 billion. In October 2008 the government introduced an emergency Budget stuffed with 'revenue-raising measures'. In April 2009 they were forced to repeat the same medicine.

In the same November 2007 report McLaughlin forecast a 'recovery' in GDP growth for 2009 to 5 per cent. The most up-to-date independent forecasts suggest that, far from growing, our 2009 GDP is set to dive by 8 per cent.

The storm was coming, but all was calm at the Bank of Ireland.

McLaughlin was not alone in his cheerful outlook. Other banks' economists took a similarly upbeat line.

Austin Hughes, the in-house economist for IIB Bank, refused to share the gloomy mood in the property market as 2008 opened. According to Hughes, 'The Irish housing market faces a tough start, but should see a steadier finish to 2008 as lower borrowing costs and reduced supply help return the market to balance . . . While a sharp turnaround may be unlikely, a lot of bad news is now "priced in" to Irish property values and less threatening news could underpin sentiment as 2008 progresses.'

In 2008 the main Irish housing index fell by 9.1 per cent.

Pat McArdle, chief economist of Ulster Bank, was another economist with his head in the sand. In March 2007 he had a brainwave. He blamed the weather for a slowdown in housing activity. His singling out of the rain and the wind bore echoes of the luckless Bank of Scotland chairman and fallen C&C boss Maurice Pratt, who blamed the weather for a failure of C&C's marketing of Magners cider in the UK. Both had unearthed a novel scapegoat.

McArdle was gung-ho about the construction industry in March 2007 – just as the property market began to decline:

Fears that the construction industry would struggle to absorb a housing slowdown are not borne out by recent Purchasing Managers Index reports. Housing activity, possibly influenced by bad weather, has contracted modestly in each of the past four months, but total construction activity has accelerated to an eight-month high, influenced by a surge in commercial. The pace of the acceleration in the latter is striking – we have not seen the likes since mid-2005. No surprise then that employment, which had tailed off, is again growing strongly and that confidence remains high. While factory closures and associated job losses in other sectors are making headlines, there is no sign that job shedding in the construction sector is imminent.

Twelve months later there were 26,800 fewer people working in the construction industry.

One or two of the bankers' economists struggled with the housing bubble. AIB's John Beggs warned in April 2006 that the 'Irish housing market has become a hot house'.

Almost in the same breath he made a prediction that his bosses would have found easy to reconcile with their own love affair with property: 'We do not foresee a sharp fall in house prices but a protracted period of stability could follow beyond 2007.' AIB could hardly claim to 'foresee a sharp fall in house prices' at a time when its lending machine was cranked up, frantically competing with Anglo to lend money to property developers.

Ireland's bankers had a line to investors through their stockbrokers and to the media through their economists. Their tentacles were everywhere. Such bullishness was one of the forces that turned a boom into a bubble.

As if that was not enough, the two major banks had powerful investment arms. AIB had Allied Irish Investment Managers (AIIM) while Bank of Ireland had Bank of Ireland Asset Management (BIAM). Even Irish Life had Irish Life Investment Managers (ILIM). These were among the biggest fund managers in the country. They managed company pension funds, large and small. They managed ordinary investment funds of all sorts. Control of these funds gave the banks huge firepower in the Irish stock market. AIIM, BIAM and ILIM all had chunky holdings in their own and each other's parent banks. Co-operating with other fund managers, they formed a cosy little association called the Irish Association of Investment Managers (IAIM). It was a lobbying group for the managers but did little to enforce high standards in the industry.

The shares which banks held in each other fostered the clubby atmosphere in the banking world. The IAIM did nothing to remedy the effects of incestuous cross-holdings. Whatever the controversy, whatever the merits of a director, whatever the wrongdoing, the banks never upset the apple cart at each other's AGMs. Invariably the pension funds controlled by their investment arms voted in favour of re-election of their rivals' board members. They cast millions of votes on behalf of pensioners whose sentiments in many cases were probably directly opposed to the managers' stance.

Frequently, small shareholders would vote against the board at an AGM while their pension fund manager would do exactly the opposite with his or her pension fund votes. The system was anomalous. Through their investment arms Bank of Ireland, AIB and Irish Life all joined in a mutual support operation guaranteed to frustrate small shareholders and preserve the power of their masters, their parent bankers.

As the banks' investment arms held so many Irish banking shares, Ireland's pension funds suffered disproportionately when the Irish market tanked in 2007 and 2008. It would have been a brave dealer at Bank of Ireland, AIB or Irish Life who, viewing his parent bank's shares as overvalued, risked depressing the price by dumping millions on the market.

Instead, bankers had created a spoofers' paradise. Spoofers flourished among their stockbrokers, among their employee economists and among their wholly owned fund managers. Full-time spoofers helped to hype the markets for too long.

Bankers' poodles were not the only spoofers hyping the property market. As spoofers go, they faced fierce competition. Indeed they were shaded in the spoofing stakes by their allies, the estate agents.

Ireland's estate agents were probably unique. To become an estate agent no qualifications were necessary. An applicant for a licence merely needed to pay a visit to the District Court. Provided an applicant was not a criminal he was almost always admitted to the industry by the judge. Then he or she could head off into the property jungle in search of victims, take booking deposits and hold auctions. I should know. I did it.

It was a doddle. And I have as much idea of how to value or sell an Irish home as an African elephant. But I can puff a property or prop up a fading boom as well as the next man.

In December 2006 I decided to find out if any old bluffer can easily secure an estate agent's licence. I filled in my application and appeared in the District Court in Bray accompanied by my solicitor. I was obliged to put a notice in the *Bray People* to warn the locals that they were about to embrace another menace in their midst! Then all I needed was a deposit of €12,700 or an insurance bond, and a tax-clearance certificate.

I gathered the necessaries and encountered no opposition from the local Gardaí, nor from an agreeable judge. All the pieces were in place. There was no requirement to be able to read, write or show evidence of numeracy. I was (and still am) an estate agent, entitled to buy and sell houses for other people, to value them and to hype their prices until kingdom come.

Each year I reapply for the licence. Each year the application sails through. I no longer bother to employ a solicitor, but turn up myself to renew the licence. If my career as a journalist or politician is ever prematurely ended I too will be able to plunder the pockets of the vulnerable people who have been exploited by estate agents for so long.

Estate agents were responsible for much of the hype surrounding the property explosion.

Many estate agents ran mortgage brokers as a sideline. First, the mortgage arm decided how big a loan a prospective buyer should be approved for. Then the auctioneering arm of the same firm sold the property to the same buyer. An RTÉ *Prime Time Investigates* programme in December 2006 revealed that some auctioneers acting for sellers were in collusion with mortgage brokers acting for the buyer. Information on the financial strength of the buyer was available to the seller. The

programme also highlighted the widespread practice of plant-
ing fake bidders in the auction room.

A leading weapon in estate agents' sales campaigns was the
quoting of nonsensically low 'guide prices' in order to entice
potential buyers into the auction room. Often the guide price
was well below the reserve price at the auction itself. It was a
device for encouraging buyers to go to their surveyor at vast
cost, to seek a loan and to consult a solicitor. Before buyers
were aware of it, they were knee-deep in a transaction well
beyond what they could afford. Either they wasted all the
money on professional fees prior to the auction or they
borrowed more than they could afford from their indulgent
banker, as the bidding invariably rose far above the guide price.

In 2004, more than two years before the property boom
climaxed, estate agents Lisney excelled themselves. They had
published a 'guide price' of €2.5 million for a large house in
Dublin's Cowper Road. The house was eventually sold for
€6.275 million. Lisney was again the culprit on a sale of 51
Terenure Road West in the same year. Once again they had
guided €2.5 million. The house sold for €5.2 million. Others
were at the same game. No one cried 'Stop'. The practice was
not discouraged by either of the two toothless auctioneers'
bodies, the Irish Auctioneers and Valuers Institute (IAVI) and
the Institute of Professional Auctioneers and Valuers (IPAV).

Why were estate agents allowed to continue with such
practices for so long? Probably because they carried huge
political clout. Many TDs were part-time auctioneers. In
2007 at least nine out of just sixty senators were estate agents.
Several TDs and scores of county councillors – responsible
for planning decisions – had acquired estate agents' licences.

Collectively, the estate agents not only misled the public
in good times with bogus guide prices; they also misled the
public in bad times with bogus sale prices. In 2008 it emerged

that certain auctioneers had been supplying the *Irish Times* with sales results figures higher than the actual price achieved. The intention, presumably, was to prop up the sagging property market: publishing higher prices gave the impression that the sharp falls were not as bad as they seemed. It also encouraged potential sellers, seeing prices holding up, into putting their houses on the market. It was a typical auctioneer's stunt.

Alan Cooke, the abrasive head of the IAVI, told RTÉ that he had no idea that some of his members were misleading the readers of the *Irish Times*. The toothless National Consumer Agency called both auctioneers' outfits in for a chat, but no prosecutions were taken. The leaders of the two groups promised to insist that their members behave better in future.

Like the banks and the stockbrokers, the leading estate agencies employed in-house economists. At the beginning of 2007 the *Irish Independent* asked estate agents' economists for their forecasts for the year. Down at CB Richard Ellis they employed nothing less than a 'Head of Residential Research'. Aodha O'Brien was up front: 'Activity in the housing market will remain strong in 2007, albeit less frantic than in recent years. On the back of strong economic and demographic fundamentals, we expect that prices will continue to rise.'

Asked what he would do with €80,000 he replied that he would 'gear up to buy a residential property'. In other words, he would advise clients to borrow buckets to buy property: exactly what the bankers wanted to hear, and exactly what they facilitated.

Sherry FitzGerald's 'Chief Economist', Marian Finnegan, predicted that 'the national second-hand market rise is likely to be in low single-digit figures with a slightly higher figure achievable in the main cities such as Dublin'. Marian's findings would not have displeased her masters in the blue-blooded firm, which is headed by Mark FitzGerald, son of the former Taoiseach Garret FitzGerald.

Alan Cooke, the head of the hapless IAVI, predicted 'modest growth in the residential sector, due in no small measure to interest rate increases'.

Bankers were in unison with auctioneers in forecasting that prospects for eternal salvation lay in the property market. Austin Hughes of IIB Bank predicted house prices would rise by 6 to 7 per cent in 2007. Hughes rounded up all the usual suspects to support his crystal ball: 'the healthy economy, favourable age profile, supportive Budget, maturing SSIAs and strong employment growth should underpin prices'.

Other estate agents' economists were equally happy to puff the market. Paul Murgatroyd of Douglas Newman Good thought it might be worth 'taking a punt on an investment property along the proposed Metro north line'. Overseas, he liked 'safe European countries like France and Germany which in my view are good areas for speculation'. Geoff Tucker of Hooke & McDonald said that 'residential property is still your best bet. The rental market is thriving and there is huge demand for good-quality, well-located accommodation. Sandyford, Kilmainham and Dublin's Docklands are my top picks.'

One wonders how many of these geniuses followed their own advice.

The other important collaborator in the property frenzy – with the banks, the developers, the stockbrokers, the estate agents and the government – was the media. As the boom heated up, property advertising became a vital revenue raiser for newspapers and magazines. Property supplements glamorizing the whole sector were published weekly by most newspapers. These supplements never carried critical commentary on any of the houses or estates reviewed. Glowing editorial pieces about a new housing estate were often miraculously accompanied by a large advertisement plugging the same estate. Unfavourable coverage of developers and auctioneers in other parts of the newspapers was regularly met by implied threats from property interests that advertising could go elsewhere.

RTÉ also pandered to the national obsession with property, putting on programmes like *House Hunters in the Sun*, *Show-house*, *About the House* and *I'm an Adult, Get me Out of Here*. But it also commissioned a documentary that opposed the general euphoria.

The word 'crash' was virtually unknown to the national lexicon before 2007. Richard Curran, deputy editor of the *Sunday Business Post*, broke the taboo in a programme he made for RTÉ in April of that year.

Curran had no axe to grind. His career spanned RTÉ, the *Irish Independent* and the *Sunday Tribune*. Unlike the outspoken economist-journalists George Lee and David McWilliams, he was not well known for sparking controversy. The programme was dynamite. Entitled *Future Shock: Property Crash*, it outlined the dangers of a steep drop in property prices to Ireland's economy. Curran spelled out the possible peril facing the country. Interest rates were rising; Ireland was too heavily dependent on the construction industry, while the United States was facing an economic storm and a weakening dollar.

Curran went to London to see if the Ireland of 2006 bore any parallels with the UK property boom of the 1980s, before the crash there. His interviews convinced him that the likenesses were alarming. The prosperous young Londoners of the heady eighties, spoilt by huge incomes from financial services, had gone property mad. Large bonuses had been spent on second and third houses. The bubble inevitably burst.

Ireland did not learn from London's experience. The Irish nation of 2007, led by the bankers, just charged forward into the property abyss.

When Curran interviewed Ireland's economists, the majority were in denial. Those employed by the vested interests nearly all spoke with their masters' bullish voices. But at least one academic economist, Alan Ahearne of University College Galway, was ahead of the posse. In the autumn of 2005, shortly after returning from the United States, where he had worked at the Federal Reserve, Ahearne wrote an article in the *Sunday Independent* warning of a property slump. He hammered away at the same theme, against the consensus view, for several years.

Others' predictions were almost universally optimistic. In February 2007 banker Niall O'Grady, the head of marketing at Permanent TSB, predicted − on camera − that property prices would enjoy mid-single-digit percentage growth every year for the foreseeable future. In the same year O'Grady won the 'Marketer of the Year' award from *Marketing Magazine*.

One or two of the less bullish forecasters pulled out of interviews with Curran. Others, fearful of their employers, laid down conditions for a piece on camera. Advance word about the programme spread rapidly in business circles. There was consternation among the bankers. An email circulated, warning that Curran was making a film about a possible property crash. The coded message was clear: shoot the messenger.

Worse still, despite several efforts by Curran to get an interview with Patrick Neary, the chief executive of the Financial Regulator declined to participate.

The programme went ahead. It caused mayhem.

The government was furious. The programme appeared just weeks before the May 2007 general election, and the timing of its release was regarded in some political circles as an act of sabotage.

Taoiseach Bertie Ahern appeared on Today FM's flagship *Last Word* programme with Matt Cooper, denouncing Curran as 'irresponsible'. The Construction Industry Federation, the mouthpiece of Ireland's builders, claimed that Curran's documentary was politically motivated. Veteran *Irish Independent* property editor Cliodna O'Donoghue – a former colleague of Curran's – wrote:

RTÉ's *Future Shock* was very much a shock tactics programme and many within the property and construction industry have already labelled it irresponsible and wholly sensationalist . . . Even if only a few people took it at face value, the programme still did much damage to market confidence, which the presenter himself acknowledged as vital for the market's health.

Business journalist Marc Coleman, who later that year would publish a book about the Irish economy entitled *The Best Is Yet to Come*, wrote in the *Sunday Independent* that the country needed Curran's programme 'like a hole in the head' and asked: 'The question is, why does RTÉ want to run down our economy?'

Even the independent economists were wrong-footed. David Duffy, of the lofty Economic and Social Research Institute, was outspoken in rubbishing the supposed doom-and-gloom brigade. At the time he said, 'We are not on course for a property crash, unless we choose to manufacture one with irresponsible comment on the state of the market.'

Official Ireland had closed ranks against Curran in a chorus of disapproval.

Although Richard Curran's intervention felt like a bolt from the blue, it wasn't the first warning about the economic storm that was brewing. David McWilliams and George Lee had taken a dark view of the property market for a long time, and as early as June 2005 *The Economist* sounded a dramatic warning: 'The worldwide rise in house prices is the biggest bubble in history. Prepare for the economic pain when it pops.' The magazine published an accompanying graph, singling out Ireland as the most vulnerable of all European countries to a fall in construction activity. Our dependence on construction was a fearsome 23 per cent; Sweden, by comparison, registered below 10 per cent.

Even further back – in 2004 – Pam Woodall, *The Economist*'s economics editor, told the *Sunday Independent* that she reckoned Irish house prices were 42 per cent overvalued based on the ratio of house prices to rents. Nobody in a position to do anything about it – the government, the bankers, the estate agents – took a blind bit of notice.

Two years later Professor Morgan Kelly, an economics lecturer at University College Dublin, strayed out of his normal specialist zone when he spotted the property figures emerging in late 2006. Kelly was so shocked by the porkies he was reading about property and the banks that he decided to enter the arena. Bemused that no one was stating what he believed was the obvious, Morgan took on the role of Jonah. Kelly not only fingered the suicidal property exposure but pointed out that the banking emperor would have no clothes if the bubble burst. Opponents tried to portray him as a nutty professor, but there was nothing arcane about Kelly's reasoning in a sequence of *Irish Times* articles.

Starting in December 2006, he looked at economic fundamentals of the housing market in Ireland that other economists strangely ignored, such as the relationship between property prices and incomes. 'There is an iron law of house prices,' Kelly wrote. 'The more house prices rise relative to income and rents, the more they subsequently fall.' He supplied a simple graph, showing that 'for every industrialized economy between 1970 and 2000 . . . a rise in house price relative to income is followed by a proportional fall'. House prices in Ireland had risen 30 per cent more than income since 2000; that rise, he argued, was unsustainable, and would be matched by an equivalent fall – plus a standard overshoot that would cause prices to bottom out at 40 to 50 per cent lower than their peak.

In September 2007 Kelly opened an article with these words: 'Irish banks are now owed almost as much by builders and developers as they are by mortgage holders and are now more exposed to commercial real estate than Japanese banks were when they crashed in 1989.' He went on to describe vividly how 'Irish banks have given speculators €100 billion to gamble with', and ended his chilling piece by deriding the Central Bank for its lack of commitment to regulation. Again, no one listened.

As business editor of the *Sunday Independent* I was, for once, on the side of the angels. A decade of observing the behaviour of the banks, and knocking them in print, convinced me that their latest antics in the property market were a product of hubris. On 27 July 2007 I wrote an article for the paper headed 'Run for Cover, Cash is King'. On that date the ISEQ index stood at 8,357. It was to drop below 2,000 by February 2009. I must admit that, having for once read the property and stock markets correctly, I never foresaw the potential perils of holding cash in unstable Irish banks.

★

Amid all the misplaced bullishness, a few sharp property investors sold out just ahead of the storm. The Doyle family – owners of a number of hotels in Dublin 4 – were maybe the biggest winners in the entire Irish property boom.

The Doyle Group had been founded by the legendary P. V. Doyle. A pal of Charles J. Haughey, he had died too young in 1988, aged sixty-five, leaving his hotel empire to his wife and children.

The Doyle family eventually sold the various elements of its birthright to go-go developers. After a series of complicated deals they disposed of the Berkeley Court Hotel and the Ballsbridge Jurys to Sean Dunne for €379 million, the Burlington Hotel to Bernard McNamara for €288 million, and the Jurys Inns chain to Derek Quinlan for €1.165 billion. The deals were sharp as a razor, just pipping the property turnaround.

A few months later Tom Roche – husband of P. V. Doyle's daughter Ann – took advantage of the buoyant Exchequer finances to sell the family stake in the West Link toll bridge on Dublin's M50. The state paid top dollar (€600 million in total, over twelve years) to buy itself out of a one-sided deal signed by the controversial Minister for the Environment Pádraig Flynn back in 1987. The 1987 deal had given Tom Roche's father (also Tom Roche) rights to monopoly ownership of the M50 toll bridge over the Liffey. The price Roche senior had paid was based on projected traffic flows of 11,000 vehicles a day, rising to 45,000 in 2020 – when the bridge was due to revert to the state. But by 2007 the Roches' company – National Toll Roads – had the state over a barrel. The traffic was running at a phenomenal rate of 100,000 vehicles a day, and the company was coining it. Better still for the Roches, the toll fee was inflation-linked. Politically, the government was under intense pressure from frustrated motorists to open the toll gates and end the daily commuter traffic jams. Long queues at the toll booths every day sometimes delayed drivers for an hour or more.

With an election looming the government buckled to a campaign (in which I was heavily involved) and bowed to huge pressure from the densely populated commuter belt. Before the polls the government, flush with money, agreed to pay the €600 million buyout payment in twelve tranches of €50 million. The Roche family left the M50 greatly enriched. The government set a date for the toll gates to be opened. The commuters were pacified, but at great cost.

The Roches and the Doyles were not the only shrewd sellers as the market started to turn. Astonishingly, in 2006 and 2007, the two biggest Irish banks began to unload their own property portfolios. Branches of banks for sale sprouted up countrywide. In the autumn of 2006 AIB sold its first tranche through auctioneers Savills to developer Gerry Gannon for around €100 million. A few months later DTZ Sherry FitzGerald sold a further 25 AIB branches in individual lots to private investors for another €100 million. At almost exactly the same time, Bank of Ireland sold 66 branches for €331 million through CB Richard Ellis; among the buyers were Bernard McNamara and Derek Quinlan.

The sensation was not the Big Two's decision to dump property in tandem, but rather the shock sale of both their Dublin headquarters. Bank of Ireland sold its HQ in Baggot Street, Dublin, for €212 million in June 2006 to a Derek Quinlan consortium. At almost the same time AIB sold and leased back its Ballsbridge HQ in two lots. The first lot was sold to a Sean Dunne consortium and leased back on a twenty-year lease with a break clause. The second lot was bought by Hibernian Life and Pensions and let to AIB for twenty years.

Even as Bank of Ireland and AIB were unloading their own

properties, they were lending wildly to high-flying developers. Did they have an in-house view on property? Were they
selling their own commercial property simply to lend the
proceeds on to builders? It was a game of contradictions.

Even more striking were the contradictions in the auctioneering world. While all estate agents were still making loud
noises about the attractions of Irish property, some were
quietly selling their firms to outsiders. In August 2005 the
Gunne family sold its commercial property division to CB
Richard Ellis for €20 million. A year later Gunne Residential was bought by its management in a €7 million deal.
Managing director Pat Gunne was cashing in his chips at
the right time.

He was not alone. Other giants, while puffing up the properties in their brochures, were selling their stakes. Hamilton
Osborne King (HOK), the largest commercial property
agency in Ireland, sold out to the UK's top-notch property
consultants Savills in June 2006. The HOK partners netted a
cool €50 million in a deal that twelve months later looked
like a stroke of genius.

Within twenty-four hours of the HOK sale, estate agent
Jackson-Stops announced the disposal of a 60 per cent stake
to Colliers CRE, one of the globe's biggest property consultants, in a deal worth €4.8 million.

And if the world needed any further warning that insiders
were deserting the Irish property market, Ireland's most
successful property enterprise of the decade changed hands.
In July 2006, six weeks after the HOK and Jackson-Stops deals,
the *Irish Times* bought MyHome.ie for a breathtaking
€50 million. Having been set up in 2001, MyHome had
achieved 300,000 users a month by 2006. Six months later the
market turned and the value of MyHome.ie plunged with it.

The identity of the sellers should have raised the alarm

bells. Auctioneers Sherry FitzGerald with 23.5 per cent, Gunne with 19 per cent and Douglas Newman Good with 19 per cent, all exited this venture with pockets bulging courtesy of the *Irish Times*, one of their main advertising outlets. The other leading shareholder, with 18 per cent, was none other than AIB. The bank took the money and ran.

Auctioneers were flogging their businesses to UK property companies, banks were selling their own assets to property developers and everybody was selling to the *Irish Times*. Did we not get the message? Insiders were speaking out of the sides of their mouths, but voting with their feet.

8. The Gathering Storm

Although the idea that the good times could last defied logic, government and bankers spent 2007 urging citizens and customers not to panic. In fact, 2007 was the year Ireland should have panicked.

One fly in the Irish ointment in 2007 was electoral politics. Two political complications obstructed the right route for the economy. The first was the general election. The second was the political ambition of the Minister for Finance, Brian Cowen himself.

Cowen was a popular member of the Fianna Fáil parliamentary party. Gregarious, a highly entertaining companion, in 2007 he was red-hot favourite to take over as party leader – and thus, if the election were won, as Taoiseach – from Bertie Ahern.

Part of the reason for his almost unchallenged position as heir apparent was his clubbable nature. The so-called 'bar lobby' in Leinster House was 100 per cent behind him. He was part of the high-living, race-going set. With an all-party group of TDs he was part-owner of an Oireachtas racehorse, a frequent winner called Arctic Copper. Cowen knew how to enjoy himself, especially in the company of Fianna Fáil TDs. His rough-diamond manner and his gruff conversational style earned him kudos with the Fianna Fáil troops. Contrary to his image he laughs a lot and people of all parties like him. He is a wicked mimic.

Yet as Minister for Finance he suffered from a fatal weakness. He wanted to be Taoiseach. To be Taoiseach, first he needed to be leader of Fianna Fáil. To be leader of Fianna Fáil, first he needed to be popular among his TDs and senators. To be popular among his TDs and senators, first he needed to be a generous Minister for Finance. He was.

Cowen's predecessor, Charlie McCreevy, was often asked if he would like to be Taoiseach. He always gave the same reply: that he would love it, but it would never happen because he could not bear to be leader of Fianna Fáil. McCreevy never curried favours with his TDs. Consequently it was easier for him to take unpopular decisions, when necessary.

The government spent at record levels in the run-up to the 2002 election. Then, the ballot boxes were hardly opened before McCreevy set about remedying the extravagance by imposing spending cuts, stymieing his fellow cabinet ministers' plans for continued extravagance. On 4 December 2002, according to *The Economist* magazine, McCreevy 'delivered the country's toughest Budget in years, raising taxes, cutting spending in real terms and keeping borrowing low'. This despite McCreevy's pre-election claim that 'no cutbacks are being planned'.

The cuts made the government unpopular. When Fianna Fáil polled poorly in the European and local elections of 2004, McCreevy was blamed by fellow ministers and backbenchers. Just three days after the results the *Irish Independent* led with the ominous headline 'Knives Out For Mac'. The media had been reliably briefed by sources close to the Taoiseach that McCreevy's refusal to loosen the purse strings was the reason. The backbenchers, jittery from the bad results, wanted Charlie out. Bertie responded and the Minister for Finance was packed off to Brussels. Brian Cowen was installed in his place.

Cowen would have been acutely aware of McCreevy's fate. He spent his four years as Minister for Finance nursing his base and mucking in with the troops. He ate in the Leinster House dining room with the Fianna Fáil rank and file; McCreevy by contrast had tended towards the cabinet dining room. Cowen's period as Finance Minister was marked by inaction at a time when the economy was boiling over. He was disinclined to upset any of the footsoldiers by introducing unpopular measures of the McCreevy type. Most of all, he did not want to annoy the champion of consensus, Bertie Ahern. McCreevy, on the other hand, had positively taken pleasure in it.

Critics accused Cowen of paralysis ahead of the succession battle. Others said he merely took his orders from civil servants in the Department of Finance in his determination to make no mistakes. In any case the leader-in-waiting's tactics of keeping the lid on the economy's problems worked, at least in terms of his own ambitions. The feelgood factor lasted until the general election of 2007 and Cowen was credited with winning the election for Fianna Fáil. Either he was blissfully unaware of the disaster round the corner or he did a good job of hiding it from the Irish people. He fought a robust campaign for Fianna Fáil at a time when Bertie had been weakened by damaging appearances at the Mahon Tribunal. For much of the campaign Cowen seized the initiative and cut a commanding figure, reassuring the nation that the economic future was bright.

By the time the election was won, the property market had already cooled. Part of the slowdown was credited to Progressive Democrat party leader Michael McDowell. Seeking an early election platform in September 2006, McDowell had proposed dramatic reductions in stamp duty for house buyers. In typical McDowell style, he had insisted that the Exchequer did not 'need' the revenue from stamp duty – quite a bold claim, as stamp duty returns from land and property amounted to €3 billion. Not a sum to be sniffed at, but the PD leader's cavalier attitude reflected precisely the nation's assumptions of predestined prosperity. The suggestion by the leader of the junior party in the governing coalition that stamp duty cuts may be in the offing did not cause property prices to fall immediately, but the volume of transactions virtually froze as buyers held back in anticipation of the change.

McDowell lost his seat in the general election, and his party was obliterated; but he had made stamp duty an election battleground. Fine Gael and Fianna Fáil felt compelled to trump the PDs' proposals. During the campaign a reluctant Cowen had been forced by Ahern to promise an end to stamp duty for first-time buyers – a move that was sold to the younger electorate as a means of bringing down prices, and to the builders as a way of kick-starting a flagging housing market.

The stamp duty debate proved a red herring. The property market was already beating a retreat as Cowen rose to his feet in the Dáil on 26 June 2007 to keep his stamp duty promise, but he was comfortable in cloud cuckoo land. His speech to the Dáil that day gave numerous hostages to fortune. He assured the assembled TDs that 'the fundamentals remain sound' in the Irish economy. They were far from it.

He declared that 'our economy will continue to outperform most of our peers'. It didn't.

The Minister for Finance went on: 'Our economy is set fair to enjoy strong growth rates over the medium term.' But the economy was already heading for the rocks. In 2008 it contracted by 3 per cent.

Cowen even declared that 'our economic success in recent years ensures that we can face any future economic challenges from a position of strength'.

Richard Curran was proved right within months. Cowen's hostages to fortune had already been shot before Christmas.

So much for the benefits of tinkering around with stamp duty. The problem ran far deeper.

Worrying developments in the world economy as 2007 progressed should have stood as a useful warning to the Irish government about how a property crash could cascade into a full-blown economic and political crisis. Instead, the global turmoil was treated as an exotic problem not directly relevant to Ireland, or, increasingly, as an excuse.

Banks in the United States, competing for business and trying to expand their markets in the middle of a housing boom, had lent money to people who wouldn't historically have been considered safe credit risks: 'sub-prime' borrowers. Many of these sub-prime loans were bundled into complex 'securities' and sold on to other financial institutions by the original lender. Securities contaminated with high-risk mortgages were treated by the credit-rating agencies as though they were the safest financial products on the planet: they generally received the highest possible safety rating. If banks wanted short- or long-term money to fund their crazy gambles, they could always borrow the shortfall from the interbank market. But when the US housing market turned, sub-prime mortgages (and other loans) went into default, and AAA-rated securities were suddenly revealed as toxic, the banks stopped trusting one another and the interbank market dried up, a state of affairs known as the credit crunch.

As far back as February 2007 HSBC bank announced larger than expected sub-prime mortgage defaults. It was an early warning sign. In April New Century Financial, one of the largest US sub-prime mortgage lenders, filed for bankruptcy. In May US Federal Reserve chairman Ben Bernanke told the world not to worry about the growing number of mortgage defaulters. By June two of Bear Stearns' hedge funds were in difficulty, but hedge funds had collapsed before and they would collapse again. No one lost much sleep.

Gradually the sub-prime problem spread. Toxic assets were popping up on the balance sheets of banks and hedge funds around the world. Major Wall Street firms like Merrill Lynch, JPMorgan Chase, Citigroup and Goldman Sachs were in trouble.

The demise of Northern Rock in September 2007 should have shaken Cowen to his roots. Northern Rock, Britain's ninth biggest bank and fourth largest mortgage lender, was the UK's first victim of the global credit crunch. Northern Rock had a small customer deposit base and depended on wholesale money markets for most of its funds. The credit crunch had almost closed this source of funding. The Bank of England was forced to ride to the rescue and provide emergency funds to keep Northern Rock going.

Northern Rock ran an operation in Ireland and had succeeded in raising €2.4 billion in deposits from Irish savers. As the crisis unfolded, Irish customers saw television pictures of fellow depositors queuing in the UK to draw their savings out of Northern Rock branches there. Queues began to form outside Northern Rock's offices in Dublin's Harcourt Street.

The British government was soon forced to guarantee all Northern Rock deposits in the UK. British depositors' nerves were soothed, but clients in Ireland remained nervous that their savings would not be covered by the Bank of England's promise. Cowen moved fast to secure an assurance from British Chancellor Alistair Darling that the Bank of England guarantee was extended to Irish savers.

In the same month that Northern Rock had to be rescued, September 2007, the International Monetary Fund wagged a finger at Ireland, forecasting a sharp reverse in Irish growth during 2008. In December, just four days before Cowen's fourth and final Budget as Finance Minister, it emerged that stamp duty receipts, a measure of activity in the property market, were projected to dive by €730 million. Total tax revenue was projected to drop by €1.75 billion. For the first time as Finance Minister, Cowen was short of cash.

Cowen appeared to be in denial. In his budget speech he admitted that the 'backdrop is challenging' but went on to insist that the 'fundamentals of the economy are still good – a point often lost by some'. He promised that 'growth will be sustained into the future'.

Such misplaced optimism allowed him to increase public expenditure by over €1.7 billion.

Cowen was in denial, and so, as 2008 unfolded, were Irish bankers.

Responding to news of the 7.3 per cent decline in property prices in 2007, Niall O'Grady, head of marketing at Permanent TSB, parroted Cowen's line:

After a decade of phenomenal growth the market finally came off the boil in 2007. However, prices today are pretty close to where they were at the start of 2006 and the fundamentals behind the market remain strong – as evidenced by rising rents. There is clearly demand for new houses albeit at reduced levels. The question is at what point buyers will take confidence that we're at the top of the interest rate cycle and return to buy.

In early February Irish Life & Permanent's normally low-profile chief executive Denis Casey rashly claimed that the falls in the share prices of Irish banks were an 'overreaction'. Even in spring 2008, two of the biggest ostriches in the business were prescribing the Cowen medicine. AIB's chairman Dermot Gleeson and his chief executive Eugene Sheehy took the opportunity of their annual report to mimic the Taoiseach's myopia.

In his chairman's statement accompanying the publication of AIB's 2007 annual report in March 2008, Dermot Gleeson conceded that 'short-term prospects are somewhat mixed' but used the f-word again, insisting that 'economic fundamentals remain solid and growth is expected to pick up again in 2009 and beyond'.

The script could have been written in the Department of Finance.

In the same report AIB chief executive Eugene Sheehy admitted that 'our bad debt provisions will rise from the very low levels of 2007'. But he asserted: 'Our lending policies and practices remain prudent.'

Within months AIB was facing bankruptcy, rescue or nationalization due to years of imprudent lending to property developers.

Meanwhile, Anglo was issuing some dodgy figures. In May 2008 it reported a 15 per cent rise in profits for the half year and made some ritually optimistic noises. In the same month Bank of Ireland hinted at profit falls for the year but proceeded to offer a dividend hike. On the last day of July AIB chief executive Eugene Sheehy followed suit, announcing that despite a profit fall of 4 per cent the bank would be paying an extra 10 per cent to its shareholders. The promise of higher dividends smelled of pure bravado. The instinct of Ireland's bankers was to brazen it out. Sheehy insisted that, 'We are not in any way concerned about capital.' This was an absurd statement, as AIB's bad-loan provisions were rocketing.

Two months later Sheehy would dismiss suggestions that AIB might seek support from the government or anywhere else, saying, 'We'd rather die than raise equity.'

Investors around the world stared in wonder. Here were

three banks – Anglo, Bank of Ireland and AIB – deeply mired in a property slump, hurling their disintegrating reserves at their shareholders.

After the world's market traders had stopped wondering what pills these Irish guys were taking, they did what they knew best: they sold Irish banking shares with a vengeance. Short selling in Anglo Irish shares peaked around the St Patrick's Day bank holiday. Dealers saw a one-way bet and sank the shares by 15 per cent. On the same day the UK's HBOS, with a weakness for property lending almost equal to Anglo's, came under fire from hedge funds.

Anglo never recovered. The market simply did not believe a word coming out of its St Stephen's Green headquarters. Sean FitzPatrick and David Drumm tried to stem the flood of disbelief, but it was overwhelming. An incensed Drumm persuaded the obliging Financial Regulator to probe the short selling activities of certain brokers, but the inquiry came to nought. An Anglo public-relations offensive flopped. Even analysts from some of the top Irish firms became non-believers.

Anglo's principal problem in the first six months of 2008 was the relentless distrust of its published figures. It was clear that Anglo was insanely overexposed to property developers, and that the property developers were getting into very deep trouble. Yet Anglo's figures assumed an implausibly low rate of loan default. The markets judged the top brass guilty of bad banking, and of gilding the lily with optimistic valuations in Anglo's scary property book.

One of the central figures in the swirl of rumours about Anglo's customers was Ireland's richest man, Sean Quinn.

Quinn, from Derrylin in Co. Fermanagh, made billions from nothing. He borrowed £100 in 1973 to extract gravel from his 23-acre family farm. Thinking big from the start, Quinn – often referred to as 'the Sandman' – founded the

Quinn Group in that same year as a vehicle for what would become an extraordinarily diverse range of business interests, including cement, hotels, glass, plastics and property.

In 1996 Quinn founded Quinn Financial Services and took the staid Irish insurance world by storm, undercutting the established companies' rates through Quinn Direct. Punters learned to love the fledgling insurance company as it played the role of a giant killer. Some of the enthusiasm for the Quinn Group's aggressive style transformed into an affection for Quinn himself.

In 2003 Quinn purchased a 20 per cent stake (later to become 25 per cent) in NCB, Ireland's third biggest stock-brokers. The quiet Quinn had big, big ideas. In 2005 a rare vanity project saw him purchase the Belfry hotel and golf course in England. He sponsored the British Masters tournament there in 2006.

By 2008 Quinn was a financial services giant; but he was also an enigma. Quinn Group was a private business; Sean Quinn was a private man. Few wealthy Irishmen have ever been able to hide so successfully from the national media. He has never owned a public company, which means that his operations have not been subjected to the reporting requirements of such companies. As he had never shown much interest in the trappings of wealth, few knew much about his tastes or his personal life. The outside world was carefully briefed that he regularly played poker with his old pals for a maximum loss of €10 a night. They knew too that he was a fiercely committed family man but, apart from that, he was an unfamiliar character. He surrounded himself with well-paid protectors from PR firm Wilson Hartnell, intent on keeping the media at arm's length. But he could not hide completely: that year *Forbes* magazine named him as 164th in its worldwide mega-rich league.

In the first six months of 2006 Quinn Direct reported prof-its of €123 million. A year later Quinn enhanced his popularity as the champion of competition in the insurance market when he bought Bupa (Ireland), a subsidiary of the UK health insurer, for €150 million. Bupa, which had broken into the Irish market as the first challenger to the state-owned VHI monopoly, was on the point of leaving Ireland after losing a court case over the terms on which the two insurers could compete. Quinn successfully appealed the decision to the Supreme Court and rebranded Bupa (Ireland) as Quinn Healthcare.

In early 2007 Quinn started building up a stake in Anglo Irish Bank. Normally a buyer of shares in a public company must declare his stake when it hits 3 per cent, but Quinn protected his anonymity by buying through 'contracts for difference' (CFDs). A buyer of a CFD in a block of shares does not purchase the shares themselves, but rather purchases the right to benefit from an increase in their price; by the same token, the holder of the CFD loses if the share price drops. Because CFD investments tend to be heavily funded by debt – most of the money involved is borrowed – gains and losses are magnified as a percentage of the investor's stake.

Anglo's falling share price in 2007 and 2008 meant that Quinn faced massive paper losses on his 25 per cent CFD position in the bank's shares. By July 2008 the Financial Regu-lator was concerned that Quinn, looking at huge paper losses that risked becoming even bigger if Anglo shares continued to tank, might decide to cut his losses by letting his CFDs lapse, causing a vast quantity of Anglo shares to flood the market and thereby causing the share price to plummet further. Quinn converted three-fifths of his Anglo CFD stake – 15 per cent of the company's shares – into a direct share-holding, taking a loss that Quinn himself says was more than

a billion euros. Presumably Quinn could not afford to convert
his entire CFD stake in this fashion, which meant the other
10 per cent of Anglo shares would be sold off – with potentially disastrous implications for the share price.

Sean Quinn was landing Anglo in the soup. No obvious
buyer of 10 per cent of a sick bank on a downward spiral was
in evidence.

The Anglo top brass caught an early whiff of Sean's intentions. The senior ranks are said to have freaked when they
realized that Sean's 10 per cent of the bank would be under
the hammer. Such a threat could be the final kiss of death
to the dying bank, already savaged by short sellers, huge
loans to property developers and rapidly escalating funding
problems.

But Anglo still had its supporters. Some were battle-
hardened veterans of the property war. At the height of the
summer of 2008 Anglo insiders secretly assembled ten true
Anglo loyalists and persuaded them to take up Sean's shares
between them. Anglo arranged to lend the ten saviours the €451
million needed to buy up the shares. Three-quarters of the
€451 million was secured against the Anglo shares themselves,
with the remaining 25 per cent secured against the individual
investors' personal assets. The Golden Circle was born.

Anglo was now treading a dangerous path. It was lending
money to clients to buy shares in itself. The whole operation
looked like a share-support scheme. Anglo was misleading
the market.

In March 2008 the collapse of Bear Stearns, the fifth largest
investment bank in the United States, set the stage for a series
of events that would leave global markets in a state of near-
permanent panic. The Bear Stearns crisis had immediate
consequences for Irish bank shares.

Back in Ireland the markets were technically open, but deadly quiet, on St Patrick's Day, the day after JPMorgan Chase offered to take Bear over at a price of $2 per share – less than one tenth of the share price two days earlier. Most Irish traders were not at their desks. This was an ideal time for the smarter hedge fund managers and opportunist dealers in Irish shares. The London Stock Exchange was open. Irish shares heavily traded in London included Irish Life & Permanent and Anglo. Anglo lost 15 per cent of its value.

Anglo had been rumbled by none other than the most influential financial column in the UK. The *Financial Times*'s Lex fingered Anglo as vulnerable to its high-wire commercial property gambles in Ireland and the UK. It bracketed the Irish bank with HBOS, widely considered the UK bank in the greatest danger. It decoupled both these banks from the US disease – sub-prime and mortgage-backed securities – and noted that on this side of the Atlantic we had our own chronic home-grown diseases. Lex was right.

Anglo reacted angrily. It protested to anyone who would listen, including the sleepiest financial regulators in Europe. Ireland's watchdog launched an investigation into dealings on St Patrick's Day, but not until the UK had given a lead by announcing its own probe into trading in HBOS, whose shares had tanked that day. It was not the first time that Ireland's regulators had played follow my leader. The investigation came to nothing, but Anglo was on the global radar: not the best place to be.

Back in the United States they waited for their next catastrophe. It came soon enough.

Fannie Mae and Freddie Mac were the two largest mortgage finance companies in the US, estimated to have a 50 per cent slice of the $12 trillion US mortgage market. By July 2008 defaulting homeowners had left the two giants virtually insolvent. The US government regarded them as an integral part of the financial system: they were a proxy for confidence in the American economy, evidenced by their debt being held by several central banks around the world. Their failure was unthinkable. But failing they were.

Treasury Secretary Hank Paulson rammed a measure through Congress allowing the government to buy shares in the two behemoths and to underwrite their ballooning debts. Freddie and Fannie were saved by the American taxpayer and nationalized in all but name.

An ideological Rubicon had been crossed. The law of the free-market jungle had been broken. State subsidies were being used to prop up pillars of capitalism. In his dying days in office George Bush had become a pragmatist.

That was early September 2008. Elsewhere around the world governments were making efforts to ensure that no big banks went bust. Takeovers, mergers, emergency funding and bailouts were the order of the day. The unwritten, and unspoken, code appeared to be simple: governments were the guarantors of last resort. The nationalization weapon would be used if all else failed.

Until 15 September. The markets woke up that Monday morning to the stunning news that the US government had allowed the giant investment bank Lehman Brothers to collapse. Lehman was filing for bankruptcy.

The fourth biggest investment house in the US, even more exposed to risky assets than Bear Stearns, had spent much of the summer swanning around the world in search of a lifeboat. Hopes that it would clinch a deal with the Korean Development Bank lifted Lehman's fortunes in early September. But on 9 September the talks with the Koreans broke down. Lehman's shares fell by 40 per cent. The next day it recorded its worst quarter ever, with a loss of $3.9 billion, and announced that it was cutting its dividend. Another possible rescue merger, this time with the Bank of America, was dashed on 11 September.

The general expectation that George Bush would do for Lehman what he had done for Fannie and Freddie proved incorrect: the government had decided that they needed at least one example 'pour encourager les autres' and to prove its macho capitalist heart was still beating. On the same day, almost unnoticed, Bank of America bailed out Merrill Lynch with a $50 billion all-stock package.

A week later the insurance colossus AIG, fearing a liquidity meltdown, received US federal funds. Hank Paulson started talks with Congress on a possible $700 billion bailout package for the entire US banking system. On Friday 19 September Wall Street rallied strongly. Despite Lehman, AIG and Merrill Lynch, the Dow actually finished ahead on the week. The market felt that if the package was agreed, the worst would be over.

On the other side of the Atlantic, the UK was having its own problems. HBOS had acute difficulties not only with its lack of capital but also because of its heavy exposure to a fast-falling UK property market. Worse still, it was possibly the most dependent of all the UK banks on the wholesale funding market, which by now had seized up almost completely. Short sellers targeted HBOS. On Wednesday 17 September Lloyds TSB, under pressure from the British government, rescued HBOS with a £15 billion sterling bailout.

The British were in US-type doo-doo. They were anxious not to nationalize another bank after Northern Rock, but they were happy to see a mega-merger creating the largest retail operation in the UK. Size was safe. Competition law was hurled out the window to facilitate this huge transaction.

For the rest of the week the market steadied. A global relief rally provided a respite. HBOS shares rose 155 per cent from their low on Wednesday.

The relief rally barely lasted the weekend. The next week the fortunes of the Dow swung wildly in tandem with the volatile prospects for Paulson's bailout. World markets followed suit. In the UK the government bit its tongue and was forced to nationalize another mortgage lender after Bradford & Bingley, which numbered ex-AIB chief Michael Buckley on its board, saw a run on deposits.

For Ireland's nervous bankers, watching these events from a distance, mergermania suddenly became the only game in town. Big was beautiful. Size was safe. Mike Soden's old idea of a Bank of Ireland–AIB marriage got a fresh outing. Others favoured the creation of a 'third force' in banking including Irish Life & Permanent, EBS and Irish Nationwide. Rumours sprouted by the hour.

Michael Fingleton's building society became the first victim of the rumour machine. On 5 September the highly respected Reuters newsagency published a sensational story. It told how the building society 'was in talks with its lenders to avoid insolvency'. Reuters posted the story on the wires at 6.14 p.m. on Friday evening, mercifully after the markets closed. Still, all hell broke loose in the Department of Finance, the bankers' boardrooms and among the media. Even the Financial Regulator showed a bit of interest.

The story was wrong. Completely wrong. Fingleton emerged fuming. He had not even been asked for a response by the journalist. He dubbed it 'an attempt to sabotage the society'. He did not try to identify the saboteur.

Reuters retracted the story at 10.45 p.m. and explained that the journalist 'had misinterpreted the source', who was never named.

The Reuters story may have been wrong, but Nationwide was in trouble. Five days later the Fitch credit ratings agency downgraded Nationwide because of its exposure to commercial and residential property in Ireland.

A few days later Sean FitzPatrick sought a meeting with Minister for Finance Brian Lenihan. A meeting was arranged between the two men, with David Doyle, secretary of the Department of Finance, also in attendance. The minister was known to be conjuring up all manner of mergers in his head at the time.

Seanie sauntered into the minister's office with a proposal. He believed that Lenihan should support a merger between his bank and Fingleton's building society. He trotted out the line that it was a perfect match. Anglo had the corporate skills, Irish Nationwide had the branches. The two combined could become a strong force in banking. All they needed was an injection of capital from the state!

Lenihan and Doyle were unimpressed. They knew that Seanie was in trouble. They knew too about Sean Quinn.

'And what about the Sandman, Seanie?' interrupted the blunt Doyle, referring to the billionaire Quinn's recent acrobatics in Anglo shares. The beleaguered chairman of Anglo shrugged his shoulders.

Lenihan and Doyle gave FitzPatrick the cold shoulder and showed him the door, but following that meeting stories kept surfacing in the media about Anglo taking over the Nationwide. The *Irish Times* gave it favourable mention. Someone was spinning a yarn. Fingleton was bewildered, insisting that he knew nothing of the moves and was not involved in any talks. This incident is believed to have soured the relationship between Fingleton and FitzPatrick.

Around the same time FitzPatrick asked for a meeting with the top brass of Irish Life & Permanent. The chairwoman,

Gillian Bowler, and the chief executive, Denis Casey, met him and David Drumm in Dublin's Westin Hotel. Seanie told them that a match of their two outfits was made in heaven. The meeting was short — it lasted half an hour — and far from sweet. At one point Seanie reassured the IL&P team that he would be willing to concede power and status in the management of the merged entity. IL&P could keep the prestige posts. He was desperate.

The following Sunday, 21 September, the *Sunday Tribune* carried a story which began:

Irish Life and Permanent (IL&P) is expected to be the next Irish financial institution to become part of a wave of consolidation set to sweep Irish banking once the deal between Anglo Irish Bank and Irish Nationwide is officially consummated.

Another story in the same day's *Tribune* stated:

The pursuit of Irish Nationwide by David Drumm's Anglo Irish is to be welcomed, although one wonders if a deal with Irish Life & Permanent (IL&P) would make more sense.

The IL&P side was furious. Bowler telephoned FitzPatrick. Their relationship was fractured.

At almost exactly the same time, FitzPatrick made frantic telephone calls to Allied Irish Banks and Bank of Ireland. AIB dismissed the approach outright. Their opinion of Anglo could be summed up by their cancellation of lines of credit to Anglo two years earlier, while Bank of Ireland remained aloof.

Sean FitzPatrick knew he was a drowning man. Unless the government bailed him out.

9. Meltdown

On 15 September 2008 – the very day, as it happened, on which Lehman Brothers went bust – John McManus, business editor of the *Irish Times*, published a column that must have touched the rawest of nerves.

He pointed out that 'the willingness of the US authorities to think the unthinkable [in nationalizing Fannie Mae and Freddie Mac] stands in stark contrast to the attitude that seems to prevail in Dublin' and observed that none of the Irish banks 'has reported a significant rise in bad debts since the start of the global credit squeeze'.

This latter fact, McManus wrote, was cited by those who claimed that the Irish banks were in decent shape and that the dim view the markets took of them was unjustified. McManus's own view was very different. The figures for bad debts did not reflect reality. Irish banks were refusing to recognize the problem. As a result, the balance sheets and profit figures of all the banks were in question.

It was powerful stuff from the *Irish Times*, a responsible paper sometimes prone to pull its punches on delicate matters of national importance. And it was on the money. Anglo Irish Bank's interim report the previous month was close to fantasy, boasting that, 'The Bank's performance in 2008 demonstrates the resilience and strength of our business model.' The statement forecast a 15 per cent growth in earnings per share and a laughably low bad-debt provision of between 0.13 per cent and 0.18 per cent. It contained the ritual pat on the back for itself: 'The Bank has no exposure to US

or other sub-prime sectors and does not sponsor any off-
balance-sheet vehicles.' There was no recognition of the
threat to Anglo posed by its exposure to a few carefully
selected property developers.

On 19 September – four days after McManus's column,
and four days after the collapse of Lehman Brothers – the
Financial Regulator responded to the carnage on the Irish
stock market by banning short selling of financial shares. This
move was accompanied with attempts at reassuring noises
– reassuring noises that reassured no one.

Meanwhile all the background noises were negative. The
previous day's *Liveline* programme on RTÉ Radio One had
revealed the nation's state of nerves at the unfolding collapse
of banks around the world. Presenter Joe Duffy's anxious
listeners rang the show to demand answers. They were
wondering if they should move their savings. They asked for
guidance about whether to minimize their risk by spreading
their nest eggs across a number of different banks or simply
to sink the lot into the state-guaranteed Post Office. Many
Irish savers wondered whether Northern Rock, now guaranteed by the British government, was suddenly a safer haven
than AIB or Bank of Ireland.

Lenihan got in a hot snot about the Duffy programme. He
rang the director general of RTÉ, Cathal Goan, and bawled
him out about the national broadcaster prompting a run on
the banks. It was a knee-jerk response from the minister and
other members of the Cabinet, who constantly overreacted
to loose media talk about the state of the banks by denouncing it as irresponsible.

Two days later, in a more constructive move, Lenihan
responded to the threat of a flight of funds from worried
depositors by raising the state guarantee on savings from a
threshold of 90 per cent of €20,000 to a clean €100,000. But

the measure was far too little, far too late. Smaller savers were already transporting their cash into the Post Office in lorry-loads because it carried an uncapped government guarantee. Depositors had lost faith in the Irish banks, and so had the markets.

I first met Brian Goggin shortly after he became boss of the Bank of Ireland in the summer of 2004.

His predecessor, Mike Soden, had just resigned after the revelation that he had surfed adult internet sites on his Bank of Ireland computer. Soden had been given a mauling by the media because of his attempts to force a merger between Bank of Ireland and AIB. He had also been involved in an unsuccessful attempt at a takeover of the UK's Abbey National. Goggin naturally wanted to avoid a similar going-over. Obviously on a public relations offensive, he asked to meet me in my capacity as business editor of the *Sunday Independent*.

I was intrigued. We met for coffee in Dublin's plushest hotel, the five-star Merrion, where you sink into comfortable sofas and drink coffee from china cups under paintings by Louis Le Brocquy and Jack B. Yeats. The hotel is partly owned by Lochlann Quinn, himself a former chairman of AIB.

Goggin was charming. He was also strangely shy, with none of the arrogance normally associated with multi-millionaire bankers. He was a dapper dresser. Not a hair was out of place, nor was there a speck of dust on his perfectly polished shoes. His trousers were creased to perfection. Altogether, he was a trifle precious. He began by politely putting me right about the Bank of Ireland, gently upbraiding me for some of the harsher charges made against his colleagues and himself in my columns, while giving me a pat on the back for taking a swipe at the Bank of Scotland, the most recent invader of his patch.

Around the same time – as a shareholder – I had visited
Bank of Ireland's headquarters in Baggot Street to have a
good snoop at Goggin's contract of employment. What I
discovered was staggering. Goggin had negotiated a deal
for himself without parallel in the history of Irish banking.
The package surpassed even Sean FitzPatrick's pay at Anglo
the year before. The new Bank of Ireland boss was set to
earn a basic salary of €1 million a year, and he was eligible
for a top-up cash bonus of €720,000 provided he reached
some pretty modest targets. In addition to his salary, Goggin
could draw up to 40 per cent of the value of his annual salary
in Bank of Ireland shares as part of a long-term performance
incentive scheme. Even more generously, he was entitled
to stock options by the barrow-full. Such options gave
Goggin a right to buy Bank of Ireland shares at the price
on the day they were granted; but he could delay exercising
that right to a future date of his choosing, hopefully when
they were much higher. Such juicy options are normal ways
of enriching bankers. If the shares rise in the intervening
months or years, the executive can exercise his right at the
lower price and sell them immediately at the market price
for a profit, having put down no money of his own. If the
shares fall in the meantime, he simply lets the options lapse.
It is a one-way bet.

If Goggin's pay was exorbitant, his perks were mouth-
watering. He was given the right to borrow the sum of his
annual salary at an interest rate of just 3 per cent – not bad
when the overdraft interest rate on the day was 11.65 per cent
– and he could borrow €4 million at 4 per cent for a new
home loan. His family would receive €4 million if he died in
office. His golf club subscriptions would be paid by the bank.
He was given an annual car cash allowance of €32,000 and
free tax advice from BDO Simpson Xavier.

It did not end there. Incredibly, he was entitled to receive a bonanza of payments from his previous post as head of Bank of Ireland Asset Management 'as if you remained CEO of Asset Management Services'. Which he didn't.

I looked at Brian Goggin and wondered what qualities this man possessed to make him worth all that money every year. Was I sitting in the presence of greatness?

Goggin had received a Christian Brothers education at Oatlands in Stillorgan, Co. Dublin. Other prominent past pupils include cabinet minister Éamon Ó Cuív and Justin Kilcullen of Trocaire. *Irish Times* political editor Stephen Collins, a contemporary at Oatlands, remembers Goggin as 'a bit of a swot; he did well but was rather anonymous'.

After school the young Brian did not head for university but went straight into the Bank of Ireland at the age of seventeen. He rose through the ranks swiftly, taking positions as chief executive of Corporate Treasury and in Wholesale Financial Services. In 1993, at the age of forty-one, he had taken an MSc in management at Trinity College. Such a career move was fashionable at the time among businessmen who had missed out on university education after school. The roll of honour at TCD's course includes Willie Walsh, later of Aer Lingus and British Airways, Cathal Magee, director of Eircom, Conor Faughnan of the AA, Garry Cullen of Aer Lingus and Aer Arann, as well as Brendan Comiskey, later to become Bishop of Ferns.

Goggin's subsequent success at Bank of Ireland Asset Management propelled him into the top job. Although he spent six years in the US and five in the UK, he never left the Bank of Ireland stable. His overall experience of banking was severely limited.

It may have been for this reason that Goggin had been passed over for the top job in 2001, when Mike Soden – a

Blackrock College boy who had worked for four different banks in six countries – was headhunted for the job. Now Goggin was seizing a surprise second chance, an opportunity brought about by Soden's shock resignation.

Goggin was appointed within a week of Soden's departure. He was the natural successor. The bank's board was in no mood for taking risks after the series of calamities under Soden's leadership. They wanted a safe insider. Goggin was their man. They gave him a golden deal.

Four years later, on the evening of Monday 29 September 2008, Goggin found himself entering Government Buildings in the company of governor (i.e. chairman) of the Bank of Ireland Richard Burrows, chairman of AIB Dermot Gleeson, and AIB chief executive Eugene Sheehy. The two chairmen sought a meeting with Minister for Finance Brian Lenihan, after the worst ever day for Irish banking shares. The four bankers entered Government Buildings at 9.30 p.m. (the following Saturday, Sean FitzPatrick would tell the nation on Marian Finucane's radio programme that at that very hour he arrived home, having had dinner out with a friend, and watched some TV before turning in at eleven).

The meeting had been initiated by a phone call from Sheehy to Lenihan's office. Although Sheehy's call was unexpected, Lenihan had been on alert since the previous Saturday, when the beleaguered minister was enjoying a rare moment of leisure at a Fianna Fáil fund-raiser at Gowran Park in Kilkenny for local TDs John McGuinness and Bobby Aylward. Lenihan was working the thirty tables of Fianna Fáil supporters, each of whom had paid €200 for the privilege, when he received an urgent telephone call. It was not a tip for the 4.30 race. It was the personal assistant to Jean-Claude Trichet, president of the European Central Bank. The minister was advised to expect an urgent message from the governor of the Irish Central Bank, John Hurley, later that afternoon.

The minister headed for the Gowran Park manager's office and rang Hurley. Trichet had been in touch, warning of banks in trouble all over Europe.

The next morning, Sunday 28 September, Lenihan slipped quietly into the Central Bank's Dublin Dame Street head-quarters to meet Hurley in his top-floor office. Hurley relayed a grim message from Trichet. European banks were in crisis. Fortis of Holland, which has a joint venture with An Post, and Depfa bank, which had headquarters in the IFSC, were in peril.

A day later, with Ireland's top four bankers in his presence, it was clear to Lenihan that he had an even bigger problem. The atmosphere in Merrion Street was far from relaxed. Top bankers are not used to seeking favours, let alone salvation. On 29 September, for once, the bankers were not in command. Their tails were deeply buried between their legs. They were desperate.

The big bank bosses were kept waiting for two hours in the celebrated Sycamore Room, so called because of its table of bleached sycamore with Fota Island yew. Playing second fiddle to the politicians was a new experience for the bankers. Spar sandwiches – the menu for the late-night crisis meeting – were not their usual fare.

The financial War Cabinet was already in situ. Side meet-ings were taking place everywhere. The principal mandarins in the Department of Finance – secretary general David Doyle and second secretary Kevin Cardiff – had been holed up all day. Central Bank governor John Hurley was in constant touch with the Financial Regulator's Patrick Neary. Lenihan and Cowen had a separate meeting.

Despite the frenzied atmosphere – the most stressful day

in the history of the Department of Finance – the minister managed to abandon the ship of state for a more important matter. September 29 was a big day in the Lenihan family calendar. In mid-afternoon Lenihan announced to his bemused staff that he was heading off for his Castleknock home to help blow out the candles on his daughter Clare's thirteenth birthday cake. The break fortified him for the long night ahead.

When all the key parties finally met in one room that evening, with the Attorney General Paul Gallagher present, Dermot Gleeson let rip. According to the AIB boss, liquidity was flowing out of the system. He embarked on a tirade against Anglo and Irish Nationwide. He made it clear that the traditional game plan – that the Big Two would take over an institution in trouble – was not a runner this time. Anglo Irish – whose shares had lost 46 per cent of their value that day – might not survive the week: deposits were pouring out of Seanie's bank. If the government did not act immediately, the whole financial system could be brought down. AIB and Bank of Ireland could tumble.

Gleeson had good reason to fear a domino effect. No bank could remain above the fray during a wholesale loss of confidence in Irish banks, as the carnage on the stock markets over recent months had illustrated. He, above all others, knew that many of the builders in debt to Anglo had huge liabilities to AIB and, to a lesser extent, Bank of Ireland. The Irish banks had common bondholders. If foreign depositors lost faith in one Irish bank, the others might see consequent withdrawals of money.

Gleeson must also have feared that if queues formed outside Anglo the next day, it would be a matter of hours before savers were assembling outside AIB branches all over Ireland. No bank would be immune from an outbreak of depositor panic. Gleeson wanted the government to nationalize Anglo or let it collapse to detach it from the others. Dramatic action was needed before seven the next morning, when the stock markets opened.

While Monday's cataclysm in Dublin markets was itself potentially lethal for all Irish banks, a second blow had been struck across the Atlantic later in the day. The shock defeat in the US House of Representatives of a $700 billion bank rescue package had caused carnage on Wall Street – the Dow was down by 777 points at the close, its worst day for 20 years – and Asian markets bombed in early trading. The four bankers feared that European bank shares would be hammered at the opening on Tuesday.

The bankers were thanked by Cowen and then ushered from the room. Little camaraderie was evident between the two sides, although one participant says that it 'probably helped that AIB's Dermot Gleeson and Attorney General Paul Gallagher were bosom buddies from the Bar library'. A surprisingly short discussion followed. Lenihan was reported to have pondered the nationalization of Anglo alone but Cowen, characteristically cautious and fearing a legal challenge, was unwilling to discriminate between Irish banks.

The combined wisdom of Ireland's top politicians and civil servants quickly settled on the cleanest choice. The government would guarantee all the liabilities – the customer and interbank deposits, and also the vast majority of bonds – of the six Irish banks. This solution had already been canvassed by David McWilliams and Dermot Desmond.

The four bankers were recalled to be told of the decision and asked to 'reflect' on it. There would, naturally, be strings attached to the guarantee, but the finer detail would be agreed later. Legislation was already being drafted by bleary-eyed civil servants. AIB's Gleeson and Sheehy were dispatched back to the Sycamore Room while Bank of Ireland's Burrows and Goggin were given their own privacy in the dining room. All four made telephone calls to senior staff so that they'd know about the new regime when the banks opened in a matter of hours.

Department of Finance officials and the Financial Regulator meanwhile made frantic telephone calls to the chairmen of the other four Irish banks – Anglo, Irish Life & Permanent, EBS and Irish Nationwide – to convey the news.

Reaching the chairmen was not the easiest task. Sean Fitz-Patrick could not be roused from his slumber, so the department settled for his chief executive, David Drumm.

Michael Fingleton, the legendary boss of Irish Nationwide, had been aware of the unfolding drama at Government Buildings as early as seven in the evening. Fingleton knew nothing of the all-night drama until he was phoned at home by his chairman, Professor Michael Walsh, at 7.30 in the morning. Walsh had been woken by a call from the Financial Regulator at 3 a.m. but saw no reason to disturb the longest-serving warhorse in the Irish banking business before the sun was up.

Patrick Neary reached EBS boss Mark Moran at around 2.30 a.m. Moran immediately rang his own chief executive, Fergus Murphy, who was only just back in bed at his Ennis-kerry, Co. Wicklow, home, having driven through the night from Donegal after holding an EBS members' meeting in the north-west. Murphy had heard rumours of dramatic action all day Monday but was relatively unperturbed as the outflow of deposits from EBS had been modest.

The decision was made; but the formalities still needed observing. Most members of the Cabinet were asleep, many unaware that they might be woken to ratify a historic deal between the Irish taxpayer and the tottering banks. An 'incorporeal' cabinet meeting was convened via conference call. Foreign Minister Micheál Martin was thousands of miles away in Newark, New Jersey; but he was far easier to contact than Green Party leader John Gormley, enjoying a deep sleep at his Irishtown home only two miles down the road. Gormley, a man notoriously keen on an early bed, had allowed his mobile to run out of juice. So the Minister for the Environment had to be woken by Gardaí and told to ring in to the cabinet meeting. Both he and his Green colleague in Cabinet, Eamon Ryan, readily agreed to the guarantee plan: Gormley had urged the guarantee route to Lenihan only a few days earlier.

Social and Family Affairs Minister Mary Hanafin had been on RTÉ's *Questions and Answers* that night, having been fore-warned that the banking topic was a minefield because 'something was going to happen'. Any answer she gave could have been overtaken by events. She acquitted herself skilfully. As she left RTÉ, Hanafin received a midnight telephone call telling her to be on standby. She went to bed and was woken at 2.45 a.m. for the cabinet meeting. She did the business from her bed. Agriculture Minister Brendan Smith had spent the day in Brussels and returned late at night to be told that he might be required for a call later on. The Cavan-based minis-ter also performed his affairs of state in his pyjamas from his brother's residence in Dublin. Cabinet secretary Dermot McCarthy briefed the politicians on the pending measures and took a few questions. The most important cabinet meet-ing for decades lasted less than thirty minutes. Lenihan was given the go-ahead to clear the next obstacles.

At 3.30 a.m. the four bankers left. They had put the gun to the government's head and the ministers had delivered. The markets would welcome the decisiveness and determina-tion of the Irish government; better still, their own jobs were not threatened. It was round one to the bankers.

At 4 a.m. Brian Cowen suggested that Lenihan take a couple of hours' rest. The Finance Minister headed home for a brief sleep.

He resurfaced at 6 a.m., just about the time that Sean Fitz-Patrick was being woken from his slumbers by Anglo chief executive David Drumm with news of the overnight drama. Back in the office, Lenihan moved quickly to cover a few danger zones. As France held the EU presidency, he rang French Finance Minister Christine Lagarde, to tell her of the Cabinet's decision. Simultaneously, Central Bank governor John Hurley contacted European Central Bank president Jean-Claude Trichet.

Even as Lenihan briefed his European colleagues, the finishing touches were being put on the formal announcement. The message from Ireland was clear: the basic decision to give the guarantee was not reversible; the Irish government was not for turning. This was a high-risk strategy for Ireland in its dealings with Europe, given the political tensions created by the country's rejection of the Lisbon Treaty.

On the home front, Cowen and Lenihan needed the support of the political Opposition, the media and the people of Ireland. Just before 6.45 a.m. Lenihan released a dramatic statement. The financial world awoke to the news that Ireland had embarked on a solo run, giving a government guarantee over the deposits and loans of all its banks. Lenihan decided to brave the country's most influential radio programme, RTÉ's *Morning Ireland*. He assured the state's small savers that their deposits were safe.

British Chancellor of the Exchequer Alistair Darling would pick up the telephone twice over the coming days to bawl out Brian Lenihan over the move. Darling told Lenihan that the guarantee was a threat to British banks already under severe pressure. He anticipated a flow of money from the UK to Ireland. The Chancellor demanded that the guarantee be dropped or, failing that, be extended to British banks operating in Ireland. These included Ulster Bank and Bank of Scotland (Ireland). Darling's calls followed two dramatic protests from Royal Bank of Scotland chief Sir Fred 'The Shred' Goodwin – one directed to the heir to the throne, Prince Charles (Goodwin was chairman of the Prince's Trust), and the other to British Prime Minister Gordon Brown. Brown rang Brian Cowen with the same message, again seeking protection for UK banks in Ireland. Neither Taoiseach nor Minister for Finance was tactless enough to mention that the UK had itself given a government guarantee to Northern Rock depositors when it collapsed twelve months earlier. If one nation's guarantee was uncompetitive, surely the same charge could be made against the other's?

International investors were initially impressed by a Lenihan tour de force. The government guarantee provided the necessary short-term relief. Money poured back into Irish banks. The exposure of the taxpayer to a €440 billion liability was hardly mentioned in the immediate aftermath, so relieved was the nation at its escape from disaster. The government was already lengths ahead in the media battle. Little opposition was emerging. Generally, commentators felt that the 'least worst' solution had been found.

Lenihan shrewdly moved quickly to square a possible critic. Fine Gael leader Enda Kenny was in the studio for an early morning TV3 interview when the minister rang, seeking his support in the national interest. Kenny says that he readily agreed 'in principle'. Within seconds he was live on the air answering questions about his party's attitude to the emergency. He took the line of responsible opposition, insisting that Fine Gael would not be found wanting if the banking system was in danger of collapse.

It was the line that Fine Gael held throughout the political chaos that followed in the next forty-eight hours.

Labour leader Eamon Gilmore was not so accommodating. He told me that he took Lenihan's call at home, responding that he would reserve his position pending the supplying of details, but would be 'mindful of the national interest'. Later that day the Labour Party opted to oppose the bill, much to the anger of the government; but many of the strongest lobby groups stood behind the guarantee. Father Sean Healy of the Conference of Religious in Ireland, the St Vincent de Paul and Age Action were all quick out of the traps to support Lenihan.

The same evening, as the government struggled with the drafting of the new law and political tempers began to fray, an impatient Kenny was to brand the procedures 'a shambles'.

The markets delivered a positive verdict on the guarantee. Shares in Anglo, by far the biggest loser when the markets hit meltdown on Monday, shot up 30 cents to €2.60 at the opening, and constant buying throughout the day lifted them to €3.84, for a gain of over 60 per cent. Irish Life & Permanent added 35 per cent before the close, Bank of Ireland a more modest 21 per cent and AIB 18 per cent.

Monday's savage losses had been recouped. Sighs of relief were heard in the boardrooms of Irish banks, the Central Bank, the Department of Finance and the Cabinet. The strategy had worked. The crisis was sorted. Brian Goggin, Eugene Sheehy and the other big bankers could join Sean FitzPatrick in a night of uninterrupted sleep on Tuesday.

Or was it a false dawn?

There were already ominous signs that all the original participants in the crisis meetings were frantically spinning an incomplete story. Indeed it is possible that they had swallowed their own propaganda. The seeds of self-delusion were buried in the last sentence of the 6.45 a.m. press release. It peddled a mantra so absolutist that it nearly became accepted as the unvarnished truth. The assertion that the government guarantee was given to 'remedy a serious disturbance in the economy caused by the recent turmoil in the international financial markets' was a convenient cover. Blaming the outside world suited all the players. Bankers, property developers, regulators, politicians and civil servants had joined forces to ram home the same message. United, they were exonerated. And now that the crisis was over they began to dream that maybe they could resume business as usual.

The truth was that while the turmoil in the international financial markets had certainly caused disruption for Irish banks, the root cause of the Irish crisis was home-grown. It was to emerge soon enough.

The legislation establishing the bank guarantee was an astonishing package giving huge powers to the Minister for Finance. Most controversial was the decision to throw competition law to the wolves and allow him to merge banks together at will. It promised 'financial support' to those in need for two years. It allowed the state to take shares in the institutions. The detailed terms of the guarantee were as yet unspecified.

Opening the Dáil debate over the guarantee legislation on Tuesday night, a tired but energized Lenihan painted the predictable picture of 'unprecedented disruption in international financial markets' and the 'extended international credit crunch'. He did a whirlwind tour of the world, calling the British, European and US problems in as cover. Offstage the bankers, property developers, regulators and builders must have been cheering. The mandarins must have been in ecstasy.

Fine Gael finance spokesman Richard Bruton spoke of the

government's 'dangerous flirtations with the property sector' and criticized the Taoiseach's constant refrain that 'the fundamentals are sound'. Otherwise he made eminently sensible suggestions about additions to the bill to protect the taxpayer. Labour Party finance spokeswoman Joan Burton took a tougher line, making it clear that her party was not going to give the government and the bankers a free run in the Dáil. Nor was she about to allow Lenihan, a constituency rival in Dublin West, to emerge as a national hero. She turned the argument away from the global crisis back to the behaviour of our bankers at home. She thundered that there should be limitations on bankers' pay written into the guarantee scheme and that none should be paid more than the Taoiseach. She attacked 'the tax breaks that fuelled the speculative bubble' and insisted that the entire price should not be 'dumped on the taxpayer'. The argument began to turn away from the global tidal wave of collapses, back to the FitzPatricks, the Goggins, the Sheehys and the Fingletons. She was not giving the government an inch. Although the bill was likely to win the support of the main opposition parties, Lenihan's hopes of all-party support for his handling of the crisis were shattered.

Meanwhile, a stone's throw away from Leinster House, three of Ireland's banks were cooking the books as 30 September drew to a close.

The last day of September happened to be the year-end date for Anglo Irish Bank's annual accounts. Although few knew it at the time, Sean FitzPatrick had been dancing rings around Anglo's accounts. He had borrowed as much as €122 million of unreported loans from Anglo at various points over the previous eight years. His gigantic borrowings never appeared under the 'directors' loans' figures in the annual report. Nor anywhere else. Each year, as 30 September approached, Sean had whipped the loan away from Anglo and transferred it to the Irish Nationwide. He left the loan there for a few weeks before returning it to Anglo. News of such unorthodox activity had never reached the media.

As politicians debated the health of Ireland's banks in the Dáil, they were blissfully unaware that they had been misled by at least one of the banks they were bailing out. The chairman and unchallenged supremo of Anglo had deliberately concealed the extent of his loans from shareholders and from all independent judges of its health. The bank's auditors, Ernst & Young, had never cried 'Foul'; they would later claim that they'd never noticed the concealment.

FitzPatrick's activities were not a one-off. A second, lethal skeleton was buried in the Anglo cupboard. Elsewhere in the same set of accounts an even more spectacular stroke was about to be pulled – and safely disguised from the eyes of shareholders.

It had always been suspected in the days before the year-end date (and the panic in Government Buildings) that there had been a heavy run on Anglo's deposits. Anglo had denied any serious impact, but rumours of big withdrawals persisted.

The rumours were spot on. Anglo rightly believed that if the truth was revealed to shareholders in the year-end report, there could be panic, further withdrawals and the destruction of an already battered share price. So Anglo contrived an audacious scam that would leave Sean FitzPatrick's hidden loans wheeze in the shade. Anglo sought a deposit of €7.5 billion from Irish Life & Permanent to cover up the haemorrhaging of Anglo's deposits. Their friends in the rival bank agreed to help, but first they demanded the money from Anglo in another form. A circular movement was devised allowing IL&P to take the money as an interbank deposit and return it to Anglo as a customer deposit. The run on the bank

was disguised. Anglo's customer deposit base had been artificially inflated for the accounts.

On Wednesday morning an exhausted Taoiseach headed
for Paris to butter up President Sarkozy. Cowen was in double
trouble in Europe. The rejection of the Lisbon Treaty was
bad enough. Cocking a second snook at our European
colleagues with a unilateral bank guarantee was possibly a
bridge too far.

On the surface the visit went well, but Cowen was reported
to be none too pleased when he jetted into Dublin that
evening to find the guarantee Bill still languishing in the Dáil.
He had wanted it passed through both houses by Wednesday
midnight.

Meanwhile the Senate had been on standby all day. Senate
leader Donie Cassidy was pacifying an increasingly irritated
flock of Fianna Fáil troops waiting for the Dáil to finish. The
bars and self-service restaurant in Leinster House stayed open
late to facilitate an all-night sitting.

The Dáil finished at 2.10 a.m. on Thursday. Green Party
leader John Gormley, who had snatched a few minutes' sleep
on a pull-out sofa in Lenihan's office, was woken to vote. The
bill was finally passed by 124 votes to 18.

The bill sped straight to the Senate. The Upper House took
nearly six hours to pass the legislation. A few technical
changes were made. They were returned to the Dáil for
approval. During the afternoon the bill headed by bike to
Áras an Uachtaráin in the Phoenix Park for an early signature
from President Mary McAleese. It was law by dusk.

Ireland's banks were saved. But were its bankers?

As Sean FitzPatrick, Brian Goggin, Eugene Sheehy, Fergus
Murphy, Denis Casey and Michael Fingleton surveyed the
situation at the end of the week they must have been smiling.
The first miracle was that they were all still in position; their

fat salaries were intact. Admittedly, there was the nasty business of the detailed terms of the bank guarantee to be thrashed out, but on balance they were well ahead. The government was on the bankers' hook. The state had underwritten their past and future behaviour. Better still, they and Lenihan were telling the same story. The government had held to the bankers' line in the Dáil debate. The run-up to 30 September had been a catalogue of financial calamities throughout the world. Ireland was a victim. Most of the Irish media was on board.

Mindful that the sensitive conditions of the bank guarantee still needed to be negotiated with government, the bankers kept their heads down. This was no time to claim victory. They had got out of jail. Diplomacy was essential.

Sean FitzPatrick, however, was no diplomat, and Seanie fancied himself for an outing on one of Ireland's most popular radio programmes. On the morning of Saturday 4 October he headed in to RTÉ's Donnybrook studios for an interview with Marian Finucane.

He blew it. In style.

Brian Goggin, Eugene Sheehy and Michael Fingleton must have been shuddering as they tuned in at their South Dublin homes. Everyone knew Seanie was a loose cannon.

He gave the now ritual line about the 'global wholesale markets' being the problem and maintained that it wasn't 'a creation of Irish bankers that this had occurred'. He did self-exoneration well.

So far so good. It was when Marian Finucane began to ask him about the Financial Regulator that he shifted on to shakier ground. Seanie graciously gave Patrick Neary the Sean FitzPatrick clean bill of health: 'Well, he regulates very closely and gets all the information that he wishes to get in relation to our lending, in relation to our liquidity, in relation to our deposits. Another thing, he comes in, because, internal audits, he looks at the top twenty loans, forty loans. He gets information about various ratios.'

Neary, listening from his home in the Dublin suburb of Ballinteer, probably stroked his moustache and purred as he heard these reassuring words. Sean made him sound positively vigilant.

There was, of course, no mention of the rinky-dink with FitzPatrick's concealed director's loans. No mention either of the €7.5 billion in deposits shooting their way between Anglo and Irish Life. And in answer to a question about whether there had been a run on Anglo's deposits before 30 September, he responded that there had been 'nothing of a very serious nature'.

FitzPatrick dismissed the charge of reckless lending to property developers, and he was angry at RTÉ commentator George Lee for saying 'the banks won't tell us what the figures are'. He riposted: 'The banks report twice a year, interim results and final results . . . And they are audited by independent auditors . . .' He was referring, in the case of his own bank, to Ernst & Young – who failed over eight years to notice that he was warehousing large personal loans from Anglo in Irish Nationwide.

Brazenly he endorsed the great work of Anglo's non-executive directors, noting that Anglo and all the other banks had 'risk committees chaired, certainly in our case, by independent non-executive directors'. So there.

Within four months, most of FitzPatrick's beloved non-executive board members were gone, his auditors Ernst & Young were under scrutiny in an inquiry into the concealment of his loans, and his regulator Pat Neary was off smelling the roses.

Perhaps the last straw for the public – in an interview of breathtaking arrogance – was FitzPatrick's refusal to apologize.

Invited by Marian Finucane to do so, the Anglo boss responded: 'It would be very easy for me to say sorry. The cause of our problems was global so I can't say sorry with any degree of sincerity and decency, but I do say "Thank you".'

That same evening FitzPatrick was the star speaker at the La Touche Legacy seminar at the Charlesland Golf and Country Club Hotel in his home town of Greystones. Also listed to speak at the dinner were developers Sean Dunne and Sean Mulryan. Both Dunne and Mulryan wisely made their excuses and stayed away: it was hardly the best of weeks for well-heeled builders to make public appearances, even if the official theme of the seminar was the benign 'Relationship Between the Local Authorities and the Business Sector'.

Seanie Fitz suffered from no such reticence. He astounded his audience with what one diner described as a 'euphoric' performance. Sean called for a review of child benefit and of the provision of free non-means-tested medical cards for the over-seventies.

His insensitivity was staggering. Here was the man whose bank had been rescued by the taxpayer just five days earlier calling for the old and the young to lose state benefits.

In less than three months he too was gone.

While the threat of vanishing deposits had been averted by the guarantee, the banks had huge problems on the other side of their balance sheets: their assets – in particular loans to property developers – were of uncertain quality. Having guaranteed the banks' liabilities, Lenihan was now faced with a more complicated task: to determine whether they were adequately capitalized and, if not, to recapitalize them. Lenihan knew that investors worldwide were now demanding that quoted banks show stronger solvency, meaning that they must carry more cash as a cushion against shocks ahead. He determined that the state would provide the cushion.

Lenihan's task was made more difficult by the fact that the chief executives of the two biggest banks – Eugene Sheehy of AIB and Bank of Ireland's Brian Goggin – were in denial, at least publicly, about the state of their balance sheets. While neither Anglo nor Michael Fingleton's Nationwide were in any position to argue the toss about their solvency, Sheehy and Goggin continued to insist that they needed no capital.

On 14 October, a fortnight after the bank guarantee, an exhausted Brian Lenihan, facing steep drops in revenues from property-related taxes and a likely need to recapitalize the banks, introduced an emergency Budget.

Budget measures included income levies of 1 and 2 per cent for everyone, depending on income; pay cuts for ministers and ministers of state; the end of the decentralization programme; and a raft of increases in taxes including VAT, betting tax, DIRT and motor tax.

The most sensational of all was political dynamite: the minister withdrew the automatic entitlement of people over seventy to a medical card. Mayhem broke out among the grey vote. The government was forced into a partial retreat.

These measures were seen as a minimum needed to bridge a widening budget deficit. But where was Lenihan to find the money to rescue the banks?

Luckily for Lenihan, Charlie McCreevy had introduced a law forcing all governments to save 1 per cent of GNP for future state pensions. The fund was a no-go area, not open to a lightning raid by politicians until 2025. McCreevy had ensured that if any of his successors wanted to pillage the nation's nest egg, they would need to pass fresh legislation.

Lenihan never had a second thought. Legislation was drafted. Ireland's future pensioners would have to be sacrificed in order to meet today's needs. He originally targeted €8.5 billion out of the pool of just under €20 billion to rescue the banks: €3.5 billion each for AIB and Bank of Ireland, and €1.5 billion for Anglo. Lenihan simply ignored protests from the Big Two that they did not need capital. When at one meeting with officials they suggested that they might raise the capital from their own shareholders, no one even bothered to argue with such pie-in-the-sky delusions. There was little hope of already badly burned shareholders subscribing towards a fund-raising exercise from two banks whose solvency was questionable.

The balance of power had now shifted in the minister's favour. Under the bank guarantee scheme he had the right to place two directors in each bank. On the Bank of Ireland he put his recently retired colleague, dyed-in-the-wool Fianna Fáil loyalist and ex-Minister for Agriculture Joe Walsh, along with former senior civil servant Tom Considine. To the AIB board he nominated one-time Labour Tánaiste Dick Spring, who had reinvented himself as a businessman after losing his Dáil seat. Lenihan raised a few eyebrows when he appointed Declan Collier, managing director of the shambolic Dublin Airport Authority, as the other AIB director. Collier happened to be the boss of Vincent Wall, whose wife Kathy Herbert was one of Lenihan's key advisers.

The resistance of Goggin and Sheehy to recapitalization dimmed as international markets demanded that quoted banks hold more capital. The alternative to state bailouts was a takeover by private equity groups, which were hovering over the carcasses of the Irish banks. If the private equity groups were allowed inside the door, the board, staff and culture of the banks would have been filleted. Recapitalization suddenly seemed a trifle more appetizing.

So far Lenihan had not succeeded in getting rid of any of

the chairmen or chief executives of the six covered banks, but as Christmas approached he was tightening the noose.

On 18 December Sean FitzPatrick swallowed the poison pill: his transferring of personal loans from Anglo to Irish Nationwide every year for eight years in order to keep the loans out of Anglo's accounts had come to light, and his position was finally untenable. Non-executive director Lar Bradshaw resigned along with FitzPatrick on the 18th; David Drumm, the chief executive, followed a day later.

David Drumm departed having set the all-Ireland banker's pay record: in the four years that he served as boss of Anglo he managed to garner €12.15 million in rewards. In 2008 he surpassed Brian Goggin's €4 million figure from the previous year, with a €4.656 million package that included a €2 million bonus. The other directors had also filled their boots before the end came. FitzPatrick managed a rise of 22.5 per cent in the year to September 2008, leapfrogging back into first position among bank chairmen at €539,000, just above the Bank of Ireland's governor Richard Burrows (€512,000). Ten thousand a week for a part-time job presiding over a failing bank. The bank's employees had an average pay of €99,000 per person in 2007, nearly double the amount taken away by AIB staff that year. Expense claims too were incomprehensible. Declan Quilligan, who was promoted to the top job in the UK in 2006, was given €335,000 for 'relocation costs'.

David Drumm departed a rich man, but he must regret that he never sold his 510,000 shares in Anglo. At one stage they were worth €9 million. When he resigned they were just about worthless.

Drumm managed to spend some of his rich pickings on two US homes. According to Ronald Quinlan in the *Sunday Independent* he paid $7.2 million for two flashy houses in the top US resort of Cape Cod. The second house was bought on 30 September, the day after the bank guarantee was signed. He had been a consistent buyer of US property during the annus horribilis for Anglo.

Anglo led the way in bankers' pay, but all of the banks paid their top people at levels that are hard to understand. The common defence for the high salaries is – or was – that they needed to be paid 'competitive' rates to retain them at home in their current positions. Richard Burrows, governor of the Bank of Ireland, was one of the stoutest defenders of the level of pay for bankers. Speaking to the *Sunday Independent* on 12 October 2008, just after the government guarantee to the banks, he was adamant that pay was at the right level. (Burrows, of course, was himself being paid €512,000 a year for his part-time job.) With an endearing lack of humility, Burrows insisted that 'we have to put in remuneration levels which allow us to retain and attract the best people to run Bank of Ireland in the interests of the shareholder. And so that means we have to compare ourselves with the pay rates not just in Ireland, but further afield.'

It is to be hoped that Burrows read the government's review of Irish bankers' pay in February 2009. It found no evidence that keeping senior staff was difficult, and pointed out that many of them came from within the organization. While bonuses had increased abroad, many of these bonuses were deferred. Irish bank executives pocketed their beefed-up bonuses straight away. The review recommended cuts of up to 64 per cent in Irish bankers' salaries.

There is not a shred of evidence that Goggin, Sheehy, Fingleton, Drumm or Casey were ever offered jobs that might have enticed them away from the happy home patch. Indeed they were all rooted to the same bank for nearly all their working lives. No one can blame them.

A comparison with international bankers might have

proved embarrassing for Burrows. Brian Goggin's €4 million package in 2007 and David Drumm's €4.7 million in 2008 appear over the top, even by the generous standards of global banking. Eric Daniels, the boss at Lloyds TSB, for example, was paid less than Goggin in 2007 despite delivering three and a half times the Bank of Ireland's profits that year.

Goggin's total package was 50 per cent more than that of Andy Hornby of HBOS, who collected €2.6 million in 2007. The Scottish giant made €6.988 billion that year compared to Bank of Ireland's €1.584 billion.

European comparisons are even less flattering to the top brass at Irish banks. Lord Terence Burns, who chaired Abbey National (a bank of comparable size to AIB and Bank of Ireland) and sat on the board of its owner, Spanish banking giant Grupo Santander, received just €135,000 for his troubles in 2007. Sean FitzPatrick, Dermot Gleeson and Richard Burrows were all paid more than three times this amount.

Comparisons with other industries also show how Irish bankers' pay had bolted out of hand. Michael O'Leary, the most successful Irish businessman of his generation, earned a basic wage of €595,000 in 2008, compared with Brian Goggin's €1.2 million. The airline chief's total take-home package amounted to €1.2 million against Goggin's €3 million in the same year.

While being a banker was a licence to print money, being an ex-banker was sometimes even better. Possibly the most outrageous aspect of Irish bankers' pay are the rewards for failure gifted to departing executives by their boards. Anglo Irish again tops the 'hard luck' league by a distance. The rationale for the pay-offs in Anglo is probably indefensible. In the years 2004–7 the bank paid €8.7 million to three executives when they left. All three appear to have been given these vast sums as comfort money, in sympathy for not being awarded the top job won by David Drumm. Tom Browne (€3.75 million), Tiarnan O'Mahoney (€3.9 million) and John Rowan (€1.1 million) were the lucky losers. Gary Kennedy left AIB with a €738,000 payment, plus €2.01 million for his pension fund, after being pipped at the post for the chief executive's job by Eugene Sheeky.

When Mike Soden, apparently voluntarily, resigned from the Bank of Ireland after breaking his own rules on viewing videos, much was made about the honourable course he was taking. He asserted that, as he had set the rules, he should be the first to obey them and to pay the penalty for breaching them. His honour was rewarded with a payment of €2.3 million and a special lump sum of €0.4 million into his pension fund.

But possibly the most sensational pay-off of all was the €1.87 million bonanza given to EBS chief executive Ted McGovern when he resigned in September 2007 after a series of board-room rows. McGovern's reign at EBS was marked by infighting and boardroom turmoil. His price for leaving a 'mutual' building society, dedicated to the benefit of its humble members, would have done Ireland's fattest bankers proud.

Just before Christmas Lenihan set up another victim for 2009. As the Oireachtas closed for the festivities, he decided finally to tackle the problem of Paddy Neary. An inquiry was set up into how the Financial Regulator had missed the transfer of FitzPatrick's loans to Nationwide over eight consecutive years. The board of the Financial Regulator appointed two of its members to find out what had happened. It was told to report in early January. There was only one possible result.

As Lenihan celebrated Christmas 2008, he must have wondered what sort of a madhouse he had inherited when Brian Cowen asked him to take over as Finance Minister. The

2008 financial and banking fortunes of Ireland had been unspeakable.

The Irish stock market, the most objective measure of the economy's prospects, had lost 66 per cent of its value. At the same time the Dow in New York had only surrendered 34 per cent despite the wholesale programme of state rescues. Irish property had slumped by an official figure of 9.1 per cent. In reality it had probably lost much more, but the glut of houses on the market was not yet reflected in the index. The market was close to a standstill.

Banking shares had suffered their worst year ever. Bank of Ireland shares, having started the year at €10.19, finished worth just 83 cents a share, a loss of 92 per cent. AIB shares dropped from €15.67 to €1.73, a collapse of 89 per cent, while Anglo's shares lost over 98 per cent of their value, tanking from €10.94 to 17 cents.

10. Heads on Plates

As 2009 opened, the action had moved decisively to the Department of Finance. The boardrooms of the banks were beginning to feel the breeze; board members were squatters, digging in, plotting resistance to their removal.

Heads on plates were high on Brian Lenihan's agenda. And his agenda was fearsome.

He had a banking system to salvage.

He had an economy to rescue.

He had a financial regulator in limbo.

He had backbenchers to calm down.

He had global investors to impress.

He had no money.

Lenihan could not even begin to tackle the economy without first stabilizing the banks. In Leinster House backbenchers had a different priority. They were screaming at him to force the banks to release loans for small businesses, many of which were teetering on the brink of bankruptcy.

As was Ireland. Lenihan desperately needed to draw water from a dry well. His October Budget had been a flop. Another, tougher one was needed.

His message, a mixture of common sense and misplaced patriotism, was being drowned by the Opposition's constant cry that Ireland's citizens were being taxed to bail out the banks. Fianna Fáil hated the charge, but it was true. The mess had been created by builders and bankers. The people were paying the bill.

Externally, global investors were giving the thumbs down

to Ireland. The cost to the state of borrowing money on global markets was increasing by the day. Our credit rating was under threat. We were the worst risk in Europe – bar Greece, where there were riots on the streets of Athens amid mounting political and economic discontent.

And on New Year's Day the jury was out on the question of the competence of the Finance Minister himself. Overseas observers were less than enamoured by the troika at the top of Irish politics. Cowen, Tánaiste Mary Coughlan and Lenihan were widely seen as tribal Fianna Fáil loyalists. Cowen and Coughlan, in particular, looked far more comfortable at local Fianna Fáil cumann meetings in Offaly and Donegal than at the tables of European leaders or when making presentations to potential investors in Ireland.

Luckily, Lenihan was as happy in Paris as in Palmerstown. He spoke French fluently. He was well equipped to understand the global angle on the crisis confronting him.

The minister had two urgent targets. First, he needed to find billions to prop up the banks' balance sheets. Second, he was determined that heads should roll.

The second should have been the easy part. Normally, business failures fall on their swords. The institutions covered by the government guarantee were all led by a chairman and chief executive. They were identifiable. They bore primary responsibility for bringing Ireland to the brink of disaster.

The two top dogs at Anglo had gone, but none of the others was showing any inclination to follow their example. As for the boards, they were chained to their chairs.

Fergus Murphy of the EBS alone was not under threat, as he was not yet in the job when the building society took the plunge into development property. The others all feared the ministerial tap on the shoulder.

On Friday 9 January Lenihan got his first break. The Financial Regulator Patrick Neary resigned.

It had been an open secret that the minister was furious
with Neary over a series of incidents, but the final straw
was the watchdog's failure to spot the movement of Fitz-
Patrick's loans from Anglo. The inquiry into how the
Financial Regulator had missed this huge transfer of funds
had been set up before Christmas. Its report found a conflict
of evidence about whether Neary had known about them
or not. One staff member told the inquiry that she had
informed him. Neary denied it. He left with a healthy sever-
ance package: a lump sum of €630,000 plus a pension of
€143,000 a year.

The inquiry into Neary's role in the fiasco painted a picture
of the Financial Regulator's office in a shambles. Staff there
had stumbled upon FitzPatrick's €87 million dodge by chance,
when checking the Irish Nationwide's returns. The report
identified a 'communications breakdown'. It even revealed
that a letter from Anglo Irish to the Financial Regulator,
confirming that the bank believed the movement of directors'
loans between it and Irish Nationwide was legal, had 'gone
missing'.

Neary's resignation marked perhaps the first time during
the crisis that Lenihan was seen to have influenced events,
not to have been buffeted about by them. The minister could
take a rare bow.

The next head on a plate was nearly Lenihan's own. Six
days later, on Thursday 15 January, I was preparing for an
RTÉ *Prime Time* programme, ready to do a run-of-the-mill
piece about the ongoing banking crisis, the prospects for
recapitalization and, above all, the future of Anglo, which
had an Extraordinary General Meeting scheduled the next
day. Small shareholders were travelling to Dublin from all

parts of the country to attend the meeting. They were worried. That Thursday had been another disastrous session on the markets for Anglo, with the shares tumbling 10 per cent to close at 22 cents. Despite the state guarantee, deposits were still flying out the door, heading for anywhere but Anglo. Some of the money was fleeing Ireland.

The only item on the official EGM agenda was a vote on the €1.5 billion of taxpayers' money destined for Anglo, but there were scores of questions to be asked of Anglo's new chairman Donal O'Connor.

Just as I was heading into RTÉ's Donnybrook studios, the telephone rang. It was the *Prime Time* producer.

Change of plan. Could I go on with Richard Bruton and discuss some breaking news? Anglo Irish was being nationalized. The nine o'clock news would lead with it.

We struggled through the programme. The implications were mind-boggling. The shares would be suspended at 22 cents, but in reality they would be worth nothing at all.

It was a grim moment for Lenihan. He had fought to keep the banks out of state ownership. His agreement to the measure was a last resort. The recapitalization plan had failed to stem the outflow of deposits or stop the collapsing share price. Lenihan insisted that it was necessary to take Anglo into the custody of the state because the bank's funding position was weakened and its reputation damaged by the scandals. The minister and the board also knew that Standard & Poor's was on the verge of downgrading the bank again. The fragile edifice Lenihan had built around all the covered banks had crumbled.

The following morning, Friday 16 January, the markets attacked AIB, Bank of Ireland and Irish Life. Even though short selling was no longer allowed the shares took a pounding. Now that Anglo was off the pitch the guessing

game began. Who was next for nationalization? AIB, with
its enormous exposure to development loans, was in the
front line.

Once again the entire banking system stood on a knife edge.

The minister decided to let the Anglo shareholders' meeting go ahead, even though it was no longer strictly necessary.
The question of whether or not to accept state recapitalization was redundant. Anglo was now fully owned by the state.

I headed for the Mansion House with broadcaster Eamon
Dunphy, a co-veteran of past AGM skirmishes. We had
fought the battle of Eircom together some years earlier. That
had been a well-organized shareholders' revolt. This time we
merely wanted to show solidarity with the battered small
investors who had little hope of salvaging anything from the
wreckage of Anglo.

The only comfort shell-shocked shareholders could have
found on that day was information about how everything
had gone so wrong. There were about a thousand of them
in the Mansion House, and their gaunt faces told it all. They
knew that they would never recoup a cent. Yet, like the
bereaved at a coroner's inquest, they wanted closure. They
felt that at least they deserved an explanation, to be told the
cause of Anglo's death.

The meeting was presided over by Anglo's new chairman
Donal O'Connor, who had been appointed to succeed Fitz-
Patrick in a mad rush on 18 December 2008. O'Connor, who
trained as an accountant, worked for many years for PricewaterhouseCoopers, eventually becoming managing partner
before retiring and hitting the boardroom circuit.

Even with the departure of Lar Bradshaw, the Anglo board
post-FitzPatrick was woefully short of directors free of the
fallen chairman's influence. Anglo's spinners tried to portray
O'Connor – who had joined the Anglo board only six months

earlier – as different, but it was a misleading picture. O'Connor had served on the panel that selected David Drumm as Anglo's chief executive in 2004, and in June 2008 O'Connor told me that Drumm had been his own first choice. In April 2007 O'Connor had succeeded Bradshaw as chairman of the Dublin Docklands Development Authority. He was on the audit committee that had approved Anglo's controversial September 2008 figures, with their absurdly low provision of €2.5 billion for impaired loans – a figure that would be revised upwards to €23.6 billion within six months. And in July 2009 O'Connor would reveal that he was a long-time pal and golfing companion of FitzPatrick. O'Connor resigned the DDDA chair when he took over at Anglo, stating that he wished to ensure that there 'can be no suggestion of conflict of interest in the various roles I have'.

O'Connor was not so concerned about possible conflicts of interest just a few months earlier when he sat on the boards of both the DDDA and Anglo. The two outfits were involved in various ventures together, the common feature being Anglo's lending to the DDDA. In one instance Becbay, a company in which the DDDA had a large stake, borrowed the bulk of a €412 million loan from Anglo. At the time the DDDA and Anglo had two common directors, FitzPatrick and Bradshaw. (The DDDA has always protested, in response to criticism of the cross-directorships, that FitzPatrick and Bradshaw left the boardroom if there was any suggestion of a conflict of interest.)

As he stood before Anglo's shareholders that day in January 2009, O'Connor was as tight as a tick. Seated behind him on the podium were most of the old directors who had presided over the FitzPatrick loans debacle – including Smurfit CEO Gary McGann, CPL chief executive Anne Heraty and Green-core chairman Ned Sullivan.

O'Connor set a template that would be followed by other banks at their AGMs: a standard apology by the chairman followed by hours of stonewalling. O'Connor coldly refused to allow any of the board members sitting behind him to reply to questions from the floor. It seemed that accountability was not to be part of the new broom of state ownership. All O'Connor needed was to survive the meeting. After that, there would be no more AGMs, no more tiresome shareholders. Anglo would have only one tiresome shareholder – the Minister for Finance Brian Lenihan.

O'Connor played the role of coroner with ease. He refused to allow shareholders to ask questions of Ernst & Young, Anglo's auditors, despite their presence in the Mansion House. Ernst & Young's senior partner Paul Smith sat uncomfortably in the front row with colleague Des Quigley. When Quigley was photographed by the *Irish Times* photographer, he refused to give his name.

Ernst & Young took €2.2 million in fees from Anglo in 2008.

Faced with stonewalling from the platform in response to their requests for information, small shareholders were reduced to speaking of the effect the collapse of Anglo would have on their lives. They left the Mansion House devastated, without hope, O'Connor's apology ringing in their ears.

Luckily for the citizens of Ireland, Lenihan's two nominees to the Anglo board under the guarantee scheme were well-chosen men who had never been on the directors' circuit: former Fine Gael leader Alan Dukes and recently retired head of the Revenue Commissioners Frank Daly. They sat on the Mansion House podium looking distinctly uncomfortable, beacons of light among the former FitzPatrick loyalists.

Within days all but O'Connor, Dukes and Daly had resigned. Five non-executive directors rolled over. Later,

those among the five who also held sensitive state appointments had to step down from them too: Anne Heraty resigned
from the Stock Exchange board, from Forfás and from Bord
na Móna, while Gary McGann gave up his post as chairman
of the Dublin Airport Authority.

Lenihan was beginning to collect scalps. He had reason to
believe he was gradually coming to grips with Anglo.

Then he blew it.

On 19 January, following the advice of the grey mandarins
in the Department of Finance, he filled one of the board
vacancies with a member of the old boys' network. Maurice
Keane had been top dog at the Bank of Ireland when
O'Connor was at the helm at PricewaterhouseCoopers. PWC
were the auditors to Bank of Ireland in 2001 when the bank
paid them a record fee of €15.4 million. Keane was a hurried
choice, probably the result of a perceived need to appoint a
banker to a board that didn't have one. It was two steps
forward with Dukes and Daly, one step back with Keane.

The press release about Keane's appointment contained an
odd omission. It failed to mention that Keane was a board
member of the publicly quoted industrial holdings group
DCC. Keane had been a loyal supporter of DCC boss Jim
Flavin, the man adjudged by the Supreme Court to have
indulged in insider dealing. Paul Appleby, the director of
corporate enforcement, had secured a High Court inspector
to probe Flavin's share dealing activities, and this investigation
was ongoing. Keane's association with Flavin should have
raised the alarm bells. It didn't.

In the week after Anglo's nationalization Irish bank shares
plunged to new depths. AIB was savaged, dropping from
€1.94 to a week's low of 45 cents before rallying to 74 cents,
while Bank of Ireland dropped from 90 cents as low as

31 cents before recovering to 42 cents at the end of the week. Investors believed these banks were in deep trouble and were terrified of a nationalization domino effect.

Time was not on the side of those wishing to save AIB and Bank of Ireland from the same fate. The big two desperately needed funding.

The Department of Finance was in a hurry. Earlier promises by both banks that they themselves would raise a proportion of the capital needed were abandoned: no one in their right mind would invest in an Irish bank that had such a dodgy balance sheet and was a candidate for nationalization. All of the recapitalization money – €3 billion for each bank – would have to come from the government. In return, the two major banks indulged in a piece of political window dressing designed to give Lenihan cover. The banks signed up to some token increases in credit to small businesses and first-time home-buyers. In the public mind the €3 billion capital – on the point of entering the two banks – would be available for lending. In reality it would not. It was simply cushion capital, there to shield them against the bad loans which they had constantly understated.

On 6 February a revised deal was struck. AIB and Bank of Ireland were both to receive €3.5 billion. Every cent of the recapitalization was to come from the Exchequer. In return senior executives of the banks would take pay cuts of 33 per cent, with no bonuses in 2008 or 2009, while non-executive directors' pay would be reduced by 25 per cent. In return the state was entitled to preference shares with a fixed dividend of 8 per cent per annum. These preference shares could be repurchased at par for the first five years of their life. The minister could also exercise warrants attached to the preference shares entitling him to purchase up to 25 per cent of the ordinary share capital of the banks at pre-determined prices.

The agreement also empowered the minister to appoint up to 25 per cent of the directors of the recapitalized banks.

It is difficult to credit today, but AIB strongly resisted state aid right up to the last minute. Bank of Ireland signed up earlier: Brian Goggin and Richard Burrows had accepted the need for more capital far sooner than AIB's Eugene Sheehy (whose statement the previous October that the bank would 'rather die than raise equity' was haunting him more and more by the day) and Dermot Gleeson.

Burrows saw co-operation with the minister as the bank's lifeline. Sheehy saw it otherwise. State aid meant state control. His resistance to state funds was a last-ditch attempt to hold on to AIB's autonomy. He had staked his reputation on it. His stance was bizarre, as AIB was even more exposed to property developers than Bank of Ireland. He seemed to believe that AIB could somehow work its way out of the swamp.

On 12 February Sheehy took to the airwaves of RTÉ's *Morning Ireland* to admit that AIB regretted some of the lending mistakes made in recent years. He even expressed gratitude to the government for the €3.5 billion, funding he had disdained only weeks earlier. Yet he was defiant. In a spirited performance he insisted that AIB was now 'well capitalized'. He parried RTÉ interviewer George Lee's questions well, admitting that bankers' pay had been too high and pleading that he was taking a 25 per cent reduction. He went on to assert that he was not resigning and that he had the full confidence of the board. As any politician would have told him, once the votes of confidence begin, unanimous support signals mortal danger.

On the same day that Sheehy publicly ate humble pie Brian Goggin was interviewed on RTÉ television by Christopher McKevitt. Asked what his salary would be in 2008 and 2009,

Goggin – apparently totally unprepared for the question – put on a hangdog look and pronounced the immortal words: 'I think my total disclosed compensation in the report and accounts, I think, was €2.9 million.' He then added, 'This year it will be less than two million.' He looked as though he expected a visit from St Vincent de Paul.

The nation was outraged. Former Labour leader Pat Rabbitte said it all in the Dáil: 'In the name of God what sort of alternative planet are these guys living on?'

Goggin had to go. He was already due to retire in June, but a few days later Lenihan announced that he would be stepping down in a matter of weeks.

Goggin will forever be remembered for his outrageous pay. The headline figure of €4 million for his overall package in 2007 is permanently embedded in banking folklore. Under Goggin, pay at the Bank of Ireland rocketed parallel with a steep upward curve in property loans. In the very year that Goggin's salary hit the €4 million mark property exposure reached 67 per cent of the entire loan book. At the same time nearly all the top executives shared in an options orgy, while Richard Burrows and the other directors helped themselves to huge fees.

A lukewarm tribute from Burrows stating that Goggin's decision was taken 'in the interests of the bank' gave the game away. In case there was any doubt Burrows went on: 'I believe that this has motivated his decision to seek retirement this summer to make way for fresh leadership to take Bank of Ireland through the challenges which lie ahead. We wish Brian well in the future.'

Gillian Bowler, chairman of Irish Life & Permanent, was at a meeting on Tuesday 10 February when her telephone rang. It was her chief executive Denis Casey. There was a spot of bother on the horizon. The media was running with a story about Irish Life having made a large deposit to help Anglo out at its year end.

Casey reassured Bowler that the Department of Finance knew about it. The implication was that if the department knew the details, the transaction must be kosher.

There was no doubt that all Ireland's financial institutions had been asked by the authorities to 'wear the green jersey' and assist their fellow Irish banks in a time of crisis. They had quietly agreed to help each other, and they had done so. Anglo was one of a number of parties believed to have provided interbank lending to Irish Life in June 2008. On the surface, the latest incident looked like a return favour. Casey initially argued that the transaction, now under media scrutiny, was simply part of this official strategy of mutual help.

Of all the bankers in Ireland Denis Casey would have seemed the most unlikely to get mixed up in a financial scandal. He was hardly visible on the public radar, and that is probably the way he wanted it to be. He started his working life at AIB in 1976 at the age of sixteen before moving to Irish Life in 1980. Having served in a number of Irish Life's divisions, he gained the pivotal position as head of the retail business in 1999 at the time of Irish Life's merger with Irish Permanent.

Casey had none of the ebullient sparkle of his predecessor as chief executive, David Went, although he is generally believed to have been Went's anointed successor when he took over in 2007. Most of the limelight was stolen by Bowler, who was easier on the eye and not as camera-shy as Casey. Now he was being introduced to the Irish public in circumstances he would never have anticipated.

That evening Casey told Irish Life colleagues that he had talked to Kevin Cardiff, the banking boss in the Department of Finance. Ominously he told them that Cardiff had said that 'structure might be a problem' with the deposit. That must have been the understatement of the entire crisis. A 'problem' with 'structure' was finance-speak for a blatant breach of the rules.

After that, Bowler moved into overdrive. Her inquiries unearthed a nightmare for Irish Life. The €7.5 billion deal was an artificial transaction. It was calculated to help Anglo, and designed to deceive the markets. It was a catastrophic failure for Irish Life, an Irish bank that had managed to keep its nose relatively clean. Irish Life's directors had not been told of the enormous transaction. That in itself would have been a sin, even if the deal had been above board. It wasn't.

The facts emerged quickly. The deal was not meant to help with liquidity, the legitimate reason for the 'green jersey'. IL&P's executives had agreed to Anglo's requests not just for the money but, crucially, for how and by what route it would be transferred. Anglo transferred €7.5 billion back into IL&P as an interbank loan; the only purpose of the €7.5 billion that went to Anglo was to give Anglo a mechanism to classify the injection as customer deposits rather than interbank funding, in order to make its year-end accounts look better. The IL&P executives would argue that they were not responsible for how Anglo chose to classify the funds, but they had assisted Anglo by using the peculiar mechanism that it had sought.

In the Dáil on Wednesday 11 February Lenihan was forced to admit that he had found out about the dodge a month earlier, in January. He conceded that he had not read the entire contents of a PricewaterhouseCoopers report, commissioned by himself and delivered in October, which had unearthed the bombshell. Somehow, no member of the Department of Finance had highlighted this explosive piece of information for the minister. He was in the soup. Opposition calls for

Lenihan's resignation, for once, carried conviction. His pleas that he could not possibly have read all 720 pages of the PWC report were ridiculed. Lenihan's position looked shaky.

On Thursday morning Bowler went to see Brian Lenihan at the minister's request. She had wanted to meet him in the Merrion Hotel for a less formal cup of coffee, but he was in no mood for cosy chats and so they met in his office. He did not explicitly demand heads but was assured that they would roll. Bowler offered Lenihan her own head, but it was refused.

That evening an emergency board meeting took place at the Lower Abbey Street head office of Irish Life & Permanent. Both finance director Peter Fitzpatrick and treasury head David Gantly accepted that they had been involved in the transactions, though they protested that they were in line with the wishes of the Financial Regulator. Casey protested strongly that he was neither aware of nor involved in the mechanism used to transfer the money. The directors were prepared to give Casey the benefit of the doubt, although there were some tough questions about how a €7.5 billion deal of this sort could be executed on his watch without board approval. Some directors were pushing for Casey to step down.

Bowler emerged at 3 a.m. with two heads on a plate for Lenihan: Peter Fitzpatrick and David Gantly. The board had refused Casey's offer of resignation.

Suddenly Lenihan faced a challenge to his authority, along with continuing calls for his resignation. He was incensed. He recalled an exhausted Bowler and other directors to his office later the same morning. He is believed to have briefed his own appointees to the board of IL&P, former finance minister Ray MacSharry and civil servant Margaret Hayes. This time there would be no mistake.

When Casey learned of the meeting of Friday 13, he knew

that his fate was finally sealed. His resignation was with Bowler before she reached Lenihan.

Poor Denis Casey did not have his feet under the Irish Life desk for long enough to sample the riches taken by other Irish bankers. His salary of €942,000 in 2008 was not in the bankers' superleague, due to the downturn. He owned 68,000 shares, worth €104,000 at his departure, and had time to accumulate only 233,000 options, none of which were of any value because the market price had sunk so low. In any case he was forced to give them up when he resigned.

Bowler herself had survived in her €288,000-a-year job, but now the three top IL&P executives had gone. Lenihan's authority had been restored.

Lenihan's cull was beginning to take shape. There had been a clearout at Anglo; Goggin was going early from the Bank of Ireland; Irish Life had shed three of its top executives. (On the same day that Casey resigned, Mark Duffy had stepped down from Bank of Scotland (Ireland). Duffy's departure coincided with massive losses in his bank's loans to commercial property.)

Three of the covered banks were still untouched. Michael Walsh and Michael Fingleton remained at the helm at Irish Nationwide; Eugene Sheehy and Dermot Gleeson were hanging on at AIB; while down at the EBS no one had yet accepted responsibility for the calamitous plunge into commercial development loans.

Four days later Michael Walsh resigned from the chair of the Irish Nationwide, citing 'unfolding events' as the reason. Most observers felt he was wisely avoiding the inevitable flak coming down the track.

The big question remained unanswered. Were these guys

token ministerial scapegoats? Or were the banks changing their culture?

The minister got his answer on 25 February. The Bank of Ireland pulled a mighty stroke. Perhaps distracted by a Gardaí dawn raid on Anglo's premises a day earlier, Lenihan let the Bank of Ireland ram a whale through his net.

In the old days – back six months – there had been two candidates jostling to succeed Goggin upon his retirement: Richie Boucher and Des Crowley. The favourite was always Boucher, the Zambian-born fifty-year-old who had joined Bank of Ireland in 2003 from Royal Bank of Scotland. He was already a board member, in pole position. Crowley, the head of Bank of Ireland's UK operations, was the dark horse.

But events were rapidly conspiring against both Boucher and Crowley. The clamour for an outsider had been growing in political and media circles. Pressure was building up for key banking positions to be filled by those who were not infected by the property bubble.

The announcement that Goggin would be departing had only just been made, but Boucher was slotted into the job with unseemly haste. Later Bank of Ireland was to maintain with little conviction that, 'Richie Boucher was the unanimous choice of the board as having the required banking and leadership experience, after an exhaustive process in Ireland and internationally, involving internal and external candidates.'

The rigour of the selection process was questionable. No outside candidate could possibly have accepted the post, as the pay package was unknown. A government committee setting top bankers' pay levels was still agonizing over how much the boss of Bank of Ireland should be paid. The appointment looked like a stitch-up.

The resistance to Boucher's appointment was initially

political. Labour Party finance spokesperson Joan Burton described it as a 'missed opportunity to signal a new development in the banking sector'.

Within a few hours I raised the appointment in the Senate. The *Irish Independent* said that, 'Senator Shane Ross described Boucher's appointment, with perhaps a touch of hyperbole, as "possibly the most disgraceful appointment in the business world in living memory".'

Hyperbole or not, it was a staggering piece of retrenchment from the Bank of Ireland board. Burrows and his boys were not beaten yet.

Lenihan was left looking lame. The next day he expressed his approval of Boucher's appointment at an Oireachtas committee. But the overriding impression was that Boucher was not his choice, that his eye had been wiped.

Powerful opposition was soon to rear its head. Billionaire Dermot Desmond, a Bank of Ireland shareholder, plunged into the fray. Desmond discussed the appointment with chairman Richard Burrows and other members of the board. He had two worries.

Firstly, he felt Boucher was totally compromised by his position as chief executive of retail, as a member of the risk committee and of the group investment committee. In a letter to Burrows he said he believed that Boucher 'must have been responsible for fatal errors of judgment, including advancing loans to developers on the strength of overstated land values and insufficient security'. Secondly, Desmond opposed an insider. 'Credibility and confidence need to be restored. This will not be achieved by promoting existing management further up the chain.' Burrows offered to meet Desmond to allay his fears, but it was a case of closing the stable door . . .

Boucher had been helped over the hurdles. The Bank of Ireland and Lenihan were saddled with him.

Richie Boucher carried some interesting baggage. The property developer Sean Dunne, in an interview with RTÉ's Marian Finucane on 15 March 2008, revealed that Richie Boucher was a 'very good friend of mine' who advised him on the financing of the enormous acquisitions he had recently made in Ballsbridge. Boucher did not fund the Ballsbridge purchases, but he had funded Dunne in other deals. In October 2007, in an unusual move for a banker, Boucher personally supported Dunne's planning application for the development he hoped to build on the Jurys/Berkeley Court sites. In a letter to Dublin City Council, Boucher stated that he believed that Dunne's plan 'will significantly benefit the city of Dublin and its citizens through helping enhance the concept of a living city and providing buildings of significant architectural merit befitting Ireland of the 21st century'.

Dunne's development was not a runner. After Dublin City Council had granted part permission in March 2008, the residents of Ballsbridge took Dunne to An Bord Pleanála. Supported by Dermot Desmond, who lodged his own objection, the residents persuaded the planning appeals board to throw out the entire project, lock, stock and barrel, in January 2009.

By the time An Bord Pleanála had turned down Dunne's application, the development was a dead duck and the banks were beached whales. Back in 2005 and 2006 all the banks would have killed for a bit of the Ballsbridge action. Today they are lucky if they are even receiving the interest payments, and the undeveloped sites in a prosperous inner suburb of Dublin are a monument to the folly of Ireland's bankers and developers.

While the Bank of Ireland was busy playing musical chairs with the pretenders, its share price was still tanking. On

5 March the shares hit an all-time low of 12.5 cents, valuing the entire bank at just €126 million: the price of two and a half houses in Shrewsbury Road a couple of years earlier. AIB bottomed out valued at €238 million on the same day. Both seemed to be heading for oblivion or nationalization. On 2 March AIB had reported the first loss in its Irish operations since it was founded. Both banks had suddenly discovered that their dodgy loans were soaring out of control.

Despite the release of AIB's awful 2008 figures Eugene Sheehy insisted that he was 'not stepping down', that he was only fifty-five and would retire at sixty. He even pointed out that his modest salary of €700,000 represented a 60 per cent cut. He was hell-bent on survival.

So was Gillian Bowler of Irish Life, still reeling from the loss of her three top executives. 'I am a fighter, not a quitter,' she declared when presenting the bank's 2008 results. At the same time she said that merger talks with the EBS were 'ongoing'. In truth they had run into the ground. Nobody wanted to be troubled with EBS chairman Mark Moran's ailing baby.

Not even Moran himself. On 10 March Moran announced his resignation along with EBS finance director Alan Merriman. Moran had been in command when the EBS had lost its nerve and plunged deeper into the property development world, chasing bigger profits. The result was disastrous. Rather than face possible humiliation in the contest for re-election as chairman at the AGM on 29 May, Mark Moran fell on his sword.

Fingleton was next, and his resignation was perhaps the most overdue. Back in 2006 he could have retired with honour ahead of the game, before the crash, once the Building Societies Bill – which allowed for the demutualization and sale of the Irish Nationwide – finally went through.

But he didn't. Instead he agreed to a board request to stay

beyond his seventieth birthday. It was madness. It only served to tee up his own crucifixion.

His extended term was notable for a series of mistakes. His profits were still healthy in 2007, coming in at €391 million, but this was a fantasy figure; many of the property development loans on Irish Nationwide's books were about to go bad. Apparently he could not see it. He had been unchallenged for too long. His board had rarely shown much sign of independence. His years of publicity and his reluctance to employ anyone who could conceivably look like a successor made him seem indispensable. The Irish Nationwide and Fingleton were inseparable in the public mind.

The government guarantee changed all that. In the grim new world of 2009 the Irish Nationwide depended on Lenihan, and not Fingers, for its survival.

Fingleton, already greatly weakened by the revelation of Irish Nationwide's role in the 'warehousing' of Sean FitzPatrick's personal loans from Anglo, had offered to leave in February. Not surprisingly, his board asked him to stay on. Not surprisingly, he accepted. It was a mistake.

After that, bad news kept spilling out of the building society's cupboard. First it emerged that Fingleton had received a €1 million bonus in 2008. The award, apparently for staying on an extra year, was particularly sensitive as it was paid after the society was rescued by the bank guarantee. His total package of €2.34 million made him the highest-paid boss of any of the guaranteed banks in 2008. Add this to his huge €27.6 million pension pot and the patriarch at the Nationwide was seen to have transgressed the spirit, if not the letter, of the guarantee.

Fingers protested that the €1 million was not a bonus, that it had been agreed prior to the 30 September guarantee, that he was entitled to it and that he was keeping it.

Lenihan was furious. At a time when taxes were being ratcheted up and spending cuts were the daily diet, the public was outraged. But Fingleton was obdurate. A battle of wills followed, one that Fingleton could not possibly win. Yet Fingers was so out of touch with public opinion that he could not see the inevitable looming. This was not February 2008, it was February 2009. His board was no longer as tame as in earlier years. Sitting beside him this year were two ministerial nominees – Rory O'Ferrall, formerly of the big accountancy firm Deloitte, and Adrian Kearns, the outgoing boss of the National Development Finance Agency. Both nominees were cursed with forensic minds, integrity and independence. They did not dance to the Nationwide agenda.

Unimpressed with Fingleton's defiant stance over the bonus, Lenihan piled on the pressure. On 27 March Fingleton finally agreed to hand back the €1 million. But his statement was grudging. It had been wrung out of him. He again insisted that he was entitled to it and was only returning it 'because of a 24-hour media siege on my home and also because of the effect it may have on the society'. He was 'pleased' to note the acknowledgement of the minister that 'he could not be compelled to return the payment'. Fingers had received legal opinion backing his view from none other than former Attorney General Michael McDowell.

Fingleton could not see that the legal opinion was a puff of smoke at this stage. The court of public opinion would not tolerate the boss of a mutual building society taking such huge sums when taxpayers were being forced to support it. All his years of cultivating the political establishment could not save him. Despite his friendship with Brian Lenihan's father, the young Lenihan would do nothing to help. On 2 April Fingleton's retirement was announced for the end of the month.

He was lucky. If he had stayed on he would have been lynched at the annual general meeting due on 12 May. Just a fortnight after he announced his retirement date, the annual report was released. It showed losses of €280 million after setting aside €464 million for bad loans, nearly all of them in property development. The top 30 customers owed 48 per cent of the loans, and 80 per cent of the loan book was to commercial property customers.

Fingleton's departure was a sad end to a sometimes stellar career. He departed quietly, refusing to allow the staff to hold so much as a farewell drink for him. Unlike some of the bankers who have been so happily relieved of their positions over the years, he received no pay-off.

The minister's headcount of bankers was now well into double figures. Still, the big one had eluded him. Eugene Sheehy remained in charge at AIB. His survival defied explanation.

It was not as if Sheehy could claim that he had personally outperformed his departed rivals. Far from it. Sheehy had managed to cling on to his lucrative job even though he had presided over one of the worst destructions of shareholder value in the history of Ireland. Shares in AIB had tumbled from a high of €23.95 in February 2007 to a low of 27 cents in March 2009. In two years, under Sheehy, they had tanked by 99 per cent. The market value of the bank had crashed from €22 billion to less than €250 million.

While his shareholders were suffering, Sheehy had done very well out of AIB. His first full year as chief executive (2006) saw him rewarded with a €2.4 million package. This included a bonus of €1.3 million.

It is a measure of the sharp climb in bonuses at AIB during the property boom that the previous boss, Michael Buckley, made only a fraction as much – €250,000 – just four years earlier in 2002. No doubt Sheehy was playing catch-up with the bulging sacks of loot being grabbed by the glory boys in Anglo.

Sheehy had adopted a cuter game plan than Goggin. He was intent on surviving. Instead of giving a suicidal interview on his pay – as the Bank of Ireland chief had done – he did a quick swerve. On 1 October 2008, seeing the danger, he waived 10 per cent of his salary. In March 2009 he announced that his pay would remain at €690,000 for his remaining four years in office.

The assumption that he would be in the job for four more years was an optimistic one at a time when most observers believed that Sheehy's days were numbered. The government was on the verge of capping his pay at €500,000 anyway.

At the same time Sheehy kept close to his board. Like him, all twelve of AIB's well-cushioned non-executive directors remained stuck to their seats, determined not to sacrifice their fees. Chairman Dermot Gleeson received a massive €475,000, while ordinary board members earned up to €153,000. At one point they felt the need to express confidence in Sheehy.

So who was this man who managed to hold on to his huge salary and position longer than all other bankers?

Eugene Sheehy was born in 1954. His father Maurice Sheehy had been head of the Irish Sugar Company. Writing in the *Sunday Independent* in 2009, editor Aengus Fanning remembered Maurice as 'diffident, steely and clinical'. He saw the son of Maurice as having 'inherited many of his father's qualities, including that of iron determination'.

Sheehy was not quite AIB's clone for Brian Goggin; as Fanning noted, he is made of sterner stuff. But the two big chiefs of Irish banking at the time of the property madness bore striking similarities. Both of them were career bankers, 'lifers' rooted for thirty-five years in the institutions where they had landed their first jobs. Sheehy was fifty when he took the top job, while Goggin was fifty-two.

Sheehy came straight to AIB at seventeen from Salesian College in Limerick, run by both the Christian Brothers and the priesthood. Like Goggin he did not initially enjoy a third-level education but – again, like Goggin – he later felt the need to take an MSc in management from Trinity College.

Cathal Magee, now chief executive at Eircom, was a fellow student of Sheehy's. He described him to me as a guy with 'no ego, a mixture of modesty and capability'. Other class-mates say that he was not the sort of guy to put his hand up but he was a man of integrity. One told me that while he was 'almost shy, you could sense a streak of ruthlessness in him. He never drew attention to himself.'

Such shyness is consistent with a man who shunned the limelight throughout his career at AIB. Like Goggin, he limited himself to media set pieces, doing interviews only where he felt it was essential. When I rang his office seeking an exchange of views for this book he did not bother to return the calls, nor even to send a message of acknowledgement.

He has always been an AIB staff man. He has never forgotten that he came to the top via the retail end, not floating in sideways like many others. He was the manager of three Dublin branches before jumping over the wall to headquarters.

He was lifted out of the branches by former AIB managing director Kevin Kelly, who spotted his talent when inquiring who was running a giant AIB technology project back in 1995. He was told it was Eugene Sheehy. After Eugene had delivered the project 'on time and on the money', Sheehy was fast-tracked. Kelly told me that he is a 'highly effective guy with no ego'. It was the first of four promotions for Kelly's protégé.

Early in 2002 Sheehy was flushed out as the bank's rising star. He was sent to the United States to sort out the mess in AIB's US subsidiary, Allfirst. In the process he extracted AIB from the scandal that had rocked the very foundations of the bank. His reward was the chief executive's job, which he gained in 2005.

The survival of Sheehy, and of his chairman Dermot Glee-son, was puzzling to observers in the spring of 2009. The AIB public relations machine had enjoyed a measure of success in portraying Sheehy as some sort of master of the universe. He was constantly being pitted against Brian Goggin, whose media appearances made him seem a plodder. When pushed, Goggin went quietly. Sheehy, who was more self-confident and articulate, could tiptoe through the minefields and dodge the missiles.

But he could not dodge the AIB numbers. They were woeful.

Long before the AIB shareholders' meeting, more bad news broke. After independent government auditors had again rummaged through AIB's books, they challenged the bank's figures. They found that AIB required another €1.5 billion, bringing its total capital needs up to €5 billion.

AIB was now in a worse position than Bank of Ireland. Its greater exposure to the property developers was recognized in the sums being put up by the government.

Reports leaked out of a fierce row in the Department of Finance about AIB's need for capital on the weekend of 18 and 19 April. Sheehy and other AIB directors were adamant that no more capital was needed, but the department would not countenance a situation where the bank was back seeking more funds within months. Sheehy's credibility on the recap-italization issue was zero.

He must have seen the men in grey coats at the door. Even

his persuasive skills could not survive the acceptance of another €1.5 billion in funding. AIB protested that it might raise the money by selling its interests in Poland or the United States, but buyers of banks were scarce in both countries. The suggestion was a face-saver.

In the following week some of AIB's biggest shareholders approached the bank. They would not be voting for Sheehy's re-election at the annual general meeting to be held two weeks later on 13 May. Lenihan himself gave no indication of support for the incumbent chief executive. Sheehy was being hung out to dry.

On Thursday 30 April AIB chairman Dermot Gleeson carried the news to Lenihan that neither he nor Sheehy nor finance director John O'Donnell would be seeking re-election.

Lenihan had now toppled the biggest names in Irish banking. Yet, once again, he bottled the succession.

A new AIB chairman had already been agreed. With a speed reminiscent of Burrows's placing of Boucher in the top job at Bank of Ireland, the AIB board had arranged for Dan O'Connor, who shared board responsibility for AIB's disastrous lending policies, to take over as chairman. He may have been a good banker in his days at GE Consumer Finance, but he was hardly a new broom. Nor was new deputy chairman David Pritchard. Both had been directors of AIB since 2007.

Lenihan could have insisted on a temporary AIB chair followed by a period of reflection, but he did not. He did, however, take a stand in the contest for Sheehy's successor.

Colm Doherty, the head of AIB Capital Markets, was hoping for a pre-emptive strike in line with Boucher's coup at the Bank of Ireland. Doherty had been a candidate in 2005 when Sheehy won the job. He and Sheehy had never been soulmates. Indeed Doherty seems to have been at pains to run his own independent republic of capital markets during the Sheehy years. He was based across town at the International Financial Services Centre, miles away from the Ballsbridge headquarters.

At odds of 7/4 against with Paddy Power bookmakers, Doherty was the leading named candidate. But Paddy Power was offering 1/2 odds on an external candidate. The money came flooding in for Doherty. Doherty moved to 8/15 when the bookies closed the book, fearing that the insider might walk away with the job.

The idea of hiring an external candidate flew in the face of the AIB tradition. The AIB board wanted to install Doherty. Lenihan was forced to instruct his nominees – Dick Spring and Declan Collier – to warn the directors against this. The move was stalled. If AIB's board had arrived at the AGM on 13 May with Doherty already slotted into Sheehy's shoes, there would have been mayhem.

The idea was dropped, at least temporarily. There was enough trouble due at the AGM without the board being deliberately provocative.

At the AGM the by now standard apology was read out by chairman Gleeson. He probably did not cut and paste Donal O'Connor's words of regret from Anglo, Burrows's from Bank of Ireland, Gillian Bowler's from Irish Life or Mark Moran's from EBS, but the speech had a familiar ring.

A few rows back from the platform lurked Gary Keogh, a shareholder from Blackrock, Co. Dublin. Keogh waited until Gleeson was in full flow, stood up and hurled an egg at the chair and at Sheehy. He missed by inches as Gleeson showed that his verbal dexterity was matched by remarkable speed when it came to ducking physical missiles. Keogh gained some satisfaction from the egg crashing into the wall behind the platform and splattering on Gleeson's sleeve.

Keogh was quietly escorted from the AGM. Unapologetic,

he gave interviews to the media, explaining that his €18,000 investment in AIB shares had been wiped out. His story resonated around Ireland.

The meeting went on endlessly. Gleeson, just like Donal O'Connor at Anglo's EGM four months earlier, refused to allow the directors to answer any questions from shareholders – a less than democratic decision, as they were due for re-election that day. Even new chairman Dan O'Connor was shielded from the shareholders. The only directors on the platform were the three in the departure lounge. The others were squatting in the front row, unaccountable for their stewardship. Eventually, under pressure from shareholders, Gleeson asked the directors to stand up. They were then re-elected on a massive vote from the big institutional shareholders, without uttering a syllable at the meeting.

Lenihan, on behalf of the taxpayer, had cast his 25 per cent vote in favour of the outgoing directors.

Three AIB heads in one day were enough for him.

A week later, on 20 May, Richard Burrows confirmed that he would be leaving his post as governor of the Bank of Ireland after the AGM in July. Burrows had held on for months as all around him were being culled; but hints were being dropped in high places that he too might not survive the July AGM. Ominously the minister had given him no assurance that he would be casting the state's 25 per cent of votes in his favour. Elsewhere institutional shareholders were again contemplating their position on the governor's future. Suddenly the re-election of bank directors was no longer automatic.

The governor of the Bank of Ireland had commanded a consistently higher fee than any other Irish bank director. Burrows's pay of €512,000 for 2008 – not bad for a year when the bank reduced the number of scheduled board meetings to seven – may explain his eagerness to stay in the job through awful times. (The bank also held two unscheduled meetings that year, to make a total of nine.)

On 17 June Irish Life slipped another 'lifer' – Kevin Murphy, head of its life and pensions division – into Denis Casey's vacated position. Murphy emerged from an 'exhaustive process of interviews of external and internal candidates'. He had been in Irish Life for thirty-seven years.

Retrenchment was on a roll.

When he was not sorting out the bankers, Lenihan had an economy to rescue. A succession of fearful figures on unemployment, recession, property prices, the budget deficit and other indicators showed the sins of the bankers pushing the economy over the precipice. An emergency Budget was called for April.

Lenihan flagged the draconian measures well in advance. Everyone expected the doubling of the income levy, the attack on social welfare payments and on the child care supplement, plus increases in capital taxes, DIRT tax and others. The entire country knew that this Budget was merely a start. There would be more of the same in December.

The minister used the emergency Budget as an opportunity to unveil his vehicle for rescuing the banks. It caused as much controversy as the entire gamut of penal measures inflicted on the taxpayer.

Lenihan had commissioned an old Bertie Ahern buddy, Peter Bacon, to recommend a solution for the banks. Bacon had a long record of writing reports for governments. Many of them were about property. He had worked in the Economic and Social Research Institute, Goodbody Stockbrokers and as economic adviser to the Department of

Finance under Bertie. Bacon had bags of ability, but his sometimes haughty manner made him few friends. Humility was not his strongest suit.

Bacon proposed a variant of the 'bad bank' solution to the toxic assets on the banks' balance sheets. Lenihan accepted his report and told the Dáil that he was setting up a National Asset Management Agency (NAMA) to acquire development loans from the covered banks.

Next day the minister, Bacon and Michael Somers, head of the National Treasury Management Agency (NTMA), held a press conference to explain how NAMA would work. The details were sketchy but the die was cast. The government had set its face against further nationalization of banks. It was heading down the Bacon road.

The basic idea behind NAMA was simple. The new agency would purchase development loans from the banks at a discount from their book value. The banks would receive government bonds in exchange. Unencumbered by bad loans, and recapitalized via the government bonds, the banks would, in theory, be freed up to lend again. Other banks too would be more willing to lend to them as they carried no toxic debt.

The NAMA plan caused consternation. Twenty academic economists wrote an article for the *Irish Times* condemning it. Hostility began to snowball as opposition politicians and even Dermot Desmond opposed the initiative. The principal objection was that, by releasing the banks, NAMA imprisoned the taxpayer. Roughly €90 billion worth of loans was on the table. NAMA would have to negotiate a discount with the banks. On past form, in a falling property market the state would pay too much. The banks might not only be relieved of their bad loans burden, but they might even wipe the government's eye in the process.

Developers too were up in arms about NAMA. They were

comfortable owing their bank millions (in some cases even billions), but they saw a transfer of these loans to an arm's-length state agency as the road to ruin. NAMA would look at the loans transferred out of the banks' hands and decide on the right path on a case-by-case basis. The builders' cosy relationship with the banker who had given them the loan was being removed. NAMA would dictate which builders would live and which would die.

Opposition from the developers was not a big deal. They were in no position to argue. Politicians posturing, even academics hurling from the ditches, were easy enough for Lenihan to brush off. But the unexpected appearance of Michael Somers, head of the National Treasury Management Agency, before the Oireachtas Public Accounts Committee (PAC) on 14 May caused an uproar.

Somers is one of the few non-elected public servants with a media profile. Successive ministers for finance have eaten out of his hands. Somers shocked the assembled TDs and media with his remarks about NAMA. He said he anticipated legal challenges and a 'bonanza' for lawyers. He related having been 'aghast' when he reviewed the banks' loan books: the scale of the development loans had shocked him. He had no idea how NAMA would be set up. His agency was not adequately staffed to deal with the challenge of running NAMA or even working on the resolution of the banking crisis. And in a sour aside he told the committee that Ireland would be lucky to hold on to its last remaining AAA credit rating, as its debt levels could surge once the state had taken on the bad loans from the banks. Standard & Poor's and Fitch had already downgraded Ireland's sovereign debt. Moody's was expected to follow (and did, on 2 July).

Lenihan was in Brussels on the day that Somers let rip, about to launch a roadshow in European capitals explaining

Ireland's strategy to would-be investors in government bonds. Michael Somers's decision to let off steam about the centrepiece of that strategy could have torpedoed the minister's mission.

Few understood Somers's outburst. A quintessential career civil servant was behaving in an uncharacteristically unhelpful way. Some suggested that he was furious that the state had pillaged his €20 billion National Pension Reserve Fund to save the banks, others that he was only six months away from retirement and was now happy to speak his mind. Certainly the highest-paid civil servant in Ireland – reputed to be on €1 million a year – had put the cat among the pigeons.

Lenihan continued on his European roadshow. He met investors in London. According to the *Irish Times* he received 'generous praise' all round for mastery of his brief and for some of the measures he was taking. On his return he took to the airwaves to defuse Somers's solo run, downplaying the NTMA boss's appearance before the committee and explaining what Somers really meant. But the relentless attacks on NAMA were undermining its credibility at home. A week later Lenihan, Bacon and the interim director of the new agency, Brendan McDonagh, put in a four-hour stint in front of another Oireachtas committee. All three of them took questions on NAMA in an attempt to persuade TDs that the government was not for turning. McDonagh put up a fine performance, releasing more details and spelling out how the agency might operate. Legislation would be ready in July. If necessary the Dáil would be recalled. Lenihan insisted that there would be no easy options for developers and that some bankruptcies would be necessary under NAMA.

For the banks the advent of NAMA could not come a day too early. On Friday 29 May Anglo Irish Bank released its interim results. They were shattering. The rogue bank revealed a pre-tax loss of €4.1 billion in the six-month period. The government promised to beef it up with €4 billion in capital. Anglo had written off €308 million for the famous Golden Circle, described in the interim report as 'ten longstanding clients', who had bought Anglo shares – now worthless – with money lent to them by Anglo after Sean Quinn unwound his CFD position in the bank. The taxpayer would pay for most of the Golden Circle's losses. (At the press briefing at which the interim results were announced, I asked O'Connor what he had known about the placing of Quinn's huge stake in the hands of these 'longstanding clients'. He said he had been quietly told about it by Sean FitzPatrick but could not remember the placing coming up at a board meeting: evidently he did not feel it was a matter worth pursuing.) The bank's losses could soar to €7.5 billion. Deposits had continued to flow out, despite the guarantee.

Some people were still doing well out of Anglo. Miraculously the auditors Ernst & Young were still in favour with the bank. They had received €2.2 million from Anglo in the previous year, even though they had failed to spot FitzPatrick's loan wheeze.

Chairman (and temporary chief executive) Donal O'Connor was drawing a healthy salary of €500,000 a year from the faltering state-owned bank. His defence of Anglo at the press conference was feeble. Far from opening up an era of transparency, the briefing was held with cameras forbidden. O'Connor's economy with information was consistent with his EGM performance. He refused to give the names of the former directors whose €31 million in personal loans had been written off by the bank. Nor could he reveal how much was known about the Golden Circle at board level. Little had changed.

Anglo was a total basket case. Capital requirements had to be waived to allow it to continue as a going concern pending EU approval for a further state injection. On that black Friday NAMA may not have been a panacea, but it was the only game in town.

11. The Abyss

Joe Higgins stood triumphant in the Royal Dublin Society at 5 a.m. on the morning of 8 June. Beside him stood his 91-year-old mother Ellen, beaming from ear to ear.

Higgins had just captured the third and final Dublin seat in the European parliamentary elections. Fianna Fáil had lost its standard-bearer in the constituency, Eoin Ryan. Ryan's father, also Eoin, had been one of the longest-serving senators in the state's history. His grandfather Dr Jim Ryan had been a minister under Éamon de Valera and Sean Lemass. His daughter Sarah had been defeated a day earlier for a Dublin City Council seat. Higgins – a hard-line socialist with virtually no resources – had toppled a dynasty spanning four generations. His posters had been printed in dull black and white, pitted against the other parties' rich technicolour. He had a small team of supporters. In the final days of the campaign the full force of the Fianna Fáil guns had been trained on him. Brian Cowen, rattled by poll figures suggesting a surge for Higgins, attacked him, suggesting that not a single job would be created by voting for a veteran of the left.

For years Higgins had called for nationalization of the banks. By June 2009 he had enlisted plenty of mainstream converts to his convictions. His views on the banks, once considered extreme, were no longer taboo.

George Lee – who had resigned as RTÉ's economics editor only weeks earlier to enter politics – had meanwhile attracted an astonishing vote in the by-election in Dublin South, one of the most middle-class constituencies in Ireland. Lee, standing for Fine Gael, received more than 50 per cent of the vote and was returned on the first count, something not achieved in a by-election for over 30 years.

Lee would probably have been elected as an independent. He was a fresh, non-political face and he was an expert in the right subject at the right time. He had been a fierce critic of the government's handling of the economy for many years, and he had been a thorn in the side of the banks. In 1998 he and his RTÉ colleague Charlie Bird had exposed an over-charging scandal at National Irish Bank.

Back in third place came Shay Brennan, son of the late government minister Seamus Brennan, the last Fianna Fáil TD for the area, whose death had caused the by-election. Shay Brennan was an unfortunate choice as Fianna Fáil candidate. Chosen by the party in the belief that a sympathy vote for a member of the deceased's family would cushion the inevitable defeat, he disappointed from day one. Shay was a banker. Not only was he a banker, he worked for the most notorious bank in town – Anglo Irish.

A well-known broadcaster who had exposed a bank scandal was going head-to-head with a banker who worked in the most infamous banking joint in town. Banking abuses were not an overt election issue, but they lurked beneath the surface.

Shay Brennan rightly protested that he should not be blamed for the sins of Anglo, but the link made for uncomfortable explaining. During the by-election campaign it was pointed out that, as Minister for Transport, his father had appointed Anglo's Sean FitzPatrick to the board of Aer Lingus. Seamus the elder had also appointed Tiarnan O'Mahoney, Anglo's head of Treasury, to be chairman of the Pensions Board after he left the bank. Young Shay had worked in O'Mahoney's Treasury Department.

George Lee had demolished another Fianna Fáil dynasty.

Many of those who backed socialist Higgins in the European elections voted for Lee, the free marketeer, in the by-election on the same day. Middle Ireland was in rebellion.

In a separate by-election, in Dublin Central, a third Fianna Fáil family brand took a blow. Maurice Ahern, the 72-year-old brother of former Taoiseach Bertie, was crushed into fifth place behind a left-wing independent winner, Maureen O'Sullivan. Fine Gael's Paschal O'Donohoe, Labour's Ivana Bacik and Sinn Féin's Christy Burke all garnered more votes than Bertie's big brother.

Maureen O'Sullivan carried the noble legacy of Tony Gregory, the independent TD for Dublin's inner city who had died in December. O'Sullivan's politics had yet to be given proper media coverage but her mentor, Gregory, had been a consistent critic of Ireland's corporate swindles.

Two independents and a novice politician running under the Fine Gael flag had routed the government. (Fianna Fáil's partners in government, the Green Party, were savaged too. They won no seats in Europe, failed to feature in the by-elections and lost 15 of their 18 seats in the local councils.) Ireland's voters were sending a solemn message: their rulers had failed them on the economy. By extension they were returning a vote of no confidence in the banks, the builders, the social partners and the other powerful forces ruling Ireland.

Labour had a good election, winning a European seat in the East constituency through Nessa Childers, the daughter of a former President of Ireland. They won another in the South constituency with a thrusting young candidate, senator Alan Kelly. They gained 31 council seats – up to 132 from 101 in 2004. Higgins's Socialist Party took six seats at local level, while the People Before Profit Alliance, another left-wing party, made a breakthrough with five seats. Elsewhere, left-leaning independents captured some of the spoils.

Ireland's centre-right government had been hammered. This could not be ascribed to global economic conditions: elsewhere in Europe the opposite happened. Incumbent centre-right parties swept the board in Germany, France, Poland and Italy – and, in contrast to Ireland, Green parties had a good election in most European countries.

Despite the recession, voters in much of mainland Europe rallied to their governments. Not Irish voters. They punished their leaders.

Ireland's electorate was slowly becoming aware that the Irish problem was different. Ireland was far worse off than the rest of Europe, for special reasons. At the time of the 2007 general election the electorate had swallowed the eternal-prosperity fantasy peddled by Fianna Fáil. They had voted the peddlers back into office. By 2009 they realized that the 2004–8 period was when the madness should have been halted, the time to tame the banks and the builders, the time to cool the economy.

Now the people knew the truth about what had been happening. The elections of June 2009 provided an opportunity to deliver a retrospective verdict on Bertie Ahern and Brian Cowen. They gave them the thumbs down.

In the European elections of 2004 Joe Higgins had trailed in with just 5.5 per cent of the vote. In 2009 his vote more than doubled to 12.4 per cent. Higgins attracted thousands of middle-class voters. The prosperous suburbs of Dun Laoghaire, even the residents of mansions in Ballsbridge, recorded number-ones for the man who had little sympathy for private property. Rich and poor alike were angry with Ireland's oligarchs.

Foremost among the hate figures were Ireland's bankers

and developers. At the centre of the banking and building oligarchy was Anglo Irish Bank. Anglo was both a symbol of the darkest days and a tangible cause of the economic disaster. Voters had made the direct link. Taxes had been raised to save Anglo, and would be raised further. Expenditure had been cut to save Anglo, and would be cut further. Borrowing had been increased to save Anglo, and would be increased further.

A week before the election Anglo's 2008 figures had been released. They showed that €308 million lent to the Golden Circle – the ten Anglo customers who had used the non-recourse loans to purchase 10 per cent of the bank's shares and prop up the share price – had been written off by the bank, in recognition of the tanking of the share price.

Who paid the €308 million?

The taxpayer.

Another €31 million was written off for former directors of Anglo who could not repay loans.

Who paid the €31 million?

The taxpayer.

As thunderstorms broke all around him, Brian Lenihan launched a fightback. His earlier commitment in the April Budget to NAMA had helped to convince investors that the minister was now dead set against nationalizing AIB and Bank of Ireland. The government's pillaging of Michael Somers's national pension fund may not have been popular with pensioners at home, but it reassured global investors that Ireland was at least confronting the depth of the problems at the banks. Gradually the stock market regained a little composure. Overseas confidence in Brian Lenihan's stewardship rose as he made more presentations to investor groups. In May and early June a tentative rally in Bank of Ireland and AIB shares lifted them both above the €2 mark.

Investors may have been picking up cheap bank shares in the hope that the banks would survive in one form or another; but the state of the real economy reflected the penal cost of the decision to bail them out with taxpayers' money.

In early June Ireland's credit rating was marked down for the second time in three months. Standard & Poor's took a dim view of our prospects. A day after the European elections S&P lobbed in a grenade: it was cutting Ireland's debt rating to a fourteen-year low. We were back to pre-Celtic Tiger levels. Worse still, S&P indicated that Ireland was on 'negative outlook', meaning that we were in danger of further falls.

Credit rating agencies have received justifiable stick in recent years because of their failure to spot the risk in the mortgage-based securities whose implosion sparked the credit crunch, and also their apparent reluctance to downgrade their big banking clients, but their influence on global markets remains strong, especially when they are rating nations rather than banks. On the international money markets Ireland's cost of borrowing increased in response to S&P's verdict. The adverse reaction on the bond markets to Ireland's lower credit rating meant that future generations would be saddled with mountains of debt. S&P blamed the Irish banks:

We have lowered the long-term rating on Ireland because we believe that the fiscal costs to the government of supporting the Irish banking system will be significantly higher than what we had expected when we last lowered the rating in March 2009, and, consequently, that the net general government debt burden will also be significantly higher over the medium term.

Our nearest neighbour, the UK, still enjoyed an S&P rating of AAA – comfortably above our own – as did France, Germany, Sweden, Norway, Finland, Denmark, the

Netherlands and Austria. Belgium, despite all its economic ills, was up there with a score of AA+. Ireland, with its AA rating, was marginally above Portugal and Italy; but they were awarded a 'stable' outlook while we were on 'negative' watch.

The situation at Anglo had deteriorated markedly since the last downgrade, just three months earlier. Ten days before the S&P statement it had emerged that the Irish government needed to find a fresh €4 billion for Anglo, on top of the other rescue packages for AIB and Bank of Ireland. Threats of huge liabilities in the event of a wind-up of Anglo were in the air; Brian Cowen stunned the Dáil with a figure of €60 billion. Anglo itself warned that it might need another €3.5 billion if property prices fell further.

Tiny as Ireland is in the context of the eurozone, the day after the country's downgrading by S&P the euro took a bath. Several global foreign-exchange dealers claimed that the scale of the banking meltdown in Ireland was being felt on the big-ticket currency markets. On 11 June Brian Kim, a foreign-exchange strategist with UBS Bank, told me, 'S&P's downgrade of Ireland was a point of pressure on the euro in the following days. The downgrade caused a pull-back in the euro.' And, even more ominously, 'If the peripheral states have issues it will only underscore the divide between the larger and smaller ones.' We were becoming a drag on the euro. Our European colleagues might not mind us being reckless at home, wrecking our own economy and impoverishing our people; but if little Ireland was pulling down Europe's treasured currency the Merkels, Sarkozys and Berlusconis would not be amused.

Our status as good Europeans had already been greatly weakened: we had rejected the Lisbon Treaty; we had caused offence to our partners by going it alone on the bank guarantee; we had breached Europe's rules on budget deficit limits by a country mile. The EU had been tolerant, giving us a derogation until 2013. At the same time we were drawing heavily on the European Central Bank to help our banks' short-term requirements. Now our bankers' wrongs were damaging the currency itself.

Europe has ways and means of dealing with errant nations. European leaders do not want any of the eurozone member nations to default on their debts. At the same time, if we continued to twist their tails in defiance of their rules we might find their support beginning to wobble.

The relative success of the rest of Europe in riding out the recession made a mockery of much of the rhetoric of Ireland's apologists for the state of the nation. The 'global' recession excuse was for gullible home consumption, but was unsustainable. The glib line that the collapse of Lehman Brothers was a source of Ireland's woes no longer fooled even the simplest soul. Our cover had been blown.

While Standard & Poor's was downgrading the nation's credit ratings, it was simultaneously reducing the ratings of our banks. The two were directly related.

The S&P report stated:

Our revised opinion follows the recent announcement by Anglo Irish Bank of losses at the upper end of S&P's expectations as well as the government's announced intentions regarding the scope of the operations of the new National Asset Management Agency (NAMA) . . . We believe the recently announced losses at nationalized Anglo Irish Bank Corp. highlight both the continued fragility of the Irish banking sector and its reliance on the government for ongoing financial support.

And the final sting:

We now believe that Ireland's net general government debt could exceed 100 per cent of GDP over the medium term – a level that is higher than for Ireland's 'AA' rated Euro-zone sovereign peers.

We were on the way to a further downgrade.

S&P was at odds with more cheerful sentiment in the stock markets. At the beginning of June, while Bank of Ireland and AIB shares were enjoying a happy rally, brokers in Dublin were reverting to type, drumming up business, suggesting that S&P were 'behind the curve', that a significant rally was in full swing. The usual form.

The bounce in bank shares was explained by the diminishing likelihood of the nationalization of AIB or Bank of Ireland, real-live possibilities when they hit rock bottom in early March. The rally was no more than a blip. Even in mid-July the prices, while way off the floor, were still as much as 90 per cent lower than their February 2007 peaks.

Just as Ireland was deemed a riskier credit bet than almost every other country in Europe, Ireland's banks trailed even the troubled UK banks in the credit ratings. Comparisons with Spain were even more depressing. Spain, often compared with Ireland as a bubble economy with a similar property boom-to-bust story, had no such banking problems. S&P rated Spain's two biggest banks – Santander and BBVA – with 'AA' rankings, better than the top UK and French banks.

The Spanish escape did not provide any cause for hope in Ireland. Spain had always been ready for the rainy day. During the years of its property bubble the Spanish financial regulator had forced the banks to put money aside for the bad times. As a result the property bust failed to plunge Spanish banks into the same life-or-death battle against bankruptcy as Ireland's. Spain had behaved responsibly, and now its banks were expanding into foreign countries, buying up troubled institutions at rock-bottom prices. The lesson was chilling.

Despite the blanket government guarantees, despite the recapitalization programme, despite the nationalization of Anglo, despite the fanfare around NAMA, Ireland's banks were still low down the European pecking order. At the beginning of June Anglo, AIB and Bank of Ireland were still regarded as the riskiest trio in the eurozone.

The possibility that Ireland might default on its sovereign debt was the elephant in the room at the Central Bank, the Department of Finance and the cabinet table. It was whispered in the corridors of Leinster House, but even the parliamentary Opposition was reluctant to spell it out in the Dáil. Such talk was considered damaging to the nation. Diehard opponents of the government baulked at denouncing the party in power for having spent the state into near-bankruptcy.

That did not stop an immediate opposition motion of no confidence in the Dáil following the series of government defeats at the polls. The government was reeling after its landslide losses. The Greens were under pressure, losing popularity because of their alliance with Fianna Fáil and facing the likely loss of all six of their Dáil seats if the government fell and an election was called. The smaller party in government held firm, along with a cabal of unhappy Fianna Fáil backbenchers and a handful of pro-government independents. The two governing parties agreed to consider a review of their joint programme.

The vote of no confidence was defeated by six votes. There were no defections from either government party. The political ship was steadied as the Cabinet set its sights on the political sanctuary of the summer recess.

Lenihan was meanwhile filling some of the vacancies in

the banks. In the early days of June it was announced that Richard Burrows was to be replaced as governor of the Bank of Ireland by Pat Molloy. Another oligarch was back.

Lenihan had been influential both in bringing an end to Burrows's reign and in the appointment – or the restoration – of Molloy. Molloy was a former Bank of Ireland lifer. He was now seventy-one, returning to old pastures, paraded by his cheerleaders as the safest pair of hands in the business.

Molloy's competence was not in question. Untouched by scandal, his tenure as a Bank of Ireland director had ended just before the property madness took off. But the appointment hardly bolstered the drive for a new image for the wounded bank. The combination of Molloy as chairman and Boucher as chief executive sent out the wrong message: that nothing had changed at the Bank of Ireland.

The almost universal approval from official Ireland for Molloy's appointment should have acted as a warning sign. Mainstream media fawned at the return of the old banker. They never stopped to ask if the appointment of a career banker as governor was appropriate. Banking at the Bank of Ireland was Richie Boucher's business. The Bank of Ireland had set its face against putting bankers in the chair: Burrows was a drinks magnate, his predecessor Lawrence Crowley was an accountant, Howard Kilroy was a paper trader and Louden Ryan an academic. For sound corporate governance reasons top bankers do not take the chair at top banks. Anglo's Sean FitzPatrick was the only other recent example of this route to the chair. Although the eleven-year gap since his departure as chief executive make Molloy's case very different from FitzPatrick's, Molloy was very much a Bank of Ireland insider. He had even taken the well-trodden directors' route between the boards of Bank of Ireland and CRH, joining Tony Barry, David Kennedy and Howard Kilroy among those who had done that double.

If Lenihan wanted Molloy's wisdom, it is puzzling why he was not installed at AIB, where he owed no past loyalties.

After news of Molloy's appointment had leaked, the Bank of Ireland made it known that its own nomination committee had been thinking along exactly the same lines: Molloy had been top of its list of candidates to succeed Burrows as governor. Under the recapitalization deal Lenihan was now entitled to appoint 25 per cent of the board. Molloy headed his list of nominees. The minister, the Department of Finance and the board of the Bank of Ireland were – not for the first time – all in agreement. Face was saved. At the AGM on 3 July Burrows handed over the governorship to Molloy.

Oligarchs old and new, but mostly old, were re-establishing themselves in the supposed new order at the banks. Boucher and Molloy were Bank of Ireland archetypes, not innovators. Donal O'Connor and Maurice Keane at Anglo were old oligarchs, now resurrected from the dead. And the quiet succession of the faceless Dan O'Connor and David Pritchard at AIB was merely a case of slotting existing board members into the positions of departing oligarchs. Many of Lenihan's appointments to the banks' boards – including Tom Considine at Bank of Ireland, Adrian Kearns at Irish Nationwide, Declan Collier at AIB, Margaret Hayes at Irish Life & Permanent and Frank Daly at Anglo – were veterans of the civil service or the semi-state sector; others – Ray MacSharry at Irish Life, Alan Dukes at Anglo, Joe Walsh at Bank of Ireland, Dick Spring at AIB – were ex-politicians. The minister, no doubt firmly guided by the permanent government, had gone for guys who could play ball with Sir Humphrey and fit in with the traditional mould.

Safe choices were precisely what the banks did not need. Irish banking was crying out for awkward bankers. It needed people who would not conform to the agenda of the

Department of Finance. It needed directors who would challenge the mandarins' role, not accept it. Irish banking and
the Irish nation itself needed people who would bring tension,
not solidarity, to the relationship between bankers and the
regulators, the department, the minister, the Central Bank
and the builders. Molloy, the competent old conformist, did
not fit the bill. Nor did most of the ageing civil servants who
suddenly found themselves on the boards of tottering banks.
The new directors oozed the aroma of official Ireland.

Lenihan and the Oireachtas committees should have been
looking far more critically at the top advisers in his department. Secretary general David Doyle, his deputy Kevin
Cardiff and dozens of higher-grade mandarins in Finance
rarely came under the public microscope. Few even realized
that the Finance Department's top mandarins were better
paid than other civil servants.

Criticism in early January 2009 from Garret FitzGerald
about the shortage of economists in the Department of
Finance seems to have prompted Lenihan to recruit the
talented Alan Ahearne from University College Galway in
early March. Ahearne had been one of the first economists
to warn of a property crash. Two weeks before his appointment to Lenihan's kitchen cabinet he had been advocating
temporary nationalization of the banks, a position strongly
opposed by the minister and his department.

When he accepted the job with Lenihan, he immediately
sacrificed his independence and took a different tack, oppos-
ing nationalization, but his reputation beefed up the Lenihan
team's credibility. Still, there was no changing of the guard
in Finance; John Hurley, governor of the Central Bank, and
Jim Farrell, chairman of the Financial Regulator, were still
in situ; departing bankers had departed rich men; their
replacements were nearly all insiders. The boom had turned

to bust but the main culprits – the top bankers – had hardly suffered.

International ratings agencies were not the sole critics of the prospects for the Irish economy. Anglo, in particular, was also being treated as a cripple by the money market dealers. During the May/June period Anglo was consistently forced to offer higher deposit rates than either AIB or Bank of Ireland, because the possibility of default or liquidation was considered higher. Liquidation of Anglo was a constant fear, leaving the government, as owner, vulnerable to a massive run on deposits. The bank consistently denied that an orderly wind-down was on the way, but the market was sceptical.

An Anglo default would mean a state default. The market feared that the Irish government might be unable to extract itself from the economic quicksands. Anyone who put money on deposit with Anglo was covered by the government guarantee, but the solvency of the guarantor was again being challenged. Not far below the surface lay the rarely spoken truth that the government bank guarantee to all the covered banks carried the most lethal threat of all: if the guarantee was called in, the government could not meet its obligations.

The alternative to establishing a vehicle like NAMA was full nationalization of all the banks. This possibility was fiercely resisted by all the oligarchs, but it attracted support from many commentators far from the Joe Higgins sphere of influence. Leading academic economists, like Professors Brian Lucey of Trinity College and Karl Whelan of UCD, favoured the nationalization road. Many wanted to see the banks taken into public ownership with a view to refloating as soon as they were cleaned up by the state.

NAMA was primarily a delaying device. Once the government, somehow, managed to issue bonds to the banks in exchange for the troubled assets, they could undoubtedly buy time. Once the time was bought, their hope was for a rise in property prices over a period.

A recovery in property prices is by no means certain. If property prices continue to fall over the next decade, or even hold steady, the government will have bought a pig in a poke.

Other uncertainties haunt the NAMA project. The government's intention to pay the banks for their loans in bonds – effectively IOUs – is full of dangers. Hopefully the European Central Bank will look favourably upon the bonds as security and lend money to the Irish banks on the back of them. Hopefully. There is no guarantee that the ECB will forever take such a charitable view of the issuing of something like €60 billion in new Irish government paper.

While the mandarins in the Department of Finance were hurriedly preparing legislation for the establishment of NAMA – the biggest property management company in the world – the real action began to move from Merrion Street to the Four Courts.

The staggering leniency of the bankers towards deeply indebted developers was possibly the most curious feature of the entire Irish banking calamity. Some big builders had gone from billionaires to bust in a matter of months. Yet they were all still living in their big houses, untouched by their creditors.

Paddy Kelly had started the ball rolling down the slippery slope when he told Eamon Dunphy in an RTÉ interview on 29 November 2008 that he owed Anglo 'hundreds of millions'. He was the first big developer to admit publicly what the nation already knew: builders were being carried by the banks; interest payments were not being made; bankers were hoping that something would turn up.

Kelly was asking for trouble. He put himself in the front

line by his public confession. So it was no surprise that a few banks – including AIB, Investec and ACCBank – soon came out of the woodwork seeking repayments from Kelly. In early March 2009 he told the Commercial Court that he was exploring bankruptcy.

Kelly's court appearances were put down to the mutterings of a maverick, not a U-turn in bankers' benign policy towards builders; no one saw his troubles as the start of a sudden developer-hunt by bankers, not least because a pursuit of the bankrupt builders might vaporize the banks' balance sheets. If builders were forced to sell their properties at knockdown prices, the whole market could collapse. The banks themselves would then crash.

The stand-off had worked wonderfully. Irish banks held tight, in solidarity behind the same sham valuations. As long as no one forced any of the big bankrupt builders to the wall, their loans from the banks could not be exposed by the open market as overvalued in the banks' balance sheets. None of the native banks broke ranks.

Sadly for Ireland's entrenched oligarchs, foreign banks could not be relied upon to share in this little conspiracy. Suddenly, in early July, ACCBank – the former Irish agriculture bank now owned by Holland's Rabobank – blew this cosy arrangement apart. The Dutch bank decided to go for the jugular. Liam Carroll, arguably the biggest of Irish developers, was in the frame. Rabobank had lost patience with Carroll, with property in Ireland and, indeed, with the entire Irish economic shambles.

Rabobank had a priceless AAA credit rating, which it did not want to lose through its exposure to the Irish property debacle. ACC, which was owed €136 million by Carroll, went on a solo run, threatening the reclusive builder with insolvency before the end of July. The Dutch meant it.

A few days earlier Carroll had been in a lesser spot of bother with Irish Nationwide, which had won a €78 million judgment against him for unpaid loans, but the skirmish with Nationwide was more a personal spat and did not threaten Carroll's entire empire. Rabo's move, by contrast, caused consternation in government circles and put the frighteners on other bankers. If successful, its court action might put Carroll's entire group of companies into receivership or liquidation. A receiver or a liquidator could flood the market with unwanted properties. The delicate balancing act, so precariously maintained between the builders and the bankers, was in peril.

As a foreign-owned bank, ACCBank was not covered by NAMA. The Dutch owners wanted their money back before NAMA started buying up loans in the autumn.

Carroll's response was predictable. On Friday 17 July he pre-empted ACCBank's action when he sought the protection of the High Court. Carroll was initially granted temporary protection for a few days to enable his Zoe companies to come up with a survival plan to satisfy his creditors. All the Irish banks were supportive of Carroll's initial protection plan. It involved the freezing of interest and a gradual sale of his properties. Judge Peter Kelly believed it was pie in the sky.

Carroll may have momentarily cheated the liquidator's weapons of annihilation, but the genie had escaped from the bankers' bottle. Carroll was forced to reveal the depth of his trouble. It made for grim reading.

The six Carroll companies that were at issue in the ACC action — a fraction of the overall Carroll empire — had borrowings from eight banks. ACCBank's €136 million was far from his worst headache. The six companies owed the banks a total of €1.2 billion. AIB was on the list for €489 million and Bank of Scotland (Ireland) for €321 million, Bank of Ireland for €113 million, Ulster Bank for €82 million, Anglo for €38 million, KBC Bank for €23 million and EBS for €8.5 million. Irish Nationwide had been lending to other Carroll companies elsewhere – as, undoubtedly, had the other banks.

It was revealing that none of the other banks supported ACCBank in its action. They nurtured a hope that something – like NAMA – would turn up. It took an outsider, a Dutch bank, to explode the Irish charade. The Irish banks had been indulging Carroll for months, if not years.

The loans were bad enough, but Carroll's summary of his six companies' net position was even worse. His lawyers told the court that his companies would be €900 million under-water if they were forced into liquidation.

According to John McManus, writing with characteristic perception in the *Irish Times*, Carroll's summary meant that he was taking a 75 per cent write-down on all his properties. If that 75 per cent write-down were accepted across the board, Ireland's banks would all be worthless.

Down at the Department of Finance the mandarins must have been paralysed. The NAMA project could be torpedoed if the Zoe chief was not granted the benefit of an examiner. NAMA's valuations, with projected write-downs of maybe 25 per cent on the properties, would have looked ridiculous. The forbidden word 'nationalization' was being whispered again in Merrion Street.

The mandarins were cheering for Carroll on his day in court. But Justice Peter Kelly rubbished his rescue plan – not once, but twice. He refused to give the developer's business plan court protection, describing Carroll's proposal as 'lacking in reality'. He dismissed the application, deriding the developer as seeking further borrowings into a 'grossly over-subscribed' commercial market and into a residential sector that is 'hardly moving at all'. According to the judge the optimistic prediction of a highly dramatic three-year turn-around in Carroll's fortunes 'borders, if not actually trespasses, on the fanciful'.

Carroll was not the only developer in the wars with the Dutch. ACCBank had already taken an action against a lesser-known Cork developer, John Fleming, to recover €21.5 million. Once again the figure owed to ACCBank was peanuts in terms of Fleming's overall indebtedness, but even such a small amount threatened a domino effect on a whole series of Fleming companies. What stunned observers was the over-all figure of Fleming's debts. Here was a company of whom few had hitherto heard, which owed over a billion euros.

On 21 July Justice Peter Kelly had replaced a receiver to the Fleming group with an examiner, giving John Fleming 100 days' protection from his creditors and a chance to find a way out of difficulty. Carroll was not so lucky.

On 28 July, even as Justice Kelly was delivering his initial thoughts on Carroll's failed bid to go down the Fleming route, the Cabinet was putting the finishing touches to the draft NAMA legislation. The Dáil was set for recall in mid-September to ensure that the bill was passed into law with respectable speed. It was important to the Cabinet that NAMA was up and running before foreign banks made further moves against developers. Forced sales of developers' assets could set a very low benchmark for valuations of all the properties held as security for the developers' loans. The appalling vista of a two-tier market in property beckoned.

On 30 July the NAMA legislation was published.

The thorny topic of how much NAMA would pay, on behalf of the taxpayer, for the banks' development loans was ducked. The minister maintained that as there was no liquidity in the market it was impossible to pay 'market value'. The

Department of Finance would work with the European
Commission on a formula combining market value and 'long-
term value'. He would give full details of the price mechanism
in the Dáil in September. 'Long-term value', the invention
of the mandarins, assumed a rise in property prices.

The banks were gleeful. On the morning of Friday 31 July,
when the stock markets opened, bank shares spiked; Bank of
Ireland finished the day up 9.2 per cent at €2 while AIB (now
known to have far more dangerous exposure to developers
– including Liam Carroll – than Bank of Ireland) rallied less
spectacularly for a gain of 2 per cent. The market's initial
judgment was emphatic. In the battle between the bankers
and the taxpayer, the bankers had triumphed.

Politicians are fond of whispering in the safety of the bar in
Leinster House – or in the corridors – that Europe will not
allow Ireland to default on its sovereign debt. Perhaps they
are right, but if Ireland has to be rescued by the European
Union, we will pay a European price. Probably the first
demand would be for an end to our 12.5 per cent corporate
tax rate, latterly so irritating to the UK and a permanent
source of anger to Franco-German leaders. We would be in
no position to resist their diktats. They would insist that we
take nasty and more immediate measures to keep within the
Stability and Growth Pact. In addition, if Europe insisted
on tax harmonization, we might not only have to retreat on
corporate tax but might also be forced to introduce a property tax at European levels, as well as more uniform income
tax rates. We might finally be compelled, in our hour of
weakness, to sacrifice the last vestiges of our economic
independence, jealously guarded for so long, with our right
to a veto on tax matters.

Alternatively we could throw ourselves at the mercy of

the International Monetary Fund. In return for the cash to keep us afloat we would take painful medicine: punitive measures such as massive cuts in public service pay, social welfare reductions across the board, further income tax hikes, the sale of state assets, a bonfire of the quangos and other penal levies. The consequences could be far-reaching. The measures might create social discontent.

Luckily for Ireland, we already have our own home-grown IMF-equivalent, known as An Bord Snip Nua.

Back in November 2008 Brian Lenihan appointed Dr Colm McCarthy, an economist with University College Dublin, to recommend spending cuts in the public sector. McCarthy, who undertook a similar exercise for Charlie Haughey and Ray MacSharry in 1987, attacked the task with relish. His small group, of six mostly anonymous experts, reported to the government on 17 July. It suggested €5.3 billion of cuts covering every department of state, including staffing reductions of 17,358 people.

The biggest targets were the three biggest-spending departments: Social Welfare, Health and Education.

A down-to-earth Dubliner, McCarthy did dozens of media interviews explaining how everyone, including social welfare recipients, teachers, doctors and members of the Oireachtas, would have to share the pain. The nation shuddered.

McCarthy's team had not been asked to tackle the political minefield of public sector pay, but they could not resist taking a swipe at the state's payroll and making it crystal clear that cuts in this area were imperative.

A political debate began immediately. Farmers and trade union leaders were first out of the traps to launch an onslaught against McCarthy and his team. Opposition politicians carefully selected which cuts to oppose while studiously refusing to produce their own programme.

The debate was useful insofar as it established that every citizen's standard of living was set to plunge.

No sooner was McCarthy's report off the presses than the knockers emerged. Some ministers sent smoke signals to pressure groups that McCarthy's recommendations were not gospel. Tánaiste Mary Coughlan asked Forfás – a government agency in her own department – to examine McCarthy's report. Forfás was unlikely to approve it as McCarthy had recommended a cut in Forfás's own budget. Additionally he had proposed chunky savings in other sections of Coughlan's department including FAS, Science Technology and Innovation, Enterprise Ireland and even the IDA. The chief executives of Enterprise Ireland and the IDA, as well as the director of Science Foundation Ireland – all targets of McCarthy – are on the board of Forfás, and the Tánaiste would have been aware of it. Cabinet members were first out of the traps to play the 'not in my back yard' card.

Everyone hoped that their own pet project, their job, their hospital or their local school would escape the minister's knife.

McCarthy's report was more a conditioning process, intended to soften the nation up for the draconian December Budget which posed the next political hurdle for Lenihan. The minister had to herd his left-leaning coalition partners, his own backbenchers, the farmers and the trade unions, and above all he needed to stiffen the resolve of his own wobbly cabinet colleagues.

The report of the Commission on Taxation, which was published on 7 September, had a similar purpose: to alert the nation that tougher taxes were on the agenda. There was no doubt that Lenihan had the stomach for the battle ahead; his main problem was his colleagues, none of whom had held office in difficult times. All had been accustomed to donating annual handouts to a grateful electorate. Among their number was the Taoiseach Brian Cowen, a long-time devotee of social partnership – a concept with which Lenihan was impatient in his crusade to remedy the nation's finances.

During those 2009 summer months many government ministers were invisible; others, like Cowen himself, often appeared paralysed. All were publicly committed to NAMA, but they left it to Lenihan to make the running. NAMA was unpopular. NAMA was complicated. Lenihan appeared to be the only minister on top of the brief.

The Finance Minister stuck doggedly to his guns, unshakeable in his belief in NAMA. He constantly insisted that it was not a bailout for the builders. He was right. It was a bailout for the bankers.

Fine Gael's woolly counter-proposals gained little backing. Indeed, two of their most distinguished former leaders, Garret FitzGerald and Alan Dukes, backed the Fianna Fáil approach. Support from such unlikely quarters gave Fianna Fáil heart, but in early autumn – just as the government launched a massive public relations campaign to convince doubters that NAMA was imperative – their coalition partners suddenly threw a few shapes. The Greens demanded legislative concessions that would cause the banks to bear more of the risk associated with NAMA. Lenihan granted his coalition colleagues this and other modest changes, including the removal over a two-year period of the bank directors appointed before 2008, a windfall tax on property developers, a pledge to make lobbying the state property agency a criminal offence, and a reduction in NAMA's borrowing limits from €10 billion to €5 billion. The Greens in turn made hay, grandstanding on the Leinster House plinth, gloating in front of the cameras about their dilution of the Bill.

A week earlier, on 3 September, the minister had signalled

his flexibility on the NAMA proposals when, needing to replace John Hurley as governor of the Central Bank, he broke with long tradition and failed to appoint the secretary of the Department of Finance to the post. Instead, he thrust greatness on an academic, Professor Patrick Honohan of Trinity College Dublin, who had been harshly critical of the performance of banking regulators in Ireland during the bubble period. More recently Honohan had played a key role in the NAMA debate, proposing a risk-sharing mechanism for NAMA that seems to have influenced the measure adopted in the final NAMA Bill.

Many of the concessions claimed by the Greens were cosmetic. The basic shape of the package remained the same. The banks were safe. So were the bankers.

But the builders were far from safe.

On the very day that Lenihan was publishing his amended NAMA legislation, Liam Carroll's fortunes were again hitting the buffers down in the Four Courts.

Judge Frank Clarke dismissed yet another of Carroll's attempts to duck the liquidator. Echoing the words of his High Court colleague Peter Kelly, Clarke described the business plan put forward by Carroll's counsel as existing 'at the further end of optimism'.

All the oligarchs had been rooting for Carroll, whose forecasts for the recovery of his companies were spiritually akin to the controversial idea that NAMA should pay more for bad loans than they were currently worth; but by the time Clarke gave him the thumbs down the NAMA train had left the station. The legislative timetable suggested that the new state asset agency would be in operation by Christmas. Bankers, mandarins, builders, stockbrokers, accountants and auctioneers were onside.

The public, however, was not onside – opinion polls showed

that NAMA was unpopular and that Fianna Fáil's public support was at an all-time low. Why had Fianna Fáil, the party with an unerring instinct for the Irish people's sentiments – a grassroots movement to its fingertips – lined up alongside the pillars of official Ireland against the popular will?

One reason was the determination of the Minister for Finance himself, who seems genuinely to have concluded that it was his duty to save the banks and that the NAMA solution was the only possible path. He was not as concerned about the political consequences for himself or for his party as were some of his colleagues. A realist, he probably saw that Fianna Fáil was destined for a long period in the political wilderness regardless of how it handled the banking crisis.

But what about his colleagues in Cabinet? How had consensus leaders like Cowen, Foreign Affairs Minister Micheál Martin and Justice Minister Dermot Ahern swallowed the oligarchs' line? Was this not, just eighteen months earlier, the party of Bertie Ahern, the softly-softly genius of keeping the peace, embracing all comers under one umbrella and pacifying warring factions? It was; but Bertie had never faced a crisis of anything like this magnitude.

The deeper truth exposed by the present crisis is that Ireland harbours more powerful forces than Fianna Fáil. The NAMA project is the brainchild of the Department of Finance and the banks. It is the oligarchs' solution, a monument to their triumph over the will of the people.

Fianna Fáil could have eyeballed the banks and the mandarins. It didn't. It was fearful that the bankers could press the Armageddon button and take the country down with them. Cowen, Lenihan and the rest recognized the realpolitik: the permanent government, conspiring with the bankers, was more powerful than the elected government. It had always been thus.

Fianna Fáil was overawed by the oligarchs. Throughout the banking crisis of 2008–9 the government was more like a passenger than a driver. They were driven by the powerful, unelected forces that held the nation in their grip. As the economy imploded, they took their cues from those who held the permanent levers of power in their hands.

The launch of the NAMA project was perhaps the bankers' greatest triumph. It had sent out a potent message: that Ireland's banks were too big to be allowed to fail; Ireland's bankers were too powerful to punish.

Epilogue

Two voice messages from David Drumm to Shane Ross

26 June 2009, 11:03 p.m.

David Drumm here, ex-Anglo, very late admittedly returning your call and I apologize for that. I moved out to the US this week so a little bit all over the place. I was very keen to return your call. I've been told many times you're a very honourable person and good old PR people have held me back at times, and I have to say I've learned a lot in the last number of months about who to listen to and who to trust but anyway, I would dearly love, you have no idea how much I'd love to be sitting down with you [*line cracks here*] to talk about everything that went on in the last couple of years but the lawyers are telling me that I cannot speak about this stuff because of the amount of, sort of, legal things going on out there and I have to be honest – at the personal level I'm a bit afraid . . . em . . . of the backlash that could come from . . . from certain quarters. But I didn't want you to think that I wouldn't return your call or that I wouldn't want to speak to you – I do. I'm hoping that your book is a bit more substantive – I know it will be – and informative than a lot of the old junk that's been out there. Irish people deserve and want to know about the complexities behind the scenes – I'm convinced of that – and the global . . . em . . . context for everything that's gone on. So, again, I do genuinely wish you well, Shane, with the book, and hopefully there will be a time when I can get a few hours with you and a cup of coffee and have a long chat about all of this. So all the best. Take care, Shane, bye bye.

3 July 2009, 12:10 p.m.

Shane, it's David Drumm here. Got your message, sorry to leave a late voicemail again. Just to reiterate, I can't get into a conversation with you at this stage. I hope . . . em . . . we will have a chance at some [*muffled*] time in the future to do that and again just, good luck with your, with your book, Shane. God bless.

Photo Credits

Credits for the inset photographs are as follows:

Tom Burke, *Irish Independent*: page 7 top left.

David Conachy, *Sunday Independent*: page 1, page 2 bottom right, page 3 top, page 5 top right, page 6 all, page 7 top right and bottom, page 8 top right.

Andrew Downes: page 4 top left.

Eamonn Farrell, Photocall Ireland: page 4 top right and bottom.

Tony Gavin, *Sunday Independent*: page 2 top.

Steve Humphreys, *Irish Independent*: page 8 top left.

Frank McGrath, *Irish Independent*: page 2 bottom left, page 5 top left, page 8 bottom left.

Gerry Mooney, *Sunday Independent*: page 8 bottom right.

Senan Doran O'Reilly, *Evening Herald*: page 5 bottom right.

Index